Legalizing Marijuana

Legalizing Marijuana

A Shift in Policies Across America

Edited by

Nancy E. Marion

Joshua B. Hill

Carolina Academic Press

Durham, North Carolina

Library of Congress Cataloging-in-Publication Data

Legalizing marijuana : a shift in policies across America / edited by Nancy E. Marion and Joshua Hill.
pages cm
Includes bibliographical references and index.
ISBN 978-1-61163-629-1 (alk. paper)
1. Drug legalization--United States. 2. Marijuana--United States. 3. Marijuana--Law and legislation--United States. I. Marion, Nancy E., editor. II. Hill, Joshua B., editor.

HV5825.L436 2015
364.1'77--dc23

2015025602

Carolina Academic Press
700 Kent Street
Durham, North Carolina 27701
Telephone (919) 489-7486
Fax (919) 493-5668
www.cap-press.com

Printed in Canada

This book is dedicated to Lynda Block Hill.
Thanks for everything.

Contents

Introduction

Nancy E. Marion and Joshua B. Hill

Laws and policies that allow for the manufacture, distribution, sale, and use of marijuana, for either medicinal purposes or recreation, are becoming more accepted across the United States. At the time of this book's publication, seventeen states and the District of Columbia have passed laws that decriminalize, or lessen the punishments, for marijuana possession and use. Twenty-three other states and the District of Columbia have opted to pass laws to legalize marijuana use by those residents suffering from medical conditions and for whom the use of the drug brings relief of their symptoms. Four states and the District of Columbia have also passed laws that allow its residents to use marijuana for recreation or pleasure.

The public support for legalized marijuana, both medical and recreational, is growing. A Gallup poll taken in October 2014 shows that 51% of respondents favored legalizing marijuana, up from 46% in October 2010, and 12% in October 1969 (Gallup Organization). In a poll by NBC News and the *Wall Street Journal*, respondents were asked to identify the most harmful substance to a user's overall health. Only eight percent of those taking part indicated that marijuana was the most harmful substance. Moreover, in a poll taken by the Pew Research Center in 2014, 47% of respondents admitted to trying the drug.

This public support for legalized marijuana has been the impetus behind the changes in the states' laws. In some states, supporters have collected enough signatures on a petition to place the issue on a state-wide ballot, at which point all voters can indicate their support or opposition. This process, called an initiative, was the process followed in states such as Alaska and Oregon. Other states, such as Colorado, have followed another path for legalization. Here, a referendum for the new law began in the state legislature. The proposal for a law allowing for marijuana use was debated and eventually passed by the elected officials in the state. In the end, the new law amended the state constitution.

Whether the state laws permitting marijuana are the result of an initiative or a referendum, they all currently violate federal law. The manufacture, use, and distribution of marijuana were made illegal when Congress passed the Controlled Substances Act in 1970, which identified marijuana as a Schedule I drug. As such, according to the US government, marijuana has no recognized medical benefits and a high potential for abuse. Other drugs identified as Schedule I drugs include heroin and LSD.

Because marijuana is currently illegal under federal law, it means that, at any time, federal law enforcement could arrest and detain any person currently possessing, growing, selling, or distributing marijuana in any fashion, even in those states with laws permitting it. Federal agents from the Drug Enforcement Administration (DEA) or the Federal Bureau of Investigation (FBI) could raid dispensaries and retail stores to arrest employees and customers, but also seize any property or profits related to the drug. While the current president has announced that he would not pursue this option, the next president may alter this policy.

In those states that have passed laws permitting marijuana use either for medical or recreation reasons, marijuana-based businesses are thriving. All types of businesses have opened and range from those that grow the plant to those that sell it, both for smoking or eating. Many of these businesses have made millions of dollars. However, because of federal laws, banks are not permitted to allow the business owners to deposit their money into an account. This makes the marijuana industry an all-cash business, leading to other problems such as a potential for more theft related offenses.

The debate over the legalization and/or decriminalization of marijuana, both medical and recreational, continues to rage. Opponents point to the dangers of marijuana use, particularly for young people as their brains continue to grow. They also point to the dangers of increased crime and violence in areas where the drug is sold. On the other hand, supporters argue that the drug is a relatively safe one, with mild effects if used safely and not mixed with other drugs. They also point out that the sale of marijuana, if taxed, could provide the state with millions of dollars of revenue, thus decreasing the burden on taxpayers.

The articles included in this text each focus on a different aspect of the debate over marijuana legalization. The first article, by Oliver, sets up the quandary over federalism. He points out that despite state laws, marijuana is illegal under the federal criminal code, and therefore, according to the supremacy clause found in the US Constitution, all state laws permitting its use are unconstitutional. A different perspective is taken by Green and Steinmetz, who take a critical look at the social construction surrounding the illegalization of the drug and how criminology has chosen to examine the topic. An international critique of marijuana use is provided by Shannon, who focuses on drug use in Portugal, Uruguay, and the Netherlands. Together, these articles provide readers with a foundation for understanding recent marijuana-related legislation in the United States.

The next set of articles focus on the growing public acceptance of marijuana use and related campaigns to legalize the drug. Hill shows how the media has covered issues pertaining to the drug and how that coverage has changed over time as public acceptance of marijuana use grows. Clearly, these changes in public opinion and associated media coverage play a large role the passage of new marijuana laws. The process by which new laws are passed, either by referendum or initiative, and the effect on implementation of the new laws, is discussed by Turner. Authors Leon and Weitzer examine ballot initiatives for marijuana legalization in more detail, identifying factors that lead to successful ballot initiatives.

The effects of marijuana legalization on the criminal justice system are the topics of the following three articles. Stohr and Foster examine the consequences of the new laws on corrections facilities and treatment programs. The impact of the new policies on law enforcement, and in particular their efforts to detect impaired drivers, is discussed by Lovrich, Christensen, and Routh. The quandary law enforcement officials face when dealing with some of the problems posed by the legalization of marijuana is outlined by Licate's article. The legal implications of the new laws are indicated by Walker, Posey, and Hemmens. Together, these three articles provide a basis for understanding the impacts of these laws on state justice systems.

The final articles included in the text, by Marion and Cronin respectively, concentrate on the effects of the new laws on other groups, namely businesses and college students. These are two populations directly affected by marijuana legalization, and can also be affected if the federal government changes its current position of "looking the other way."

In total, the articles in this book present a variety of perspectives on the constantly changing realm of marijuana legalization in the United States. These laws are controversial and have been the basis of copious debate by practitioners, lawmakers, and citizens alike. There is no doubt that these debates will continue as more states consider legalizing marijuana for either recreation or medical reasons. The articles contained in this book will provide a basis for that debate.

Legalizing Marijuana

1

Federalism and US Marijuana Laws: A Constitutional Crisis

Willard M. Oliver

Introduction

As of the start of 2015, seventeen states and the District of Columbia have decriminalized the use of marijuana, twenty-three states and the District of Columbia have legalized medicinal use of marijuana, and four states and the District of Columbia have legalized recreational use of marijuana. Despite all of these new laws that legalize the drug, the national government in Washington, DC, continues to enforce the federal law that lists marijuana as a Schedule I narcotic, making its use illegal and criminal regardless of the reason it is being used. If the national government's laws are the supreme law of the land, then the state legalization or decriminalization of marijuana would be illegal. The fact that these states and the District of Columbia, the very seat of the national government, have flaunted the laws of the national government has created the most significant federalism crisis in modern times.

The statement that this is a crisis may sound overstated, but many leading scholars have not minced words over this issue. One explained that "the struggle over marijuana regulation is one of the most important federalism conflicts in a generation" (Chemerinsky, Forman, Hopper, and Kamin, 2014: 1). Another stated, "Marijuana legalization represents the most pointed federal–state policy conflict since racial desegregation," (Schwartz, 2014) and elsewhere argued, "Marijuana legalization by the states presents the most pressing and complex federalism issue of our time" (Schwartz, 2013). Addressing this constitutional crisis and the issue of federalism is the purpose of this chapter.

In order to deal with the issue, this chapter presents some contextual historical information on the historical development of marijuana policy in the United States, as well as the relationship between the national and state government in regard to intergovernmental relations. It then turns to the more modern development of the decriminalization of marijuana and the legalization of marijuana for both medicinal and recreational purposes. Finally, it will present the dilemma the United States now faces in regard to federalism and the impact it is having on this country.

History of Marijuana in the US

The use of marijuana in American history dates back to the colonial era. At the time, however, it was not smoked for either enjoyment or medicinal purposes, but was, rather, used as a food product and for making ropes and fabrics (Deitch, 2003; Marion, 2014; Robinson, 1996). The hemp plant, from which marijuana is derived, is indigenous to Central and South Asia and was brought to the Western Hemisphere by the Spaniards (Courtwright, 2001; Lee, 2012; Marion, 2014). It became a standard crop in the New World, with the early House of Burgesses requiring farmers to plant hemp, and its growth was common among the early Puritans in New England (Deitch, 2003). There is evidence that even the Founding Fathers—George Washington, Thomas Jefferson, James Madison, and James Monroe—all grew hemp plants on their estates (Booth, 2003).

The early use of marijuana for recreational purposes appears to have been derived from the Spaniards and their descendants who grew hemp in Central and South America (Lee, 2012; Marion, 2014; Robinson, 1996). The use of the drug migrated north in the early twentieth century with Mexicans laborers into the American South (Courtwright, 2001; Jonnes, 1996). The prevalence of marijuana in the South is also believed to have been influenced by it being brought to the United States by those in the Caribbean, both free islanders and African slaves (Courtwright, 2001; Jonnes, 1996). By the late nineteenth and early twentieth centuries, marijuana was largely associated with two groups: Hispanics and blacks (Bertram, Blachman, Sharpe, and Andreas, 1996; Courtwright, 2001; Jonnes, 1996). More specifically, it was associated with Mexicans, practitioners of Voodoo, and those associated with the jazz movement (Booth, 2003; Lee, 2012; Courtwright, 2001; Deitch, 2003). This was largely seen as a cultural and underground phenomenon until the late nineteenth century when concerns over mass immigration fundamentally changing American culture became a growing concern (Daniels, 2002; Bertram, Blachman, Sharpe, and Andreas, 1996; Kraut, 2001).

The first action by the federal government to address the early "marijuana problem" was the passage of the Pure Food and Drug Act of 1906 (Jonnes, 1996; Oliver and Hilgenberg, Jr., 2010). In the late nineteenth century, marijuana was increasingly being labeled as a poison which clashed with the notion of people smoking it for recreational purposes. Congress thus addressed the problem when it added cannabis to a list of "dangerous" drugs and required the labeling of all prescription drugs, including marijuana, detailing their contents and the dosage. This law launched the regulation of the drug, but because the federal government did not have the necessary structure to enforce the law, states began regulating the drug.

Although the first jurisdiction to regulate marijuana was Washington, DC, in 1906, the first state to do so was California, when it passed the Poison Act in 1907 (Deitch, 2003; Lee, 2012). California law listed marijuana as a poison and regulated it like all other poisons. The first state, however, to outlaw marijuana outright was Massachusetts in 1911 and soon other states followed suit, including New York (1914), Maine (1914), Wyoming (1915), and Texas (1919) (Chemerinsky, Forman, Hopper, and Kamin, 2014; Deitch, 2003; Marion and Oliver, 2014; Marion, 2014). State after state continued to regulate the use of marijuana throughout the 1920s. This decade, however, became one of growing tension as the jazz movement, long associated with marijuana use, went mainstream, and people were looking for an alternative recreational drug as alcohol had been made illegal by Prohibition. Because every state was different in how it regulated marijuana, with some making it illegal while others simply listed it as a poison with no enforcement, there were many calls for a uniform policy.

A confluence of two meetings set the stage for a uniform policy in America. In 1925, the US participated in the International Opium Convention, where the central issue was the shared problems of heroin. However, because Indian hemp was known as hashish (which had a high THC content—the chemical with the intoxicating effect), there was a call for an international ban on this type of hemp. Soon thereafter, a National Conference of Commissioners on Uniform State Laws was convened in 1925, and after seven years a final draft of the Uniform State Narcotic Act was finally issued (Marion and Oliver, 2014; Oliver and Hilgenberg, Jr., 2010). Congress then accepted the final draft as model legislation for the regulation of drugs, including marijuana.

At first the states were not interested in the uniform standards for drugs. States were typically leery of any uniform policy coming out of Washington, DC. However, the Roosevelt administration became active in the policy change by focusing on the uniformity of both food and drugs to prevent harmful effects (Jonnes, 1996; Marion and Oliver, 2014). Roosevelt wrote to Congress calling for "the setting up and careful enforcement of standards of identity and quality for the food we eat and the drugs we use, together with the strict exclusion from our markets of harmful or adulterated products" (Roosevelt, 1935). The plea for uniformity worked and by 1935, every state in the nation had signed on to the uniform standards (Courtwright, 2001; Marion and Oliver, 2014; Oliver and Hilgenberg, Jr., 2010).

At the same time Congress was developing the uniform policy, they were also working on the enforcement mechanism. Despite having their own laws on the books regulating drugs, including the Pure Food and Drug Act of 1906, the Harrison Narcotics Tax Act of 1914, and the Narcotic Drugs Import and Export Act of 1922, the federal government only had limited enforcement mechanisms, including the Federal Narcotics Control Board and the Narcotics Division of US Treasury (Marion and Oliver, 2014; Oliver and Hilgenberg, Jr., 2010). On June 14, 1930, Congress consolidated these two existing bureaucracies and created the Federal Bureau of Narcotics (FBN). Armed with new powers of enforcement, the FBN fundamentally changed the regulation of marijuana in the United States (McWilliams, 1990; Oliver and Hilgenberg, Jr., 2010).

Harry J. Anslinger, who had made a name for himself in the Bureau of Prohibition, was selected as the commissioner of the Federal Bureau of Narcotics and he assumed the position with the passion of a zealot (McWilliams, 1990; Marion and Oliver, 2014). Although dealing with a variety of illicit drugs, Anslinger focused much of his time on marijuana (Bertram, Blachman, Sharpe, and Andreas, 1996; McWilliams, 1990). In order to enforce marijuana laws more fully, Anslinger needed a stronger federal law to legitimize his enforcement, and in order to achieve that, Anslinger launched a very public campaign designed to demonize marijuana, garner the support of the American people, and force the hand of Congress to pass the laws he needed to target what he saw as a scourge of American society (Marion, 2014; McWilliams, 1990).

The public campaign worked and many civic and church groups became actively involved. One of the most popular aspects to come out of this campaign was the use of the film medium to convey an anti-marijuana message. Dwain Esper's production of *Marihuana* in 1936 and Elmer Clifton's *Assassin of Youth* in 1937 were intended to scare and mobilize Americans against marijuana. The most popular of these was *Tell Your Children* by producer George Hirliman, which was later titled *Reefer Madness*. Today considered a cult-comedy, it was originally intended as a serious treatment of the problems of marijuana (Jonnes, 1996; Marion and Oliver, 2014).

Anslinger's successful campaign led Congress to pass the Marihuana Tax Act in 1937 (Chemerinsky, Forman, Hopper, and Kamin, 2014; Marion, 2014; Oliver and Hilgenberg, Jr., 2010). The bill, first drafted by Anslinger, did not criminalize the possession or use of marijuana, but rather placed a tax on anyone selling marijuana and imposed heavy fines for anyone violating the law. Thus was Anslinger able to expand his agency's budget. Armed with the new federal law, Anslinger then began targeting mostly minorities. Relegating his agency's enforcement to populations that were already marginalized, Anslinger's political astuteness avoided raising the ire of the political elites (Bertram, Blachman, Sharpe, and Andreas, 1996; Jonnes, 1996). He continued to successfully grow the Federal Bureau of Narcotics and target marijuana use in the United States, as he remained the head of that federal law enforcement agency from his appointment in 1930 until 1962 (Bertram, Blachman, Sharpe, and Andreas, 1996; Deitch, 2003; McWilliams, 1990).

The decade of the 1960s saw a cultural transformation in the United States. The end of World War II had created a stable America and produced the baby boom, the largest generation the nation had ever seen. Beginning to head off to college in the early 1960s, this generation began challenging the institutions of their parents that had provided America's stability. A significant change began to affect the American way of life. The baby boomers openly flaunted the laws against marijuana and the smoking of cannabis became a symbol of their generation (Jonnes, 1996; Marion, 2014). However, the more that generation smoked marijuana, the more the older generations began to dig in their heels. The late 1960s and early 1970s, especially under the Nixon administration, witnessed a hard-line approach to marijuana (Baum, 1996; Bertram, Blachman, Sharpe, and Andreas, 1996; Marion, 2014; Oliver and Hilgenberg, Jr., 2010).

This resulted in the passage of the Controlled Substances Act, Title II of the Comprehensive Drug Abuse Prevention and Control Act (PL 91-513), which was signed into law by President Nixon. This new law placed drugs into different categories, called Schedules, based on their medical usefulness and potential for abuse. Marijuana was identified as a Schedule I drug, meaning that it has no recognized medical benefits and a high potential for abuse. This angered many who argued just the opposite—that marijuana has many potential medical uses and little abuse potential. Thus, while the older generations were still in power, the baby boom was a force to be reckoned with and looming on the horizon was a conflict over the legality of marijuana.

Federalism

The conflict that arose, beginning in the 1970s and reaching its crisis stage in the 2010s, is between the national government and the state governments.

It is an issue of federalism. Understanding the relationship between these two government entities—intergovernmental relations—is key to understanding the issue that America now faces with marijuana policy.

In the United States' system of government, there are two levels of government, the national government in Washington, DC, and, today, the 50 state governments. Based on the Constitution, the supreme law of the land, the national government is given certain enumerated powers that are their responsibility alone, such as the creation of a military and the printing of US currency. The Constitution also reserves certain powers to the state governments, such as the conduct of elections and the establishment of local governments. In addition to the enumerated powers relegated to each level of government, there are also shared powers of governance such as the establishment of courts, chartering of banks, and making and enforcing of laws.

Before addressing that, however, it is important to note that the framers of the Constitution could not possibly allocate responsibility for every issue at the time or for the future (LaCroix, 2011). They recognized that the best they could do was to provide a framework of governance for how the national and state governments would relate to one another. Many people at the time pointed out that the Constitution was rather vague in specifying which government would be responsible for most issues (Robertson, 2012). When the Bill of Rights was drafted, the 10th Amendment was designed to address this deficiency by specifying that "the powers not delegated to the United States by the Constitution, nor prohibited by it to the states, are reserved to the states respectively, or to the people" (US Constitution, Amendment X).

In the case of marijuana laws, since the Constitution mentions nothing about regulating drugs for medicinal or recreational purposes, it should be left to the states to decide. However, the United States Constitution, under Article VI (clause 2), states that "This Constitution, and the Laws of the United States which shall be made in Pursuance thereof; and all Treaties made, or which shall be made, under the Authority of the United States, shall be the supreme Law of the Land" (US Constitution, Article VI). This is known as the "supremacy clause," which states that when the laws of the national and state governments come into conflict, the national laws will reign supreme.

The supremacy clause and the reserved powers clause clearly can find themselves in conflict with one another as they have in the case of marijuana laws. If the federal government passes a law, as it has, that says marijuana is illegal and has no medicinal value, then regardless of what laws the states pass, under the supremacy clause, the national government's law rules supreme. However, because the US Constitution does not explicitly give the authority to the national government to regulate drugs for either medicinal or recreational purposes, then under the 10th Amendment's reserved powers clause, this policy area is under the purview of the states. So, it is the question of which government triumphs in this case that has brought on this Constitutional crisis of federalism (Nagel, 2002).

Making of a Modern Crisis in Federalism

At the end of the 1960s, a generation of young people had adopted the smoking of marijuana as part of an overall cultural movement, despite the fact that marijuana was illegal in all 50 states individually and the nation under federal law. That changed in 1973, when Oregon became the first state to decriminalize marijuana (Garvey, 2012). The decriminalization of the drug did not make it legal, but rather, it just simply made small amounts no longer criminal. This is akin to a speeding violation where speeding is illegal, but it is not considered criminal behavior. Like a speeding ticket, however, anyone caught with small amounts of the drug could be issued a ticket. This became the issue of the decade—the decriminalization of marijuana.

A number of states began to consider the decriminalization of marijuana and within five years, eight more states followed suit. Eventually, seventeen states and the District of Columbia decriminalized the first time possession of small "personal" amounts of marijuana (see Box 1). The decriminalization of marijuana created a crack in the federalism agreement that marijuana was against the law, but the Drug Enforcement Administration reaffirmed that marijuana was still illegal and would be treated so by the federal government. Decriminalization also surfaced as a campaign issue in the 1976 presidential campaign and although Governor Carter backed off from the issue, he was still elected to the presidency. However, not much went well for the Carter presidency and by the end of his one term in office, the move toward decriminalization of marijuana had been turned back.

The decade of the 1980s witnessed the tide not only turn, but the fight against illegal drugs strengthen. The presidencies of Ronald Reagan and George

Box 1. Jurisdictions Where Marijuana Has Been Decriminalized

Alaska	Mississippi
California	Nebraska
Colorado	Nevada
Connecticut	New York
District of Columbia	North Carolina
Maine	Ohio

H.W. Bush made the fight against illicit drugs a centerpiece of their presidencies and the so-called "War on Drugs" was launched in America (Marion, 2011; Marion and Oliver, 2014; Marion, 2014). Marijuana policy under the federal government, like all drug policies, created a law enforcement mechanism that supported the targeting of producers, carriers, and users of the drug. Federal funding was provided to states and local governments to create drug task forces, thus funding the enforcement of federal laws against drugs at the state and local level. Federal dollars were provided for those states and local jurisdictions that maintained laws prohibiting marijuana.

For those states that had decriminalized marijuana, there was a strain on intergovernmental relations. For many, the War on Drugs was believed to have gone too far and some states did not approve. Where the issue truly came to a head, however, was in 1996, when California became the first state to pass a law, by way of a proposition, to make the use of marijuana for medicinal purposes legal (Chemerinsky, Forman, Hopper, and Kamin, 2014; Garvey, 2012; Schwartz, 2014). By legalizing marijuana for medicinal purposes, California had allowed for not only the legal sale of marijuana, but also the legal growth of the plant throughout the state. Despite the government regulating both the growth and sales of medicinal marijuana and mandating that it has to be prescribed by a doctor, this was still, according to federal law, illegal (Garvey and Yeh, 2014).

Funded under a new federalism task force, the Drug Enforcement Administration and the Butte County Sheriff's Department, in a joint drug task force, targeted one of the growers of medicinal marijuana in California. Although the drug was legal to grow in the state for medicinal purposes, it was still a Schedule I narcotic under federal law and illegal for any purpose. The joint task force raided the small pot farm and destroyed the plants. A lawsuit ensued and it reached the United States Supreme Court as the case of *Gonzales v. Raich* (2005) (Chemerinsky, Forman, Hopper, and Kamin, 2014; The Federalist Society, 2013; Gostin, 2005).[1]

The issue of federalism was the centerpiece of the Supreme Court case and whether the supremacy clause or the reserved powers clause dominated. In addition, because of the fact that the case had to do with the growth and sale of a product, by its very nature commerce, the issue also arose as to the national government's right to regulate commerce (*Gonzales v. Raich* 2005).

The Supreme Court reached their decision and explained that the national government had the right to regulate commerce and that the supremacy clause

---

1. Note: The case was formerly titled *Ashcroft v. Raich* as the Attorney General for the United States at the time of the case began was John Ashcroft.

Box 2. States That Legalized Medicinal Marijuana

Alaska	Michigan
Arizona	Minnesota
California	Montana
Colorado	Nevada
Connecticut	New Hampshire
District of Columbia	New Jersey
Delaware	New Mexico
Hawaii	New York
Illinois	Oregon
Maine	Rhode Island
Maryland	Vermont
Massachusetts	Washington

meant that the national government's laws on drugs trumped California's law on medicinal marijuana (Garvey and Yeh, 2014; Gostin, 2005). Marijuana, by federal law, was illegal, and California's law on medicinal marijuana did not nullify federal law (Garvey, 2012; Gostin, 2005).

Despite the fact that the national government essentially won the case, other states ignored both the ruling and federal law and began passing medical marijuana laws. The growing crack in federalism had widened into a great chasm. State after state passed laws until, by 2014, twenty-three states and the District of Columbia had laws allowing the sale of medicinal marijuana (see Box 2) (Chemerinsky, Forman, Hopper, and Kamin, 2014; Marion, 2014). This created a quandary for the federal government as it tried to figure out whether to enforce the national laws in states where marijuana had become medically legal. At first, it appeared that President Obama's administration and Attorney General Eric Holder were going to hold to the law and its enforcement, but in an announcement in 2009, Holder stated that the DEA would no longer raid stores that sold medicinal marijuana. The federal government had backed down from enforcing its laws (Chemerinsky, Forman, Hopper, and Kamin, 2014; Garvey, 2012). Yet this only created a temporary pause in the issue of federalism.

The issue of states allowing for medicinal marijuana in the face of the national government's laws stating that marijuana was illegal for any purpose could be justified to a degree. If marijuana was a drug that could be used to treat certain ailments and a licensed physician prescribed the drug, then perhaps the state laws for medical purposes could be justified in the face of the blanket federal law that said marijuana was illegal for any purpose (Garvey, 2012). However, when Colorado and Washington placed initiatives for the legalization of recreational marijuana on the ballot in 2012, that justification was removed.

Box 3. Jurisdictions That Legalized Recreational Marijuana

Alaska	Oregon
Colorado	Washington
District of Columbia	

When the 2012 elections were held, Colorado had Amendment 64 on the ballot and Washington State had Initiative 502 (Chemerinsky, Forman, Hopper, and Kamin, 2014; Garvey and Yeh, 2014; Schwartz, 2014). Both of these ballots allowed the citizens of those states to vote on whether to make recreational marijuana legal. When the votes were counted, both states had passed their initiatives with 55% of the voters supporting passage. Colorado became the first to implement the law, and Washington State soon followed (Garvey and Yeh, 2014; Schwartz, 2014). Then, in 2014, two additional states were added to the list, along with the District of Columbia (see Box 3). The modern relationship of federalism, where the national government essentially dictates to the states their policies, had just been undermined (Garvey and Yeh, 2014). In short, the legalization of marijuana has created a federalism crisis in America (Gostin, 2005; Kamin, 2013; Schwartz, 2014).

Marijuana and the Federalism Crisis

The current status of marijuana policy in the United States has created a federalism crisis (Schwartz, 2013). This modern crisis in federalism has created a policy dilemma between the policies of the national government and those of the state governments. The national government has a law that states that marijuana is a Schedule I narcotic, a drug that is illegal, regardless of why it is used. A growing number of states have either decriminalized marijuana, passed laws that have allowed its use for medicinal purposes, or, more recently, allowed its use for recreational purposes. In these circumstances the question to ask is, which law stands?

The supremacy clause of the US Constitution would suggest that the national government has the final say for it is the "supreme law of the land" (US Constitution, Article VI). Taken to its extreme, however, that would suggest that the national government could pass laws that regulate everything in American life, thus making state and local governments irrelevant. This makes little sense, for then why would the Founding Fathers pass the Bill of Rights, which included the Tenth Amendment, reserving the right of the state governments (and the people) to regulate those things not found in the Constitution? This reserved powers clause would suggest that because the US

Constitution says nothing about the national government regulating marijuana, specifically, or drugs, generally, than this would be a power reserved for the states. Much of this debate centers on the powers delegated to the national government, and this debate traces itself back to the Founding Father's themselves, for Madison argued that the powers were "few and defined," while Hamilton argued that they were highly expansive (Rossiter, 1961).

The idea that the state can allow you to sell marijuana and you can smoke it openly, but the national government (DEA) will arrest you for the same behavior seems anathema to an American's sense of fairness. Since it does not seem to fit any of the old styles of intergovernmental relations, marijuana policy appears to have placed American in a new era of federalism. This new era suggests a major conflict where each level of government is moving to assert its authority, but that in the end, is about asserting authority over the other. The national government is moving toward preemption of state laws when they do not conform with the supreme law of the land (Chemerinsky, Forman, Hopper, and Kamin, 2014; Garvey, 2012; Garvey and Yeh, 2014; Schwartz, 2013). State governments, by the very nature of passing legislation that decriminalizes marijuana or allows its use for medicinal and recreational purposes, has moved toward the nullification of the national government's law related to marijuana (Garvey, 2012; Schwartz, 2013). This stand-off between the two forms of government has created the crisis of modern federalism, and this crisis has consequences.

The marijuana debate has created a major policy issue that has divided American society (Marion, 2014). Executives, legislators, and even the judiciary, do not readily agree on which side should predominate (Schwartz, 2013; Schwartz, 2014). Many governments, especially the national government, have built up an extensive law enforcement mechanism to target illegal drugs, while at the same time, interest groups concerned about the criminalization of marijuana, its medical value, or simply the right of Americans to use the drug at their leisure, have been created in opposition. In addition, since the legalization of marijuana in some states, an entire industry has been created to grow, market, and sell marijuana. The reality, however, is many of these entities get caught in the middle of the mixed policies on marijuana (Chemerinsky, Forman, Hopper, and Kamin, 2014).

A couple of examples of this dilemma may suffice. A local police officer or deputy sheriff from the state of Colorado may not use marijuana, even though it is legal, for their employment within the agency bans the use of something that is now legal (Schwartz, 2013). They are no longer required to make arrests for marijuana per se, but if someone is driving under the influence of marijuana and poses a danger to other drivers, can they arrest that individual? Like the use of Blood Alcohol Content (BAC), at what level of THC is an individual considered to be impaired? (Wong, Brady, and Li, 2014). Also, if that local officer works with a federal drug task force, can they participate in an arrest for marijuana when it is legal by the state laws they enforce, but illegal by the drug task force's laws?

The cannabis industry faces similar dilemmas. In order to operate a business, an individual must meet certain federal and state regulations, have appropriate licenses, and adhere to tax code laws (Chemerinsky, Forman, Hopper, and Kamin, 2014; The Federalist Society, 2013; Garvey and Yeh, 2014; Schwartz, 2014). If the store owner sells a substance that is illegal by federal government standards, the national government may not permit them to operate the business, despite the fact that it is legal within the state. Where this has become very evident is when individuals desire small-business loans from banks and other institutions in order to open a cannabis store. Because the banks are federally insured, the loans must meet certain federal standards, and as the loan is to operate a business that is considered criminal by federal law, the loans cannot be approved (Chemerinsky, Forman, Hopper, and Kamin, 2014; Garvey and Yeh, 2014). In fact, a bank could face money laundering charges if they engaged in banking transactions for marijuana businesses (Chemerinsky, Forman, Hopper, and Kamin, 2014; The Federalist Society, 2013). The same issue applies to the tax code, for while businesses must pay federal taxes, to do so on the sale of something that is illegal by federal law also amounts to potential money laundering charges (Chemerinsky, Forman, Hopper, and Kamin, 2014; The Federalist Society, 2013). The answer to these types of problems is usually to bring in an attorney, however, the attorney faces the same dilemma, since they are bound to respect federal laws as well, thus placing them in the awkward—and illegal—position of advising a client on illegal criminal behavior (Chemerinsky, Forman, Hopper, and Kamin, 2014; The Federalist Society, 2013).

Finally, the legalization of marijuana can also create a dilemma in something as simple as the purchase of a gun (Garvey and Yeh, 2014). Due to the Brady Bill, background checks are required for the purchase of a handgun. A Bureau of Alcohol, Tobacco, & Firearms (ATF) firearms transfer form is also required to be completed at the time a person picks up their firearm. One question on the form is "Are you an unlawful user of, or addicted to, marijuana or any depressant, stimulant, narcotic drug, or any other controlled substance?" (US Department of Justice, 2012). Assuming a person attempts to answer the question truthfully so as not to face legal issues in the future, if that person lives in a state where marijuana is legal and has smoked it legally, because the transfer form is a federal form, that person would have to check "yes" on the form and would thus be denied the right to purchase the handgun. This same issue can arise with those who live in federal assisted housing, work for a company operating under a federal contract that must adhere to the Drug-Free Workplace regulations, or for a school or institution of higher education which must follow regulations under the Drug-Free Schools and Communities regulations (Chemerinsky, Forman, Hopper, and Kamin, 2014; Garvey and Yeh, 2014).

Conclusion

America is truly at a crossroads in regard to the development of intergovernmental relations as a result of states decriminalizing and legalizing marijuana. While the national government maintains a law that criminalizes any use of marijuana regardless of the purpose, states are defying that law and passing legislation that legalizes marijuana for medicinal and recreational purposes. This has created an oppositional form of federalism between the national and state governments. The national government may well argue that under the Constitution that it is the supreme law of the land it can preempt state law that defies it. The state governments can counter argue that under the Tenth Amendment they have the reserved powers act, which gives them the right to regulate areas not specified or enumerated in the US Constitution, hence allowing them the right to nullify national laws. Although states move forward and the national government has backed off from its enforcement efforts, this uncooperative federalism is nonetheless affecting many citizens, businesses, and government agencies—creating a crisis that must, at some point, be resolved.

References

Baum, D. (1996). *Smoke and mirrors: The War on Drugs and the politics of failure.* Boston, MA: Little, Brown, & Co.

Bertram, E., Blachman, M., Sharpe, K., & Andreas, P. (1996). *Drug war politics: The price of denial.* Berkeley, CA: University of California Press.

Booth, M. (2003). *Cannabis: A history*. New York, NY: Picador.

Chemerinsky, E., Forman, J., Hopper, A., & Kamin, S. (2014). Cooperative federalism and marijuana regulation. Legal Studies Research Paper. Irvine, CA: University of California, Irvine, 1.

Courtwright, D. T. (2001). *Forces of habit: Drugs and the making of the modern world.* Cambridge, MA: Harvard University Press.

Daniels, R. (2002). *Coming to America* (2nd ed.). New York, NY: HarperCollins.

Deitch, R. (2003). *Hemp—American history revisited: The plant with a divided history*. New York, NY: Algora Publishing.

The Federalist Society. (2013). *Marijuana and the states: How should federalism principles inform the federal government's response to state marijuana initiatives?* Retrieved from http://www.fed-soc.org/multimedia/detail/marijuana-and-the-states-how-should-federalism-principles-inform-the-federal-governments-response-to-state-marijuana-initiatives-event-audiovideo.

Garvey, T. (2012). *Medical marijuana: The Supremacy Clause, federalism, and the interplay between state and federal laws*. Washington, DC: Congressional Research Service.

Garvey, T., & Yeh, B. T. (2014). *State legalization of recreational marijuana: Selected legal issues*. Washington, DC: Congressional Research Service.

Gostin, L. O. (2005). Medical marijuana, American federalism, and the Supreme Court. *Journal of the American Medical Association*, 294, 842–844.

Jonnes, J. (1996). *Hep-cats, narcs, and pipe dreams: A history of America's romance with illegal drugs*. Baltimore, MD: The Johns Hopkins University Press.

Kamin, S. (2013). Medical marijuana in Colorado and the future of marijuana regulation in the United States. *McGeorge Law Review*, *43*, 147–167.

Kraut, A. M. (2001). *The huddled masses: The immigrant in American society, 1880–1921* (2nd ed.). Hoboken, NJ: Wiley-Blackwell.

LaCroix, A. L. (2011). *The ideological origins of American federalism*. Cambridge, MA: Harvard University Press.

Lee, M. A. (2012). *Smoke signals: A social history of marijuana—medicinal, recreational, and scientific*. New York, NY: Scribner.

Marion, N. E. (2011). *Federal government and criminal justice*. New York, NY: Palgrave Macmillan.

Marion, N. E. (2014). *The medical marijuana maze: Policy and politics*. Durham, NC: Carolina Academic Press.

Marion, N. E., & Oliver, W. M. (2014). *Drugs in American society: An encyclopedia of history, politics, culture, and law*. Santa Barbara, CA: ABC-CLIO.

McWilliams, J. C. (1990). *The protectors: Harry J. Anslinger and the federal bureau of narcotics, 1930–1962*. Newark, DE: University of Delaware Press.

Nagel, R. F. (2002). *The implosion of American federalism*. New York, NY: Oxford University Press.

Oliver, W. M., & Hilgenberg, J. F., Jr. (2010). *A history of crime and criminal justice in America* (2nd ed.). Durham, NC: Carolina Academic Press.

Robertson, D. B. (2012). *Federalism and the making of America*. New York, NY: Routledge.

Robinson, R. (1996). *The great book of hemp: The complete guide to the environmental, commercial, and medicinal uses of the world's most extraordinary plant.* Rochester, VT: Park Street Press.

Roosevelt, F. D. (1935). Message to Congress on pure food and drugs. *The American Presidency Project.* Retrieved from http://www.presidency.ucsb.edu/ws/index.php?pid=15025&st=Drugs&st1.

Rossiter, C. (Ed.). (1961). *The federalist papers.* New York, NY: New American Library.

Schwartz, D. S. (2013). High federalism: Marijuana legalization and the limits of federal power to regulate states. *Cardozo Law Review, 35*, 567–641.

Schwartz, D. S. (2014). Presidential politics as a safeguard of federalism: The case of marijuana legalization. *Buffalo Law Review, 62*, 599–657: 601.

US Department of Justice, BATF. (2012). Firearms transaction record Part I—Over-the-Counter. Retrieved from https://www.atf.gov/files/forms/download/atf-f-4473-1.pdf.

Wong, K., Brady, J. E., & Li, G. (2014). Establishing legal limits for driving under the influence of marijuana. *Injury Epidemiology, 1*, 26–33.

2

Up in Smoke: Marijuana, Abstract Empiricism, and the Criminological Imagination

Edward L. W. Green and Kevin F. Steinmetz[1]

> *Let us underline the fact that the modus vivendi of orthodox criminology is in all of its aspects, the very opposite of the sociological imagination proposed some fifty years ago by C. Wright Mills. For orthodoxy offers the disconnection from power, the loss both of structure and meaning, and acts bereft of the context of history. It is to restore these things that critical criminology must set as its central task.*
>
> Jock Young (2011b, p. 198)

Over the previous decades marijuana has been a veritable political minefield. The substance has been historically mythologized as a scourge of society despite the presence of (less influential) competing narratives. Indeed, the politics of pot have been so divisive that even scientific research on it has been shunned to varying degrees as a result of its stigma as a harbinger of delinquency and urban decay. Inciardi summarizes this trend as:

> [M]any people typically seem to ignore the treasuries of evidence descriptive of drugs, drug users, and drug taking that the fields of pharmacology, medicine, and the social and psychological sciences have provided, in favor of many prevailing mythical systems (Inciardi, 2008, p. 181).

---

1. The authors would like to thank Tammy Castle and Carl Root for their comments and criticisms on earlier drafts of this manuscript.

As the legal tide shifts toward legalization, marijuana is once again rendered problematic for many policy makers and other moral crusaders who found marijuana an easy target as part of the strategy to garner votes through "tough on crime" rabble-rousing.

Marijuana is classified by the US government as a "Schedule I drug (i.e., no medical value and a high potential for abuse)" (Leon & Weitzer, 2014, p. 193). Despite this classification, medical marijuana (MM) is now ignored as a federal crime in at least five states which have allowed dispensaries, and with the results of the 2014 election, Oregon and Alaska have legalized the sale of marijuana for recreational use and have decriminalized personal consumption. Colorado and Washington pioneered decriminalization decisions in 2012. Public support for pot "rose from 12% in 1969 to 25% in 1980 to 31% in 2000, and has now passed halfway mark: hovering between 55% and 58% [citations omitted]" (Leon & Weitzer, 2014, p. 193). While the political topography of marijuana is shifting, the tension between competing demands for criminalization, legalization, and decriminalization persists. Various interests still stand against marijuana legalization, thus creating a tense political climate in some circles.

Criminology has endured its own shifts in the areas of empirical research and theoretical development on marijuana. Early criminological work in this area was heavily influenced by the sociological domains of symbolic interactionism and social constructionism, which viewed marijuana as a phenomenon subjected to the shifting forces of deviance and social control. Becker's (1963) study of marijuana smokers is a key example where the creation of marijuana use as a problem behavior worthy of control occurred not along objective lines, but as a result of moral entrepreneurialism and perceptions of race. Like plate tectonics, the academic landscape has gradually shifted away from such analyses, becoming more positivistic over time. Recent mainstream criminological research on marijuana use has tended to remain relatively unreflexive on these issues. For instance, marijuana research published in criminological journals over the past several years has tended to examine topics that cast marijuana as a social problem. These studies have included examinations of supposed relationships between jurisdictional drug policies and youth marijuana use (Terry-McElrath, McBride, Chriqui, O'Mally, VanderWaal, Chaloupka, & Johnston, 2009), prosecutorial decision making towards juvenile marijuana cases (Terry-McElrath, Chriqui, Bates, & McBride, 2014), the relationship between childhood sexual abuse and later-life marijuana use (Chu, 2011), and the relationship between intimate partner violence and prior marijuana use (Reingle, Staras, Jennings, Cranchini, & Maldonado-Molina, 2011), to name a few. Many of these studies seem content to view marijuana use as a problem behavior (or potential problem behavior) largely divorced of the social forces which have generated such perceptions.

Despite marijuana's ubiquity as a social phenomenon and a key point of intersection between deviance, public opinion, politics, and social control, very few criminological analyses seem to take pot seriously.[2] When these analyses are conducted, marijuana use is often relegated to a control measure. When pot is a *dependent* variable, it is usually investigated as a phenomenon caused by various negative predictors, such as peer delinquency. In other words, criminology seems to have become comfortable with adopting and perpetuating the negative connotations surrounding the substance.

Indeed, looking at the top five criminology journals as of August 20, 2014, we can plainly see a dearth of research on marijuana.[3] Examining all articles published from the beginning of 2010 to August 20, 2014, only 12.84% out of 802 articles even *mention* the terms "marijuana" or "cannabis." Of these articles, only 7.61% (of the total article pool) incorporate marijuana in their analyses or arguments. When marijuana was included in a study it was largely done so wrapped within a broader aggregated variable such as substance use and delinquency (5.36%).[4] Articles which made marijuana their *explicit* phenomenon of interest were few and far between, comprising only .5% of the 802 articles analyzed—2.24% if we also count analyses which made marijuana use *one* of its primary dependent variables among many. Of all of these analyses, not a single one looked at marijuana in its broader social context—instead examining the substance through behavioral or attitudinal prediction models. Considering the rich social, cultural, and historical context surrounding marijuana, such treatments of pot within the literature echo Young's (2011b) statement that "the lens of orthodox criminology not only distorts, *it leaves out*" (emphasis added, p. 189).

---

2. There are notable exceptions to this claim—though they are few and far between—such as Leon and Wietzer's (2014) study.

3. To determine the top five journals in criminology, the ISI Journal Citation Report for Criminology/Penology was used. The top five journals ranked by impact factor were *Criminology, Trauma Violence & Abuse, Theoretical Criminology, Journal of Criminal Justice,* and *Sexual Abuse: A Journal of Research & Treatment.* Each article was electronically scanned for any mention of the keywords "marijuana" or "cannabis." As each mentioning was isolated, these were then analyzed as to their context—if they are mentioned off-handedly, constitute an independent variable, serve as the main thrust of analysis, etc.

4. Only articles which *explicitly* stated that marijuana/cannabis was included in an aggregate variable were counted as many articles used variables like "substance abuse" without detailing the substances which comprised the measure, thus making it impossible to determine if marijuana was included.

Shifting public opinion on marijuana only excavates old issues of social conflict and consensus surrounding the symbolic nature of illicit substance use, particularly marijuana. The social moorings of pot as a problem substance are loosened—to borrow nomenclature from the late Jock Young—to remind us that the social constructivist issues originally at the fore in criminological thought on marijuana have not gone away. A return to theories and perspectives sensitive to these shifting social dynamics thus seems warranted—a return of what Young (2011b) terms the "criminological imagination" in research and theorizing on marijuana and other drug "problems."

Drawing from C.W. Mills' (1959) work, Young (2011b) endeavors to temper the rise of abstract empiricism within criminology by promoting the criminological imagination:

> The sociological imagination proposed that sociology, if it is to be of any significance, must link the inner lives of people to the structures of power and ideology and the historical period in which they live ... any social analysis worth its salt must do this (Young, 2011b, p. 3).

Part of embracing the criminological imagination, then, is recognizing the importance of situating phenomena within their evolving social and historical context. Conversely, such insight also involves the recognition that an impoverished social science considers objects of inquiry largely *divorced* of this context. Regarding marijuana, our contention is that "[w]e are confronted at this moment with an orthodox criminology which is denatured and desiccated" (Young, 2011b, p. 84). In other words, orthodox criminology has reduced marijuana studies to abstract empiricism removed from the substance's historical, political, and symbolic construction.

As criminological research investigating marijuana has often derived legitimacy for the idea of pot use as a problem behavior through (1) law and (2) the popular consensus notion of substance abuse as negative, attention is then given to discussing the necessity of criminology to embrace imaginative thinking in order to remain relevant in the discussion of marijuana in contemporary times. The organization for the following analytic essay is as follows. First, a brief history of marijuana is provided. This temporal context helps us understand the shifting social constructions—often hinging on power inequalities—which have underpinned pot's illegalization. Within this historical backdrop is also a description of the rise and proliferation of counter-narratives to these demonizations. We then revisit the problems of orthodox criminology in its handling of marijuana—pointing out how arguments for its consideration as an anti-social substance are tenuous at best. The history and contemporary state of marijuana—as a constructed deviance—is dissected, drawing from moral panic theory/cultural criminology. Finally, this chapter will end with a call for a criminological imagination, one that guided marijuana research for so many years, lest criminology risk reducing itself to irrelevancy in the study of this often vilified plant.

A Brief History of Reefer

> *Deviance is not inherent in an action but a quality bestowed upon it: the ascription of deviance demands both actors and reactors.*
>
> Jock Young (2011b, p. 202)

The Rise of Cannabis

According to the *Pharmacopoeia*, in 1936 "cannabis" is defined as:

> Cannab.—Cannabis indicae herba P.I. Cannabis consists of the dried flowering tops of the pistillate plants of Cannabis sative Linne (Fam. Moraceae). It contains not more than 10 per cent of its fruits, large foliage leaves, and stems of 3mm. in diameter, and not more than 2 per cent of other foreign organic matter. It yields not more than 5 per cent of acid-insoluble ash (Musto, 2002: 407).

The above description originated under "Hemp Growing for Farmers" and was introduced to farmers in 1920 as a "drug yielding plant crop." This was before federal regulation of the plant that we have come to know as marijuana. The farmers were encouraged to grow cannabis mostly for hemp rope. This humble plant has been used throughout history for textile fabrics. In addition, up to this point, marijuana had "been used therapeutically for 5,000 years" (Kappeler & Potter, 2005, p. 198).

Like many drugs at the time, marijuana was largely introduced through snake oil salesmen and make-shift medicine of all types in the latter half of the nineteenth century. At this time marijuana was primarily grouped into hemp, hashish, or cannabis. Such linguistic categorization is understandable as hemp and marijuana come from the same plant. The difference between hemp and marijuana is between species, concentration of select chemicals, and use of the plant (West, 1998). Inciardi reports, "By the middle of the 1880s, every major US city had its clandestine hashish clubs catering to a rather well-to-do clientele" (Inciardi, 2008, p. 31). The plant lost favor with apothecaries due to the insolubility of the leaves, its inability to be injectable, and general ineffectiveness when taken orally (Inciardi, 2008). Despite its declining popularity in more legitimate arenas, marijuana use flourished in the periphery.

In the early 1900s public awareness of health standards, packing processes, and various other industrial practices and issues became inculcated in the social consciousness. For example, Upton Sinclair's book *The Jungle* generated enough public outcry that new legislation was created as a result. Sinclair's exposure of the unsavory methods of meat packing to the public sparked a shift in governance, and reform known as the Pure Food and Drug Act passed in 1906 (Inciardi, 2008). Ultimately this required patent medicines to report their ingredients and eventually led to the demise of the clandestine industries of snake-oil salesmen. The Food and Drug Act did not criminalize substances, rather it was a law governing preparation, labeling, and packing—in short, this was a quality standard that listed what constituents were in a substance. In 1914, the Harrison Act was passed and enacted a federal tax on all cocaine and opiates. Inciardi (2008) stated, "It was a revenue code designed to exercise some measure of public control over drugs rather than to penalize the estimated 200,000 users of narcotics in the United States" (p. 28). Herein, through the FDA, started the legal regulation of food and drugs.

With marijuana eschewed by apothecaries and its production/distribution increasingly regulated, marijuana was deemed unviable as a commercial product during this period. In some underground circles, however, marijuana's effects were still appreciated. As a result, by the 1920s marijuana was largely associated with musicians and minorities (Becker, 1963; Inciardi, 2008; Musto, 2002). Soon after, a national crusade emerged to sever any permissive attitudes towards the substance (Musto, 2002). The language surrounding the once innocuous substance also changed as marijuana became classified as a drug. Pejorative tropes and euphemisms described what soon became "dope" to the federal government.

The implications of marijuana use seemed to have emerged spatially and culturally from Mexico. It is largely agreed upon that marijuana flowed into the United States from the southern border states. The use of the drug was quickly racialized and demonized and, as Inciardi (2008) described, "not only was marijuana an 'intoxicant of blacks and wetbacks' that might have a corrupting influence on white society, it was considered particularly dangerous because of its alien (Mexican) origins" (p. 31; See also: Becker, 1963). In other words, not only had marijuana been largely rejected as a viable commercial product, it had also become increasingly associated with immigrants and racial/ethnic minorities and their supposed dangerousness and/or criminality, thus creating a connotation which upset some of the xenophobic and racist attitudes of the time. With minimal capital interest and the image of marijuana pejoratively associated with marginalized minorities, the ground-work had been laid to legitimate the implementation of social control.

"Reefer Madness": The Criminalization of a Plant

With the tide of distrust ebbing against marijuana, a new legal force would be needed to control popular opinion and law enforcement. The formation of the Federal Bureau of Narcotics (FBN) was a watershed moment in history for the constructed narrative and criminalization of marijuana. In fact, the tone with which the substance was described in FBN reports evolved from a "matter-of-fact description in the first selection to the dramatic warnings in the last reports" between the years 1931, 1933, and 1937 (Musto, 2002, p. 422). The construction of this narrative culminated in further legislation and, arguably, the most famous public decry describing the dangers of marijuana addiction. The Marihuana [sic] Tax Act of 1937 imposed what Musto (2002) described as "an occupational excise tax upon certain dealers in marihuana [sic] to impose a transfer tax upon certain dealings in marihuana [sic], and to safeguard the revenue therefrom by registry and recording" (p. 430). The political (and cultural) impetus to create a monstrous "other" (comprised of individuals associated with marijuana in various capacities) was in place.

A smear campaign ensued, perhaps beginning with a 1938 *Reader's Digest* article penned by US drug czar H. J. Anslinger and Courtney Ryley Cooper titled "Marijuana: Assassin of Youth." The first paragraph of Anslinger's manifesto is clearly rooted in public deterrence:

> The sprawled body of a young girl lay crushed on the sidewalk the other day after a plunge from the fifth story of a Chicago apartment house. Everyone called it suicide, but actually it was murder. The killer was a narcotic known to America as marijuana, and to history as hashish. It is a narcotic used in the form of cigarettes, comparatively new to the United States and as dangerous as a coiled rattlesnake (As cited in Musto, 2002, p. 433).

Persons who not only consumed marijuana but *distributed* the substance were regarded as menaces. Distributors/dealers were portrayed as "depraved sociopaths—people who must be stopped before they corrupt the innocent" (Kappeler & Potter, 2005, p. 176). The tone was clear (though the content distorted and warped) and the message influenced US governance and interdiction efforts for the following seventy years. This history of marijuana prohibition, it seems, laid the groundwork for what would become the War on Drugs that drastically shaped US crime control and society generally.

It was through such forces of social construction that marijuana became a problem in the public mind *and* in legal codification. During the 1970s, the vitriol directed at marijuana diminished via top-down reform throughout the United States, notably with the creation of the Comprehensive Drug Abuse Act of 1970 which "eliminated mandatory-minimum penalties, reduced maximum sentences, eliminated a provision preventing convicted offenders from being eligible for suspended sentences or probation, and provided treatment for first-time offenders arrested for drug possession" (Leon & Weitzer, 2014, pp. 194–195). The scrutiny towards marijuana increased in the 1980s with the onset of the War on Drugs in tandem with a shift in law enforcement practices (what became known as order maintenance policing) (Inciardi, 2008; Nguyen & Reuter, 2012)—driven by right-realist perspectives in criminology as well as ideology. These trends contributed to large-scale drug arrests. For instance, in 2008 it was estimated that of the 14,000,000 arrests that occurred, 45% were for possession of marijuana (Nguyen & Reuter, 2012). This effort has not been shown to reduce drug use, however, as there were "estimates that the rates of past year use had risen from 6,520 in 1991 to a rate of 9,797 per 100,000 in 2008" (Nguyen & Reuter, 2012, p. 881). The realities of marijuana dealing and use have not lived up to the murderous substance that Anslinger constructed.

These facts bring up several points. First, minor offense-oriented or "order maintenance policing"—which became popular alongside the development of the War on Drugs—does not decrease offending. A negative feedback loop has resulted in minority arrests leading to overrepresentation in the criminal justice system, and racially fueled policing practice (Alexander, 2010; Barak, Leighton, & Flavin, 2010; Kappeler & Potter, 2005; Tonry, 2011). For example, Gelman, Fagan, and Kiss (2007) measured "stop and frisk" searches among racial/ethnic minority populations in New York City, finding that they were disproportionately stopped as a result of the NYPD's "stop and frisk" policy. Furthermore, a focus on outdoor drug activity and police perceptions also contributes to minority overrepresentation in drug arrests (Beckett, Nyrop, Pfingst, & Bowen, 2005; Nguyen & Reuter, 2012). Such minority representation is particularly troubling because it fails to align with the reality of drug use, as Kappeler and Potter (2005) explain:

> The drug war, and particularly intensive street level drug enforcement, has been blatantly racist. In 2002, 32.5% of all drug arrestees were African American [citation omitted]. Yet, only 15% of the nation's drug users are black, compared to 72% who are white [citation omitted] (p. 186).

In addition, African Americans are also more likely to gain prison sentences for drug violations compared to whites (Kappeler & Potter, 2005; Tonry,

2011). According to these findings, perceptions of racial association and marijuana remain strong. The history of marijuana use and control has created an unsavory cocktail composed of one part social inequality and two parts social construction.

Contradicting Mythology: A Counter-Narrative of Marijuana

Dominant political narratives surrounding marijuana were largely pejorative—propelling and being propelled by various moral entrepreneurs (Becker, 1963) who advocated political, cultural, and policy changes to "protect" the people from pot as an alleged enemy of the public. Despite such constructions, voices in the periphery have sought to combat such narratives. Since 1971, various organizations have advocated for the legalization and rescheduling of marijuana. Over a forty-year campaign, these efforts have contributed to, at least to some degree, social and policy changes despite the mythologization of pot. Perhaps the most noteworthy of these changes was the legalization/decriminalization of marijuana in two US states. In the November 2012 election, Colorado's Amendment 64 and Washington Initiative 502 passed by democratic vote. In 2014 Alaska and Oregon opted for similar legislation. These bills made personal consumption and possession of up to 1 ounce of marijuana legal for persons aged 21 and above.

The most well-known group of marijuana advocates is known as The National Organization for the Reform of Marijuana Laws (NORML). Founded in 1972, NORML advocated changing marijuana from a Schedule I to a Schedule II narcotic. The current Schedule I classification places marijuana in the same category as cocaine and heroin. From the 1930s until quite recently, this legal classification has prevented legal medical research on marijuana (Musto 2002).

The Supreme Court agreed on January 15, 1975, that there were medical reasons to reform medical marijuana laws (Zeese, 1999). The Drug Enforcement Agency (DEA) was against marijuana law reform of any kind (Zeese, 1999). In the mid-1970s, advocate Robert Randall defended smoking pot on a medical basis. Randall and his partner, Alice O'Leary, lobbied and, between the years of 1978–1982, 33 states passed laws allowing the availability of marijuana to seriously ill patients. Because of these arguments and other similar efforts, the USDA had recognized the anti-emetic properties of marijuana (Zeese, 1999). In the ensuing thirty years, research conducted found that 90% of patients overall prescribed to smoke marijuana reported relief from nausea and vomiting with no major side effects. Reporting on six states, and using experimental samples, Zeese (1999) found overwhelming support for use of marijuana as an anti-emetic for the seriously ill in New Mexico (90%), Michigan (71%), Tennessee (90.4%), and 100% for inhalation therapy. New York reported 92.9% success in North Shore and 89.7% at Columbia, while Georgia (76%) and California (74%) also reported high rates of success (Zeese, 1999). In general, the most common side effect reported for medical marijuana was sleepiness. Ultimately, the author states "After 14 years (1986) of litigations, three reversals of the agency (DEA) by the US court of appeals ... NORML finally got hearings on the medical use of marijuana" (Zeese, 1999, p. 325).

Despite the continuous subversion of these scientific findings with political agendas, by 1998 a coalition of six states, including Alaska, Arizona, Colorado, Nevada, Oregon, Washington, and Washington, DC, voted on medical use for marijuana (Zeese, 1999). This effort was spearheaded by the organization Americans for Medical Rights (Zeese, 1999), and some legal leeway had been made for further research on medical marijuana (MM) dispensaries (Cerda, Wall, Keyes, Galea, & Hasin, 2012; Kepple, Freisthler, 2012; Miller, Kuhns, 2012; Vickovic & Fradella, 2011). Boggess, Perez, Cope, Root, & Stretesky (2014) conducted a spatial analysis in Denver, Colorado, hypothesizing that dispensaries would be considered an undesirable land-use, however, they did not find any evidence of negative community perceptions of MM dispensaries.

The purpose of detailing the medical marijuana research and its associated advocacy is to show how counter-narratives concerning pot have begun eroding the previously prescribed political discourse villainizing the plant (and those who chose to smoke it). That such research and advocacy have contributed to—at least to some degree—public opinion reflecting the subjective and symbolic nature of marijuana. In addition, highlighting the history of these counter narratives also reveals another point of damage wrought by the negative construction of marijuana as a social problem, "The mythical demonization of marijuana injures not only users caught in the law enforcement net but also those who could find relief from serious ailments if marijuana were decriminalized" (Kappeler & Potter, 2005, p. 202). The current trend of decriminalization will lead to further knowledge about marijuana. Unfortunately, little criminological work will have had much value toward the process of legitimization.

Beyond the policy changes, research has begun to show symbolic shifts in both media rhetoric and public opinion in favor of marijuana. For instance, Vickovic and Fradella (2011) conducted an ethnographic content analysis of a random sample of news articles from around the country that mentioned marijuana, and coded the articles as positive, neutral, and negative. One of the significant findings was that overall 64.2% of the articles were positive. Vickovic and Fradella (2011) suggested, "In addition to national coverage of political rhetoric on major policy issues, the news content of regional and local media outlets can similarly manifest local political attitudes and outcomes" (p. 70). It seems that all of the rhetoric used to fuel the moral panics of marijuana are culturally beset by decades of differing, and arguably, positive experiences. In other words, people have been ignoring the illegal status of pot for decades on a normative basis during adolescent experimentation. Few people have not been around or tried marijuana.

In terms of public opinion, this conclusion is further supported by the national level Quinnipiac Poll, of which the *Chicago Tribune News* reported, "Majority of Americans support legalizing marijuana: poll" (Whitesides, 2012). The finding was 51% support to 44% opposition with the primary differences manifesting themselves on the variables gender and age; 59% of men support, while 52% of women polled oppose the legalization of marijuana and the majority of people over the age of 64 opposed the legalization of marijuana. It appears that younger Americans oppose the legalization of marijuana less than older generations that experienced the propaganda of the past.

It is at this critical juncture that we turn to criminology. Up to this point, the reader may have been curious about how this history of conflict and construction is relevant to criminology as a disciplinary issue. As demonstrated in the following section, the surge of regression-based analyses often devoid of any theory sensitive to larger macro-structural dynamics becomes problematic for conceptualizing marijuana. The problem therefore rests on a lack of theory and focus, an explication to which this analysis now dedicates itself.

Moving Toward a Criminological Imagination: Steering Criminology Away from an Atheoretical Iceberg

Criminology tends to have a predilection towards quantitative regressional analyses that are plagued by a poverty of theory and, when theory is in place, it is often a kind of abstract empiricism incapable of addressing macro-structural, symbolic interactionist, or social constructionist matters. In other words, it often lacks what Young (2011b) describes as a "criminological imagination." As the apparent anti-sociality of marijuana seems to wane in light of its increasing public acceptance, marijuana represents a kind of moving target with which positivistic studies of marijuana struggle to grapple—becoming questionable or even obsolete shortly after publication.

For instance, take the study by Reingle et al. (2012) which "found that any use of marijuana during adolescence and young adulthood increases the risk of intimate partner violence" and concludes, "any marijuana use during adolescence nearly doubles the risk for intimate partner violence perpetration and both victimization and perpetration" (pp. 1571–1573). Perhaps implicitly hiding behind the excuse that it is simply a single regressional analysis, this study fails to incorporate even the slightest hint of sensitivity to the historical, political, and economic forces that have served to shape individuals' relationships with both inter-partner violence and marijuana use. Indeed, not even a citation hinting at such possibilities was given.

By not situating itself in an analytic manner sensitive to broader discursive shifts around marijuana, the associations between the substances and violence become reified. If more people begin consuming marijuana as it becomes increasingly acceptable, will marijuana use begin to lose its correlation with the anti-social behavior described? Perhaps not, but by not situating itself within its historic and social context—as Young (2011a) and C. Wright Mills (1959) advocate—the study risks sliding down a gradual slope into irrelevancy shortly after its publication.

Of course, the intrepid positivist may rally a defense against such criticisms, pointing out that regardless of the history of the substance, there are objective detrimental anti-social or physiological outcomes associated with substance use/abuse, marijuana included. As such, it does not matter how marijuana changes as a social problem because it can still be scrutinized as an empirically objective issue. Perhaps, the researcher may argue, if the marijuana were legalized/decriminalized and the underground market dissipated, the substance could still be understood as a social problem. While such claims have generally been problematic across the board with drugs, such assertions are particularly untenable regarding marijuana (Kappeler & Potter, 2005). For instance, there have been no reported overdoses on marijuana, a claim that cannot be made of regularly used over-the-counter medications, like aspirin (Kappeler & Potter, 2005). Indeed, most negative claims associated with marijuana—including brain damage, reproductive system damage, its status as a "gateway drug," its lethality, etc.—are problematic at best, and outright falsehoods at worst (refer to Kappeler & Potter, 2005, for more detail).

Of course, the orthodox criminologist may then assert that problem behaviors could still be associated with marijuana. Links between marijuana (and other drugs) and crime, however, still have yet to elevate themselves above the level of association (Kappeler & Potter, 2005). Indeed, "the only drug for which a clear causal link with crime has been established is alcohol—a drug that is legal" (Kappeler & Potter, 2005). In fact, the substances themselves—including marijuana—are far less problematic than the laws which seek to regulate them, breeding illegal markets and associated violence as buyers and sellers must compete among each other in an underground economy away from the prying law enforcement eyes, having little alternative other than to take matters into their own hands when necessary (Kappeler & Potter, 2005). As Henry (1987) elaborates:

> It is important to recognize, then, that informal economies can be transformed by redefinition from activity that was previously no more than innocent trading into a criminal enterprise. Although some of the original substance of the activity may remain—in the case of the hidden economy the original substance is that of an intimate and associational network of exchange—this interpretation is publicly suppressed, and the illegality and corresponding avaricious motives are drawn out as the significant dimension (p. 142).

Any associations marijuana may have with crime, therefore, appear to be more of a product of *crime control efforts* (driven by the social construction and history underpinning the substance) rather than any real innate characteristics of pot itself.

Further still, not all informal economic transactions surrounding criminal activities are necessarily even avaricious and/or malicious. An example of an often more benign illicit, informal economic approach regarding drug-use is "stash dealing," where a recreational user pedals just enough to get a price reduction in her or his own use (Adler, 1993). Immersive qualitative research such as *Outsiders* (Becker, 1963) and *Wheeling and Dealing* (Adler, 1993) show the diversity of social relationships that can occur among users and distributors of prohibited substances. Not every behavioral outcome associated with the informal economy of marijuana is inherently anti-social—a nuance lost in the oversimplification of orthodox criminology.

A criminology that clings to the idea of marijuana as an agent of anti-social behavior finds itself in a curious position. At the same moment that it asserts overly simplistic correlations between marijuana use and alleged problem behavior, it runs against evidence to the contrary as well as indications of greater social ills wrought by its stigmatization/criminalization. We contend that to continue considering pot a kind of anti-social substance means that mainstream criminology then seems to be considering any pleasurable activity beyond going to a sock hop and getting a drink from a soda shop as somehow anti-social or otherwise problematic. This is a criminology of prohibition—and prohibition, particularly against culturally enshrined behaviors, traditionally creates more problems than it solves. In addition, this is a criminology that upholds socially constructed perceptions of marijuana while simultaneously obscuring the nuance and complexity found within social relations among participants in such informal economies (see: Becker, 1963; Adler, 1993). The result is that one hand points toward a particular perspective on marijuana while the other blocks alternatives from sight.

Having articulated that criminology should avoid the de facto assumption that marijuana use is a problem behavior seemingly *because* it is a mind-altering substance and has been prohibited, we now turn to the argument that the perspective best adopted by criminology is one attuned to its socio-cultural, historical, and political economic context.

Marijuana and Moral Panics: Jump-Starting the Criminological Imagination

Considering the detrimental potential of abstract empiricism to detach both theory and methods from the phenomena it claims to examine—mainstream criminology would benefit from a little criminological imagination and reinvesting itself in the theoretical core sensitive to social changes and symbolic nuances. To this end we argue how culture and perceptions of marijuana have changed over time. Culture, as a conceptual apparatus, has changed in the decades since Becker's (1963) work in *Outsiders.* These alterations have largely arisen out necessity to account for the collapsing of space and time through new media and communication technologies, which have augmented the social landscape. Scholars have argued that these changes have emerged at least partially as a result of neo-liberal governance and geopolitical strategies as contemporary mechanisms have contributed to the restoration of class power through global media networks (Harvey, 2006; Ferrell, Hayward, & Young, 2008; Hayward, 2012; Cohen, 2011; Young, 2011a). Cultural impulses, as well as corporate culture industries, are amazingly elastic systems networked through modern technology. The end results are massively diverse and rapid systems of cultural generation, remediation, commodification, and consumption. These are the funhouse mirrors in which crime, deviance, and crime control take shape—their images becoming warped and distorted (Ferrell, Hayward, & Young, 2008). These are the mechanisms that mill the political rhetoric and image of marijuana.

To make sense of this tumultuous setting, we turn to one of the most influential theoretical bodies of thought surrounding the construction of crime and crime control, Cohen's (1972; 2011) moral panic theory. After describing the details of moral panic theory, we then elaborate on additional insights borrowed from cultural criminology regarding cultural transmission and mediation in late modernity.

Moral Panic Theory

While the "labeling perspective" advanced by Becker (1963) has been invaluable for understanding the conflicts underpinning the creation of a social "problem," Becker's emphasis was on the symbolic interactionist level of analysis. Arguing that broader social structural dynamics are at work beyond those indicated by Becker, we now turn toward Cohen's (1972) moral panic theory. In particular, we look at moral panic theory in the broader context of cultural criminology, an emergent area of critical criminology influenced heavily by phenomenology, symbolic interactionism, radical criminology, and perspectives on late modernity. Connecting the historical, social, and cultural geographies of state control are rooted micro-sensitivities and critical structural awareness—never far from material conditions. Cultural criminologists Ferrell, Hayward, and Young (2008), heavily influenced by Cohen's work, explain that moral panic theory extends Becker's labeling approach as it helps to make sense out of what is described as "ill conceived and irrational reactions to deviance by authorities and the wider public" (Ferrell, Hayward, & Young, 2008, p. 47). Before using the insights of cultural criminology to explain how moral panics operate in late modernity, a brief overview of moral panic theory as articulated by Cohen and his predecessors is provided.

A moral panic arises when an event—often of little consequence—occurs and is subsequently reported and exaggerated by the mass media (Ferrell, Hayward, & Young, 2008). These reports connect such events to an often marginalized population, thus constructing the group as dangerous to the moral order in the public imagination; they are transformed into *folk devils*. The presence of such folk devils then encourages denigration of the marginalized population believed to be responsible for the assaults on common decency, often leading to knee-jerk reaction policies to address the perceived problem (Ferrell, Hayward, & Young, 2008). These panics seem to occur in times of social instability where the "searchlight of panic and *ressentiment* scours the social structure for cases of faux injustice and springboards of moral outrage" (Young, 2011b, p. 256). These morals outrages often and arguably drive political wills and contribute toward a treadmill-like production of social control.

The origins of the concept are often attributed to Stan Cohen's (1972) *Folk Devils and Moral Panics* where he examined the creation of the mods and rockers into *folk devils*, a process stemming from social anxiety (mis)directed towards populations which allow for people to cast their concerns outward—thus rendering these groups as somehow the sole groups responsible for the erosion and degradation of the moral order.[5] These perceptions then trigger social reactions, often in the form of calls for crime control, which are often disproportionate to the actual (if any) threat posed. In this way, the social terror over marijuana qualifies as a moral panic because it triggered a response grossly disproportionate to any real hazard presented by the substance. In this manner, the reactions are said to be *irrational* in that they fail to address the actual underlying problem. For instance, when marijuana was demonized amidst panics such as *reefer madness,* the panic was underpinned by broader social concerns stemming from racism and social insecurity (Becker, 1963). Moral panics also require the creation or presentation of a negative deviant other—a person that society most certainly *does not want to be or become.* Marijuana users were cast as sexual and violent deviants, with these connotations often being attached to marginalized racial/ethnic others. Young (2011b), reflecting on his early days as a budding academic, encapsulates all of these dynamics around marijuana in the 1960s succinctly:

> I was fascinated by the nascent hippie culture, the interface of bohemian, West Indian and ne'er-do-well life, the strange pantomime of police and drug users, the extraordinary venom, repulsion and attraction that such an innocuous drug like cannabis and such a quiescent subculture evoked (p. 146).

The 1960s counter-culture moved against racism, misogyny, classism, and imperial state power. Part of this counter-culture moved against inequality by engaging in the experimentation of previously denounced substances.

Marijuana is important to consider from a moral panic perspective because, its origins are firmly entrenched in tales of "reefer madness" and the projection of social fears onto marginalized populations. These social fears are often intentionally propagated by smear campaigns of social control. The effect has been enduring and, indeed, persists today in the same way that Garland (2007) describes moral panics generally:

> Moral panics often seem ephemeral but over time their cumulative effect can be to create social divisions and redistribute social status as

5. There is some contestation as to whether Stan Cohen or Jock Young came up with the concept of moral panic first (Jenks, 2011).

> well as building infrastructures of regulation and control that persist long after the initial episode has run its course (p. 16).

In this way, panics over the effects of marijuana—and subsequent panics over other substances—have helped erect massive ideological apparatuses surrounding substance use as well as the growth of the largest social control system ever erected: the American criminal justice system. These systems have continued to persist despite changing attitudes towards drug use, most notably marijuana, over the years. In this way, the moral panics have a permanency that outlasts the original panic—perhaps even becoming culturally enshrined within the agencies of the state.

Part of this persistence is a result of a stain the panic leaves on the cultural imagination of many in society; webs of meaning are created extending beyond the initial moral panic. The symbols of danger become connected to others. Marijuana, as a symbol, is connected to the eroding moral health of society and dangerous marginalized others. These meanings are then juxtaposed to the legitimation of various social control efforts. As the moral panic ebbs, many of these meanings and associations may persist, though their relational configurations may change over time. Such webs of meaning or discourses are often self-perpetuating, echoed, and amplified through various channels, notably media (Critcher, 2011).

Moral panics are also more likely to manifest in a culture oriented toward fear, into which late modern America has transformed over the course of the latter half of the twentieth century and into the twenty-first (Critcher, 2011). In a culture of fear, society becomes risk adverse as it looks for perceptibly blameworthy parties who threaten safety (Critcher, 2011). In the management of risk and the dangerous other, the culture of fear also encourages a reliance on experts and professionals to protect us, the "helpless victims likely to be traumatized by our exposure to harm" (Critcher, 2011, p. 265).

These messages of fear, risk, and professional protection are transmitted rapidly in our hyper-mediated society, through what cultural criminologists defines as "loops and spirals" through which collective endeavors are derived. Loops are:

> The saturation of social situations with representation and information suggests that the linear sequencing of meaning is now mostly lost, replaced by a doppelganger world where the ghosts of signification circle back to gaunt, and revive, that which they signify ... Importantly, this looping process suggests for us something more than Baudrillard's postmodern hyper-reality, his sense of an 'unreality' defined only by media images and cultural obfuscation. Quite the opposite: we

> mean to suggest a late modern world in which the gritty, on-the-ground reality of crime, violence, and everyday criminal justice is dangerously confounded with its own representation (Ferrell, Hayward, & Young, 2008, p. 130).

Many objects of moral panics are thrown into loops of signification, as part of the process of social construction, where the boundaries between reality and representation become blurry at best, indistinguishable at worst.

On the other hand, loops are seldom entirely recursive symbolic processes. Instead, these loops also tend to *spiral* as well. In this manner:

> ... the next loop of meaning never quite comes back around, instead moving on and away to new experiences and new perceptions, all the while echoing, or other times undermining, meanings and experiences already constructed. As with Cohen's mods and rockers, today's spirals of crime and culture continue to wind and unwind—only faster and more furiously (Ferrell, Hayward, & Young, 2008, p. 131).

This ability of moral panics to be carried forward through loops and spirals in late modernity is at least partially a function of what Virilio calls the "logic of speed" (Ferrell, Hayward, & Young, 2008, p. 129). Speed, according to Virilio (1986; 1991; as cited in Ferrell, Hayward, & Young, 2008), has a capacity to warp and distort phenomena; as meaning travels faster and space and time collapse on themselves, the loops and spirals of meaning spin tighter, faster, and more violently than before. Considering, for example, how fast a tweet or Facebook post can spread information and go "viral," facilitates an understanding of how fast the logic of perception moves in the technologies of our late modern existence.

It is our contention, then, that marijuana was packaged early in its genesis as a social phenomenon in a manner that cast it as a dangerous substance tied to dangerous people worthy of social control. Over time, the loops and spirals of crime signification have altered its meaning without ever entirely becoming untethered from this original framework. Marijuana now has become more socially acceptable but is also still linked in the social imaginary with marginalized others, ontological insecurities, or plain old fashioned xenophobia. Marijuana is often cast as a substance used by poor layabouts, slackers, and ne'er-do-wells. Pot is regularly seen smoked on the big screen by various racial/ethnic minority and marginalized groups. Even youth is inextricably connected to marijuana use symbolically as many users are portrayed as immature dimwits—ubiquitous examples being Cheech and Chong and *Animal House*, among others. Of course, marijuana has often been held as associated with youth subcultures but it is interesting how its effect is not to sort of *infantilize* individuals portrayed imbibing the substance.[6] Marijuana and drug culture generally is then also drawn into the consumer culture—marijuana is hip and edgy. Perhaps one could argue that over the past twenty years the "trustafarian" (white upper-middle-class) has become largely associated with casual and habitual marijuana use. Even further speculation may address how and why counter-culture has continued to embrace pot (i.e., the hit television series *Weeds*).

All the while, the well of meaning social control efforts have derived their legitimacy from has sprung a leak, with much of the meaning flowing into other areas. As a result, law and justice has less to draw from to justify mass sanctioning of marijuana users. But, some of the meaning has lingered, and old perceptions of marijuana as dangerous—a gateway drug that will pull a person into seedy social circles—persist. In this manner, the loops and spirals of mediated meaning in our society has generated conflicting and contradicting grounds for marijuana to remain banned. Its legitimacy is sustained seemingly only by sheer force of will as its symbolic contexts spirals onward and, seemingly, away.

What does this all mean for reefer? As marijuana was originally constructed as a dangerous substance because of the threat it poses to the moral order and its connections to racial others, the substance has taken on more complex dimensions through the loops and spirals of late modernity. It has taken on multiple popular connotations. On the one hand, many media depictions, common political rhetoric, and advocacy groups continue to insist marijuana is still a social bane. For example, the federal government's outspoken stance against marijuana is said to have played a large part in the failure of decriminalization in California in 2010 (Leon & Weitzer, 2014). Even if unintended, this is where we find many treatments of marijuana in mainstream criminology. While marijuana is no longer a problem because of its racial and moral associations *per se*, it has now been rejoined to other problem behaviors and seems to be assumed problematic on the basis of correlation. On the other hand, other media depictions, political rhetoric, and advocacy groups have crafted a counter-narrative of pot, which is equally symbolic in its connections to marijuana.

An important caveat to remember with the loops and spirals of moral panics is how fear can be dislodged through marijuana's symbolic connection with non-marginalized populations. For instance, recall that the federal govern-

---

6. For a more thorough discussion of culture, commodification, and infantilization, refer to Hayward (2012).

ment reduced its punitivity toward drugs, including marijuana, during the 1970s (Leon & Weitzer, 2014). This reduction was a partially a result of "increasing arrests of middle- and upper-class youths coupled with the interests of law enforcement agencies, seeking more efficient use of limited resources" (Leon & Weitzer, 2014, p. 195). While pragmatic concerns played a role, the association of marijuana with less *othered* groups seems to have made a difference. Currently, one of the reasons for the waning of fear associated with pot may be a result of media connections of pot with medical use and an increasing realization that *most* people have used marijuana, not just racial others, without a complete erosion of society.

Conclusion

So the question remains, how will criminology contribute to the policy directions and regulatory discourse of a possible legal marijuana future? We contend that a return to a more sociological-centered criminology would produce more lasting insights into fluid behaviors that, like marijuana, may change in legitimacy. Criminology needs to produce knowledge that will change with the social landscape. Ken Tunnell (2014) argues, "Stand out portions of *Outsiders* are the marihuana use and dance musicians chapters; the stuff of legend. Those four are as relevant today as they were when Becker was engaged in the research (ca. late 1940s and early 1950s)" (p. 189). Continuing with a myopic scope of analysis does not seem the most effective direction for moving criminology forward.

National arrest rates suggest that regardless of extensive efforts in "order maintenance," or proactive policing, pot's demand, use, and availability have increased for marijuana users nationwide. Conversely, while enforcement efforts have evolved and become more aggressive over the past forty years, marijuana remains the single highest substance for convictions, post arrest, in drug suppression. Consider this war on pot in spite of the fact that a majority of the US public, when polled, supports the decriminalization of marijuana.

A multi-level analytic approach seems most productive to understand the phenomenon of marijuana use and its future in the United States. A cultural approach seems to explain a more theoretically rich side of the social construction and criminalization of marijuana. On the other hand, a historically and materially aware structural perspective, such as moral panic theory, explains the erosion of propaganda perpetuated by smear campaigns and political will toward criminalization. What seems evident is that marijuana is a piece of the cultural fabric in modern American society. What is yet to be uncovered, politically, is whether we will continue to research marijuana as a *crime* or from a legal, social *deviancy* position? More specifically will contemporary criminology still be employed in fifty years like Becker's *Outsiders*? Backpedalling through decades of propaganda and the social construction of a substance as a crime means teasing through the threads of science, prejudice, and state-level rhetoric in order for the discipline of criminology to contribute anything meaningful toward the newly legal substance of marijuana. Since marijuana helped to grow the criminal justice apparatus, will the transition into a non-criminal substance leave criminology up in smoke? Perhaps a criminological imagination is exactly what will lead to timely and lasting knowledge as the social landscape evolves.

References

Adler, P. A. (1993). *Wheeling and dealing: An ethnography of an upper-level drug dealing and smuggling community* (2nd ed.). New York, NY: Columbia University Press.

Alexander, M. (2010). *The new Jim Crow: Mass incarceration in the age of colorblindness.* New York, NY: The New Press.

Barak, G., Leighton, P., & Flavin, J. (2010). *Class, race, gender, & crime: The social realities of justice in America* (3rd ed.). Lanham, MD: Rowman & Littlefield Publishers, Inc.

Becker, H. S. (1963). *Outsiders: Studies in the sociology of deviance.* New York, NY: The Free Press.

Beckett, K., Nyrop, K., Pfingst, L., & Bowen, M. (2005). Drug use, drug possession arrests, and the question of race: Lessons from Seattle. *Social Problems, 52,* 419–441.

Boggess, L. N., Perez, D. M., Cope, K., Root, C., & Stretesky, P. (2014). Do medical marijuana centers behave like locally undesirable land uses? Implication for the geography of health and environmental justice. *Urban Geography, 35*(3), 315–336.

Cerda, M., Wall, M., Keyes, K. M., Galea, S., & Hasin, D. (2012). Medical marijuana laws in 50 states: Investigating the relationship between state legalization of medical marijuana use, abuse and dependence. *Drug and Alcohol Dependence, 120,* 22–27.

Chu, D. C. (2012). The links between religiosity, childhood sexual abuse, and subsequent marijuana use. *International Journal of Offender Therapy and Comparative Criminology, 58*(9), 937–954.

Cohen, S. (1972). *Folk devils and moral panics.* Great Britain: MacGibbon and Kee Ltd.

Cohen, S. (2011). Whose side were we on? The undeclared politics of moral panic theory. *Crime Media Culture, 7*(3), 237–243.

Critcher, C. (2011). For a political economy of moral panics. *Crime Media Culture, 7*(3), 259–275.

Ferrell, J., Hayward, K., & Young, J. (2008). *Cultural criminology: An invitation*. Thousand Oaks, CA: Sage.

Garland, D. (2008). On the concept of moral panic. *Crime Media Culture, 4*(1), 9–30.

Gelman, A., Fagan, J., & Kiss, A. (2007). An analysis of the New York City Police Department's "Stop and Fisk" policy in context of claims of racial bias. *Journal of the American Statistical Association, 102*, 813–823.

Hayward, K. (2012). Pantomime justice: A cultural criminological analysis of 'life stage dissolution.' *Crime Media Culture, 8*(2), 213–229.

Henry, S. (1987). The political economy of informal economies. *Annals of the Academy of Political and Social Science, 493*, 137–153.

Inciardi, J. A. (2008) *The War on Drugs IV: The continuing saga of the mysteries and miseries of intoxication, addiction, crime, and public policy* (4th ed.). New York, NY: Pearson A & B.

Jenks, C. (2011). The context of an emergent and enduring concept. *Crime Media Culture, 7*(3), 229–236.

Kappeler, V. E., & Potter, G. W. (2005). *The mythology of crime and criminal justice* (4th ed.). Long Grove, IL: Waveland Press, Inc.

Kepple, N. J., & Freisthler, B. (2012). Exploring the ecological association between crime and medical marijuana dispensaries. *Journal of Studies on Alcohol and Drugs, 73*(4), 523–530.

Leon, K., & Weitzer, R. (2014). Legalizing recreational marijuana: Comparing ballot outcomes in four states. *Journal of Qualitative Criminal Justice & Criminology, 2*(2), 193–218.

Miller, R. N., & Kuhns, J. B. (2012). Exploring the impact of medical marijuana laws on the validity of self-reported marijuana use among juvenile arrestees over time. *Criminal Justice Policy Review, 23*(1), 40–66.

Mills, C. W. (1959). *The sociological imagination*. New York, NY: Oxford University Press.

Musto, D. F. (Ed.). (2002). *Drugs in America: A documentary history*. New York, NY: New York University Press.

Nguyen, H., & Reuter, P. (2012). How risky is marijuana possession? Considering the role of age, race, and gender. *Crime and Delinquency, 58*(6), 879–910.

Reingle, J. M., Staras, S. A. S., Jennings, W. G., Branchini, J., & Maldonado-Molina, M. M. (2012). The relationship between marijuana use and intimate partner violence in a nationally representative, longitudinal sample. *Journal of Interpersonal Violence, 27*(8), 1562–1578.

Terry-McElrath, Y. M., Chriqui, J. F., Bates, H., & McBride, D. C. (2014). Do state policies matter in prosecutor-reported juvenile marijuana case disposition? *Crime & Delinquency, 60*(3), 402–426.

Terry-McElrath, Y. M., McBride, D. C., Chriqui, J. F., O'Malley, P. M., VanderWaal, C. J., Chaloupka, F. J., & Johnston, L. D. (2009). Evidence for connections between prosecutor-reported marijuana case dispositions and community youth marijuana-related attitudes and behaviors. *Crime & Delinquency, 55*(4), 600–626.

Tonry, M. (2011). *Punishing race: A continuing American dilemma.* New York, NY: Oxford University Press.

Tunnell, K. (2014). Historical book review: Howard S. Becker, *Outsiders: Studies in the sociology of deviance. Journal of Qualitative Criminal Justice and Criminology, 2*(1), 184–192.

Vickovic, S. G., & Fradella, H. F. (2011). Medical marijuana in the news. *The Southwest Journal of Criminal Justice, 8*(1), 67–96.

Virilio, P. (1986). *Speed and politics.* New York, NY: Semiotext(e).

Virilio, P. (1991). *The aesthetics of disappearance.* New York, NY: Semiotext(e).

West, D. P. (1998). Hemp and marijuana: Myths and realities. Retrieved from www.naihc.org/hemp_information/content/hemp.mj.html.

Whitesides, J. (2012, December 5). Majority of Americans support legalizing marijuana: poll. *Chicago Tribune News.*

Young, J. (2011a). Moral panics and the transgressive other. *Crime Media Culture, 7*(3), 245–258.

Young, J. (2011b). *The criminological imagination.* Malden, MA: Polity.

Zeese, K. B. (1999). History of medical marijuana policy in US. *International Journal of Drug Policy, 10*, 319–328.

3

Decriminalization of Cannabis in Portugal, Uruguay, and the Netherlands: Lessons Learned

Brooke Shannon

This chapter begins with an overview of the decriminalization of marijuana in three countries: Uruguay, the Netherlands, and Portugal. The overview also includes a discussion of the major challenges and facilitators of implementing the drug policy in each country. The chapter concludes with lessons learned for each country that might be applied to decriminalization efforts in the United States.

Background

Each of these countries was chosen because of their unique experiences and policy choices to decriminalize cannabis. Decriminalization of cannabis is a practice that recognizes cannabis as illegal while also establishing clear guidelines for the use, possession, cultivation, and distribution of the drug as well as how the criminal justice system will address these issues. Legalization is an alternative concept that would allow some aspect of use, possession, cultivation, and distribution of the drug to the free market and outside the purview of the criminal justice system.

Country Case Studies

Portugal

In 1998, the government of Portugal appointed the National Commission for the National Strategy to Combat Drugs. The commission issued a report recommending policy changes in many different areas. One policy area recommendation was to decriminalize personal use, possession, and acquisition of all illegal drugs. Personal use was defined as up to a ten-day supply of the substance. Criminal penalties would still be imposed on growers, dealers, and traffickers. The report was approved in parliament and became the framework for the 1999 National Strategy for the Fight Against Drugs. The legislation went into effect in July of 2001.

The goal of the legislation was two-fold. First, the commission wanted to shift the focus of legislation from criminal penalties to regulation. Second, they wanted to focus law enforcement efforts on traffickers and distributors rather than personal users. These shifts stemmed from a humanistic philosophy of dealing with drug users that would help rehabilitate addicts and a pragmatic approach that would reallocate government resources to areas that mitigate the more socially destructive criminal activity (Moreira, Trigueiros, & Antunes, 2007).

Prior to the 2001 legislation and according to Decree-Law 15/93, the courts could impose a fine or a sentence of up to three months for the possession of a List I substance, which included marijuana (EMCDDA, 2011). The sentence could be as long as a year if the amount was more than a three-day supply. Decree-Law 15/93 differentiated the occasional user, for whom the penalty could be waived, from an addict, who could be sentenced to treatment rather than imprisonment.

As with previous legislation, the new law framed trafficking as a more socially destructive offense as evidenced by the penalties for trafficking of List I substances being greater than for personal use. For example, trafficking could result in imprisonment for a range of four to twelve years; however, imprisonment could be reduced to between one and five years if the crime was considered "traffic of minor importance," which takes into consideration circumstances, modalities of the crime, quantity of the substance, and nature of the substance (Article 25). This clause allowed for greater flexibility when determining what is best for both the individual and society. Finally, the law also allowed for a reduced sentence of three years or fewer if the trafficker sold drugs "to finance their own consumption." Again, this considers the individual's personal situation, specifically, the state of addiction.

In practice, when a law enforcement officer finds a person to be in possession of marijuana, the officer must determine if the type of use seems to be occasional or dependent, or in other words, recreational use versus addictive use. The law officer can then fine an occasional user, and conversely refer a dependent user for treatment. The type of treatment is decided by a local, district Commission for the Dissuasion of Drug Addiction (CDT), comprised of a panel of three people: a legal advisor appointed by the Ministry of Justice, and two other members with a social services or medical background (e.g., psychologist, physician, social worker) appointed jointly by the Minister of Health and governmental coordinator of drug policy (Greenwald, 2009). Within 72 hours of the infraction, the CDT meets with the offender, evaluates the individual's circumstances, and recommends an appropriate sanction or treatment and rehabilitation plan. In response to occasional users, the CDT may issue a sanction, such as community service or a fine. Those considered dependent users are offered a treatment and rehabilitation plan. If the dependent user completes the treatment without further infraction, then they incur no criminal charges. If the dependent user recommits a violation or offense of the drug law or does not complete the prescribed treatment program, they can again be charged with the full sentence and penalties recommended by the law.

To implement the law, Hughes and Stevens (2007) pointed out several areas of institutional change which occurred within the Portuguese system. The leading change was the establishment of CDTs in each of Portugal's 18 regions to handle referrals. Between July 2001 and October 2007, these CDTs handled over 520 cases per month, 62% of which involved cannabis. A second institutional change was the addition of a central support department created to help support the CDTs and maintain records. Also, more treatment and rehabilitation programs were established to provide support to dependent users. Drug awareness and addiction prevention programs within schools additionally increased. Finally, law enforcement agencies refocused their efforts on disruption of trafficking operations rather than targeting or enforcement efforts focused on individual drug users.

Measuring the impact of the law is difficult because surveys were not administered before decriminalization; however, Hughes and Stevens (2007) suggested that since 2001 in Portugal, there has been an increased use of cannabis, a decreased use of heroin, an increased uptake of treatment, and an overall reduction in drug-related deaths. Greenwald (2009) found that overall drug use has declined, and the percentage of addicts seeking and receiving treatment doubled between 2001 and 2007. If treatment of addiction is the goal, then this finding is a positive indicator of success. Such findings led Greenwald to claim that decriminalization "has enabled the Portuguese government to manage and control the drug problem far better than virtually every other Western country does" (Szalavitz, 2009).

Importantly, Hughes and Stevens argued that the shift in drug policy provided some relief to an over-burdened criminal justice system. For example, the number of people charged with drug consumption significantly decreased from 7,597 criminal charges in 2000 to 6,026 administrative referrals in 2002, a 20% decrease. Furthermore, the number of drug-offence sentences declined by 28% in the four years following decriminalization.

Since implementing the new drug law, Portugal has faced several challenges. Hughes and Stevens (2007) explained that implementation has varied across districts. For the law to be effective in practice, CDTs, police departments, and health sectors needed to coordinate their efforts across district borders and jurisdictions. Delays in training and the lack of an effective communication strategy that articulate the differences between decriminalization and legalization are two results of the lack of coordination that districts have experienced.

Adding to the challenge, Greenwald (2009) observed that police officers were conflicted due to a perceived futility of the new enforcement strategy. In some cases, officers stopped issuing citations because they continue to apprehend or encounter the same offenders. Other officers embraced the new strategy and more enthusiastically issued citations due to their belief in the treatment and rehabilitation programs as a more effective solution. Essentially, this philosophical difference that motivated varying citation practices among law enforcement officers made pre- and post-comparisons difficult (Greenwald, 2009). Without such comparisons of data, identifying the most effective practices and rehabilitation resources remains difficult to categorize or assess.

In addition, the prioritization of funding throughout the life of the program may have falsely represented the importance of the law. Specifically, funding was greater in the beginning and then trickled off as the program progressed. This gave the generalized perception within the public that the overall objective declined in importance or did not achieve the desired impact or end state (Hughes & Stevens, 2007). This point cannot be totally separated from another challenge, which is that if the implementation strategy is to have a chance to be successful, then more national resources must be allocated and funneled to prevention and treatment programs or options. Essentially, Portugal's new drug strategy did not necessarily reduce the overall strain on national resources; it actually created more resource-dependent programs in new sectors.

Uruguay

In Uruguay, cannabis has been legal since 2013, although the law has not been fully implemented. The primary purpose of the current drug law, Decree-Law No. 19.172, is harm reduction. As stated in the legislation, the Government of Uruguay believes "that it is in the public interest to protect, promote and improve the health of the general population through policies oriented towards minimizing the risks and reducing the harm of cannabis use, which promote accurate information, education and prevention of the consequences and damaging effects associated with its consumption as well as the treatment, rehabilitation, and social reintegration of problematic drug users" (Article 1).

The legislation is the result of a presidential and congressional proposal (Faubion, 2013). With the introduction of this new law, the state assumes all responsibility for regulating the cannabis industry in Uruguay, including all "importing, exporting, planting, cultivating, harvesting, producing, acquiring under any title, storing, commercializing, and distributing cannabis or its derivatives, or hemp in corresponding circumstances" (Article 2). A few exceptions are noted. For example, the Ministry of Public Health is still in control of planting and cultivating cannabis specifically for use in scientific research.

One issue the new law addresses is possession for personal consumption. Personal consumption of marijuana has always been tolerated in Uruguay; however, previous drug laws, such as Decree-Law No. 14.294 instituted on October 31, 1974, and Decree-Law No. 17.016 passed in 1998, did not specify what amount constituted personal consumption (Faubion, 2013). Therefore, the judge was responsible for subjectively determining what amount was considered for personal use and what amount was considered as trafficking. The new law states that "the quantity intended for personal use will not exceed 40 grams of marijuana" (Article 7).

Another complication that arose and caused modification of the law was that, although personal use is legal, any cultivation is still deemed illegal. This, as Faubian (2013, p. 2) explains, "is a tenuous position difficult to explain or justify." Two paragraphs in the legislation address cultivation for personal consumption. Article 5 (para. E.) defines cultivation for shared domestic consumption as "up to six psychoactive cannabis plants and their resulting yield, up to a maximum of 480 grams" (Article 5, para. E). The same article also allows marijuana membership clubs, which may have between fifteen and forty-five associates, to "plant a maximum of ninety-nine psychoactive plants and acquire as a product of their cultivation a maximum yield proportional to the number of associates" (Article 5, para. F.) Clarifying both personal consumption and the amount of cannabis that is allowed to be cultivated for personal consumption has resolved the discrepancy between illegal cultivation and legalized personal use. Competent judges are responsible for determining what is considered illegal personal consumption, cultivation, selling, or trafficking.

The legislation also created a new regulatory body, the Institute for Regulation and Control of Cannabis (IRCAA). Its responsibilities are outlined in articles 27–28. The IRCAA monitors compliance of membership clubs and domestic cultivation. They also grant licenses to private entities, such as pharmacies, for distribution. The IRCAA determines whether or not violations have occurred and can issues penalties, give warnings, confiscate or destroy material, disqualify a licensee or member, or even close the establishment (Article 40).

The legislation has distributed other duties to relevant bodies. For example, the National Integrated Health System (SNIS) assumes the role of preparing policies and strategies to promote public health and devising an "adequate mechanism for the assistance, guidance and treatment of problematic cannabis users who may require it" (Article 9, para. 1). In cities of more than 10,000, the National Drug Council (JND) oversees the "management, administration and operation" of various mechanisms "established to provide information, counseling, diagnosis, referral, care, rehabilitation, and treatment and social reinsertion of problematic drug users" (Article 9, para. 2). The JND is also responsible for public outreach and awareness campaigns for the general population (Article 12).

Another important facet of the legislation is that addressing educational programs aimed at children and youth. The National Public Education System (SNEP) is charged with preparing education policy that focuses health promotion and reduction of problematic usage of cannabis (Article 10). The SNEP is in charge of implementing relevant policies and programs in primary, secondary, and vocational schools.

A primary challenge facing implementation of the new drug law is the creation of a new regulatory body, the IRCAA. The IRCAA is a non-governmental body that is administratively controlled by the executive branch through the Ministry of Public Health. It obtains funds through fees charged for licenses and permits, inheritances and donations, title funds, and fines and sanctions (Article 32). The drug industry in Uruguay is huge, generating about 75 million dollars annually, with a bureaucracy comparable in size to that of an airline or the power industry (Faubion, 2013). This simply means that function and efficiency must be carefully balanced to achieve any effective outcomes.

Perhaps, the greatest facilitator of the new law has been government buy-in from multiple political parties, including presidential buy-in. South American leaders realize that the US model has not been successful and that they must find a new methods or approaches to drug control, trafficking, and abatement. For example, the government of Uruguay was quite aware of and in agreement on the need to respond to the alarming rise in violent crime associated with drug trafficking activities (Padgett, 2012). Ultimately, Uruguay was losing their war on drugs—consumption was increasing, drug seizures were not curbing drug use, little to no emphasis had been placed on demand, investment in the "war" had diverted much-needed funds away social services, and the trafficking business as a criminal enterprise was too lucrative of a business to deter criminal entrepreneurs (Faubion, 2013). A new strategy, even if experimental, was needed.

The Netherlands

The Netherlands' first drug law, the Opium Act, was enacted in 1919. This law satisfied the terms of the 1912 International Opium Convention, which was signed by the Netherlands, 11 other nations, and several British territories. This convention was the first international drug law and focused specifically on the regulation of opium, morphine, cocaine, and heroin (UNODC, 2014). In 1919, the convention was incorporated into the Treaty of Versailles and, therefore, gained much wider acceptance.

The Opium Act of 1919 was first amended in 1928, and this prohibited all psychotropic drugs, including cannabis (Leuw, 1991). In 1976, the law was amended to separate hard and soft drugs. One of the primary changes included distinguishing between hard drugs, such as heroin, which posed "unacceptable risks," and soft drugs, such as cannabis (Leuw, 1991). This distinction was recommended by a governmental report prepared by the Working Group on Narcotic Drugs, or the Baan Commission.

Similar to Portugal and Uruguay, the drug law is based on harm reduction and takes a pragmatic, humanistic approach to drugs (Leuw, 1991). Grapendaal, Leuw, and Nelen (1995) summarize the law: the central aim of the law is the prevention or alleviation of social and individual risks caused by drug use; there must be a rational relation between those risks and policy measures; a differentiation of policy measures that take into account the risks of legal recreational and medical drugs; repressive measures against drug trafficking (other than trafficking of cannabis) as a priority; and the inadequacy of criminal law with respect to other aspects (i.e., apart from trafficking) of the drug problem must be recognized. Overall, the policy is considered a "normalization" policy. Drug use is considered a social problem, and Dutch law does not use criminal law to address social problems.

Possession of marijuana for personal use (five grams or fewer) is legally considered a minor offence but is not prosecuted. While cannabis use is not a crime, it is prohibited in certain contexts or venues, such as in schools or on public transportation.

Possession by "coffee shops" is a more serious offense that can be prosecuted if the coffee shops violate specific criteria: no more than five grams per person may be sold in any one transaction, coffee shops are not allowed to keep more than 500 grams of cannabis in stock, no hard drugs may be sold, drugs may not be advertised, coffee shops must not cause any public nuisance, coffee shops are not allowed to sell alcohol, drugs cannot be sold to minors (those under 18) nor may minors enter the premises, and, the maximum penalty for production and sale for personal consumption of more than 30 grams is 1 month imprisonment and/or a fine of 3,350 Euros. In 2007, the Opium Act was amended with the Democles Bill (Article 13b), which allowed local authorities to close both public and private premises used for the sale of illegal drugs. The tolerated sale of cannabis in coffee shops falls outside the scope of this article.

About 80% of the cannabis produced in the Netherlands is exported (MacCoun, 2010). In addition, most Dutch criminal organizations deal and traffic cannabis—and only cannabis (Laar, et al., 2013). The maximum penalty under Dutch law for importing or exporting any quantity of cannabis is 4 years of imprisonment and/or a fine of 67,000 Euros. The Dutch drug law does not explicitly mention "trade" as a punishable act. Although the penalties for import/export on the one hand and sale on the other are different, all these acts must be considered to constitute drug "trade."

In the Netherlands, criminal investigation and prosecution are founded on what is called the expediency principle. This means that prosecution authorities carry out prosecution only if it is expedient and is in the public's best interest. Prosecution of cannabis has not been viewed as serving the general interests of society because doing so might stigmatize and alienate the nation's youth (Korf, 2008). Under this same principle, many distributers also have not faced prosecution as long as the dealer met the following criteria: no overt advertising, no hard drugs, no nuisance, no underage clientele, and no large quantities. A common practice that emerged under these guidelines was the establishment of "coffee shops," or café-like cannabis shops. Licensing regulations were introduced in the 1990s and resulted in the closing of an estimated 50% of these shops, dropping from an estimated 1,500 in 2000 down to approximately 737 in 2004 (Korf, 2008); the actual number is difficult to gauge due to variations in regulation and enforcement efforts at the local level. Finally, the law granted local communities the authority to disallow coffee shops in their area, and a large majority of rural areas or local governments have chosen this option.

Two major challenges the Netherlands must address are complaints from local residents about noise violations caused by coffee shops and alleviating the worry of neighboring countries concerned about drug tourism and cross-border trafficking (MacCoun & Reuter, 2001). The former challenge was more easily addressed than the latter by tightening the regulations governing coffee shops. Of course, the issue remains complicated and confusing as the sale of cannabis at coffee shops is not actually legal. Satisfying neighboring countries affects international treaties, and many nations are on the verge of considering the Netherlands as a narco-state, a sponsor of soft drug use and sale; however, the Netherlands does not consider themselves in violation of any international treaties currently in effect (Korf, 2008). Instead, the Netherlands view their drug reform policy and efforts as necessary and exemplary acts that delineated the necessary separation of the hard and soft drug markets. To address concerns with drug tourism, the Netherlands introduced the resident criterion, which requires a coffee shops patron to provide proof of residency (Laar, et al., 2013). Implementation of the criterion is left up to local authorities and is practiced primarily in border regions. How long this measure will last or how it will continue to be implemented is questionable because residents are concerned about privacy issues.

Despite an inability to accurately assess whether or not the existing drug policy has been successful, Dutch authorities appear to have no intention of reversing the law or reverting to more strict regulations than those currently in effect (MacCoun & Reuter, 2001). Cannabis use varies widely across the nation, with the largest divergences being those in locale, especially those between urban and rural areas (MacCoun, 2011), as well as the demographics of users, primarily the use within certain age groups. Comparison of Dutch drug statistics to those of other nations is made difficult due to the use of different types of survey instruments (MacCoun & Reuter, 2001). No standard measure has been established by the international community or drug monitoring agencies that would allow easier identification of "best practices" by those nations enacting a variety of drug abatement or control legislation. Likewise, reaching an assessment on the reduction or prevention of harm caused by drug use, sale, and trafficking challenges statistical measurement efforts. Furthermore, whether or not Dutch policy has successfully separated the hard and soft drug markets is difficult to gauge (MacCoun, 2011). The very nature of the two markets and Dutch oversight of the soft drug market, and in particular, the coffee shops, will make it difficult to confirm or refute the resulting state of affairs.

What This Means for the US

Admittedly, legal, governmental, and social institutions in the US provide a framework that differs significantly from those of Portugal, Uruguay, and the Netherlands. Nonetheless, important lessons can be learned about translating a similar policy in the US.

Drug policies in each of these nations were the result of a failing War on Drugs. This same war is being lost in the US. Furthermore, the most detrimental type of drug in each of these countries was not cannabis; rather, "hard" drugs, like heroin and cocaine, were the issue. Addiction to these harder drugs is considered a disease in the case countries, yet, in the US, addiction is treated like a crime. The philosophical underpinning of each perspective is important. Portugal, Uruguay, and the Netherlands have adopted a humanistic, pragmatic approach to dealing with drug offenders. In contrast, the US has adopted a moralistic, puritan approach that dehumanizes, and even demonizes, addicts (Gray, 2012). The result is a zero-tolerance approach that alienates people, who are often youth, who need help and, if treated, might actually become functioning members of society. Instead, the US has criminalized their behavior, and addicts have become a constant strain on society and its resources.

One of the lessons learned from the Portuguese model has been that an effective communication strategy might help curb some difficulties encountered when implementing a new drug policy (Hughes & Stevens, 2007). First of all, drug policy discourse has evolved to include many concepts and legal terms that need to be clarified for the general public and relevant stakeholders, such as health officials, politicians, and law enforcement agents. For example, decriminalization does not mean legalization. Law enforcement agents must also know both their options in enforcing relevant policies and the impact of their enforcement options. Perhaps, greater understanding of the goals, options, and impact will result in greater coordination and positive attitudes among police officers and other coordinating bodies.

Identifying who plays what role in the strategy has been a major challenge for Portugal and Uruguay. For example, in Uruguay, the IRCAA, which reports to the executive branch through the Ministry of Public Health, has been charged with regulating the drug industry, a vast industry that Faubion (2013) has described to be as potentially bureaucratic as the airline industry. Likewise, Portugal's CDTs have become highly bureaucratic and inefficient (Hughes & Stevens, 2007). Even if the US establishes a new agency or incorporates this mission into an existing agency, such as the Drug Enforcement Agency, a high level of bureaucracy will inevitably be the case. As a result, coordinating resources to get help to dependents in a timely matter will be a challenge. Greater local autonomy for social and legal services seems ideal; however, this may not work in the US model when equity of services also has to be a priority.

Importantly, changing directions cannot necessarily be seen as a way to save resources. While the current strategy is likely wasting resources, more funding and the creation of alternative resources will have to be created to emphasize treatment and rehabilitation. This alternative approach might actually be more expensive; however, the return might be greater as addicts are rehabilitated and prepared to become employable and active members of society (Gray, 2012).

A vital part of drug prevention is educating US citizens. A national organization has to take the lead in developing an education policy that mandates drug awareness and prevention education into curriculum in primary, secondary, and vocational schools. In addition, a strategy must be developed for public outreach and awareness. Again, this curriculum and awareness campaign would need to complement the communication strategy implemented in training and coordination among health, governmental, and law enforcement personnel.

Finally, the US must have buy-in from neighboring countries. Any decriminalization of marijuana will affect neighboring countries. Mexico's President Mujica admits the global strategy to combat drugs has been an economic and moral failure (AFP, 2013). For example, he recognizes that "Uruguay, a small country with just 3.3 million people, spends upwards of $US80 million a year on combating drugs but seizes just $US4 million–$US5 million worth of contraband." In Mexico, the impact in number of lives lost and cost is as significant. Mr. Mujica is in favor of regulation, not legalization, and especially for stricter sentences for unregistered cultivators.

References

Agence France-Presse, (2013, August 7). Uruguay considers legalizing marijuana as 'experiment', says President Jose Mujica. Retrieved from http://www.news.com.au/world/uruguay-wants-to-legalise-marijuana-as-experiment-says-president-jose-mujica/story-fndir2ev-1226693125631.

EMCDDA. (2008). A cannabis reader: global issues and local experiences, Monograph series 8, Volume 1. Lisbon: European Monitoring Centre for Drugs and Drug Addiction. Retrieved from http://www.emcdda.europa.eu/html.cfm/index5174EN.html?pluginMethod=eldd.countryprofiles&country=NL.

EMCDDA. (2011). Drug policy profiles—Portugal. Lisbon: European Monitoring Centre for Drugs and Drug Addiction. Retrieved from http://www.emcdda.europa.eu/publications/drug-policy-profiles/portugal.

Faubion, J. (2013). Reevaluating drug policy: Uruguay's efforts to reform marijuana laws. *Law & Business Review of the Americas, 19*(3), 383–408.

Grapendaal, M., Leuw, E., & Nelen, H. (1995). *A world of opportunities: Lifestyle and economic behavior of heroin addicts in Amsterdam.* Albany, NY: State University of New York Press.

Gray, J. P. (2012). *Why our drug laws have failed and what we can do about it: A judicial indictment of the War on Drugs* (2nd ed.). Philadelphia, PA: Temple University Press.

Greenwald, G. (2009). Drug decriminalization in Portugal: Lessons for creating fair and successful drug policies. Washington, DC: Cato Institute.

International Opium Convention, (1912, January 23). 8 L.N.T.S. 187. Retrieved from https://treaties.un.org/doc/Publication/UNTS/LON/Volume%208/v8.pdf.

Korf, D. (2008). An open front door: The coffee shop phenomenon in the Netherlands. In S. R. Sznitman, B. Olsson, & R. Room (Eds.), *A cannabis reader: Global issues and local experiences.* Lisbon: European Monitoring Centre for Drugs and Drug Addiction.

Leuw, E. (1991). Drugs and drug policy in the Netherlands. *Crime and Justice,* 14, 229–276.

MacCoun, R. J., & Reuter, P. (2001). *Drug war heresies: Learning from other vices, times, and places.* New York, NY: Cambridge University Press.

MacCoun, R. J. (2010). What can we learn from the Dutch cannabis coffeeshop experience? (Working Paper No. WR-768-RC). Retrieved from RAND website: http://www.rand.org/content/dam/rand/pubs/working_papers/2010/RAND_WR768.pdf.

MacCoun, R. J. (2011). What can we learn from the Dutch cannabis coffeeshop experience? *Addiction, 106,* 1899–1910. doi: 10.111/j.1360-0443.2011.03572.x.

Moreira, M., Trigueiros, F., & Antunes, C. (2007). The evaluation of the Portuguese drug policy 1999–2004: The process and the impact on the new policy. *Drugs and Alcohol Today, 7*(2), 14–25.

Padgett, T. (2012, June 26). Uruguay's plan to legalize marijuana sales: Should the rest of the world follow? *Time.* Retrieved from http://world.time.com/2012/06/26/uruguay-wants-to-legalize-marijuana-sales-should-the-rest-of-the-world-follow/.

Szalavitz, M. (2009, April 26). Drugs in Portugal: Did decriminalization work? *Time.* Retrieved from http://content.time.com/time/health/article/0,8599,1893946,00.html.

United Nations Office on Drugs and Crime. (2014). The 1912 Hague International Opium Convention. Retrieved from http://www.unodc.org/unodc/en/frontpage/the-1912-hague-international-opium-convention.html.

van Laar, M., Cruts, G., Van Ooyen-Houben, M., Meije, D., Croes, E., Meijer, R., & Ketelaars, T. (2013). The Netherlands drug situation 2012: Report to the EMCDDA, Lisbon. Ultrecht: Reitox National Focal Point. Retrieved from http://www.emcdda.europa.eu/html.cfm/index213775EN.html.

4

Marijuana and the Media: Changes in Bias

Joshua B. Hill

Introduction

Given the recent political issues surrounding marijuana, it is unsurprising that it has become a frequently covered topic in the news. With the number of states now having legalized recreational use of marijuana rising to 4 (plus the District of Columbia) and the number of states now allowing medical use of marijuana standing at 23 (plus the District of Columbia), it is perhaps to be expected that the drug has been under scrutiny. Making the subject even more exciting to news organizations, the issues of federalism (elsewhere discussed in this book) and banking (also discussed in another chapter) have created a climate where newspapers and other media organizations can reliably use marijuana stories as leads.

Despite this deluge of legalization (in its various forms), there is still considerable debate within society about whether or not legalization is appropriate. Mass media, and in particular, those media elements that reach a large and politically involved audience, have waded into this debate regularly. In particular, since the vote to legalize recreational pot use in Washington and Colorado, there have been a set of stories that examine the potential downsides of marijuana usage.

One example of this type of story was Maureen Dowd's unique coverage, which involved her trying THC-laced edibles in Colorado. She accidentally ingested nearly six times the recommended dosage, and wrote about her experience for the *New York Times*, in largely negative terms, describing her hallucinations and paranoia (Dowd, 2014). Significantly, this type of media coverage in the mainstream would have been simply impossible prior to the passage of the legalization initiative. Also importantly, Dowd's piece was not the only negative depiction of marijuana to surface subsequent to the legalization of recreational use.

Given the potential impacts of media coverage on public opinion, examination of media coverage of issues surrounding marijuana use and legalization are important. In a 2011 article, Vickovic and Fradella examine the coverage, finding that, generally speaking, coverage in the years 2008 and 2009 was positive. However, given the large number of states that have recently legalized marijuana usage, it is appropriate to revisit that finding and examine whether or not coverage has remained positive.

This study builds on the work of Vickovic and Fradella (2011) by both bringing the analysis up to date, as well as examining changes in the tone and content of the articles after the passage of pro-marijuana policies in Oregon and Colorado. Additionally, it broadens the scope of the original article by examining not just medical marijuana, but all forms of marijuana legalization.

Literature Review

The history of marijuana is elsewhere accounted for in this book, so there is little need to rehash it. It does bear repeating, however, that the history of how marijuana has been depicted in the media has been contentious (Musto, 2002). From the early reports by the Federal Bureau of Narcotics and the widely distributed movie *Reefer Madness*, there was a significant negative bias in the media presented to the public regarding marijuana use (Marshall, 2005). The depictions in this early media were specifically used to instill fear in the public over marijuana use. Henry Ainslinger, the Commissioner of the Federal Bureau of Narcotics, was a major figure in prohibition and penned several reports maligning marijuana as likely to cause psychological breaks and even suggested the drug would cause suicide (Ainslinger & Cooper, 1937).

The negative portrayal was not the only image found in the media, however. By the late 1960s, marijuana had moved from an illicit substance associated with minority use (Bertran, Blachman, & Sharpe, 1996) to a significant part of the counter-culture movement (Bonnie & Whitebread, 1974; Matthew, 2009). This demographic shift was not only played out in terms of the use of marijuana, but was also played out in the context of the media—with public depictions of marijuana increasing and the figures associating with it changing (McEwen & Hanneman, 1974).

This positive shift in general public perception was actively combatted by the government. Beginning with the Controlled Substance Act of 1970 (CSA), there was an active attempt by various presidential administrations to control the public narrative about marijuana. For instance, in 1973 President Nixon indicated in a radio address regarding drug abuse and law enforcement that he

> "... oppos[ed] the legalization of the sale, possession, or use of marijuana. The line against the use of dangerous drugs I now draw on this side of marijuana. If we move the line to the other side and accept the use of this drug, how can we draw the line against other illegal drugs? Or will we slide into an acceptance of their use as well? My administration has carefully weighed this matter ... there must continue to be criminal sanctions against the possession, sale, or use of marijuana" (Nixon, 1983).

This narrative from the government was, however, inconsistent. In 1977, President Carter called for decriminalization, but suffered politically for that call (Marshall, 2005). Additionally, states began to act to decriminalize marijuana, with 12 states having done so by 1978 (Vickovic & Fradella, 2011).

This depiction of marijuana as linked to other drugs was solidified as the government began its drug war in the 1980s under President Reagan (Benavie, 2009). The development and continuation of the War on Drugs was the occasion for a great deal of media originating from the government, especially in terms of presidential speech (Hill, Oliver, & Marion, 2012). By the turn of the twentieth century, the media campaigns mounted by the government had shifted. The National Youth Anti-Drug Media Campaign, funding by the Office of National Drug Control Policy (ONDCP) represents an attempt to directly target youth in order to reduce drug use (Southworth, 2004). The ads specifically targeted marijuana and were shown across all major network news channels. Similar public service announcements are familiar to many, including the now infamous "this is your brain on drugs" image of a fried egg.

More recent examinations have focused on the changing narrative behind marijuana coverage, focusing specifically on medicalization. Indeed, there is good reason to believe that the recent rash of states that have decriminalized medical use of marijuana have impacted the type of coverage the media has given the overall topic of marijuana usage (Leon & Weitzer, 2014). This change in framing has potentially had important effects on subsequent coverage of marijuana use, as well as potentially impacting the public agenda.

While the government was using mass media markets to attempt to influence viewers regarding marijuana usage, there was also continuous coverage of marijuana in the news media. In a 2003 study examining media coverage regarding marijuana and its potential impact on adolescent marijuana usage,

Stryker found that there was support for the idea that news coverage directly affects marijuana usage. Specifically, she found that the type of coverage mattered; in cases where aggregate news coverage was negative, marijuana use among adolescents went down. In addition, the study found that the marijuana coverage partially explained the beliefs adolescents had regarding marijuana (Stryker, 2003).

Stryker's (2003) finding is somewhat unsurprising given what we know about the media's impact on public perception of drugs. Hill, Oliver, and Marion (2012) found that the relationship between the public and the president was mediated by the media when it came to the topic of drugs. Additionally, other studies (Whitford & Yates, 2011) have examined the impact of media, not directly on use, but on politicians and the public agenda. These findings tend to support the importance of media as a factor in determining how public policy is developed, even if it is not the only cause.

It is therefore particularly important to determine how the media is framing marijuana as it impacts both the use of marijuana (Stryker, 2003) as well as the public perception of marijuana (Hill, Oliver, & Marion, 2012). Moreover, we know that the media helps determine the public agenda (Whitford & Yates, 2011), making the question of how marijuana is portrayed even more significant. This chapter, therefore, attempts to fill a gap in the literature by comparing the tone and content of media coverage before and after the passage of Washington and Colorado's legalization initiatives.

Methods

In order to examine the question of national media coverage of marijuana both before and after the decriminalization of recreational use in Washington and Colorado, articles from the *New York Times* were analyzed using content analysis. The sampling period was from 2011–2015. A Lexis-Nexus search was conducted using the term "marijuana" with the source limited to the *Times*. A total of 228 articles were identified with marijuana appearing in the title. These were in various sections of the paper, including the op-ed sections.

The content of the articles selected was examined in terms of two major characteristics. The first of these, themes, was determined by examining each article's contents, and identifying the major approach to marijuana within the article. These individual article themes were then grouped topically to identify any larger themes within the dataset. The second characteristic examined was the tone of coverage. This was assessed by examining the content of the article in terms of arguments made for the use of marijuana or against it, or a third category was possible if the article was neutral.

In addition to those characteristics coded for in the content analysis, the article date is relevant in terms of whether or not themes or tone change before and after the passage of the Colorado and Washington initiatives. These were considered important because they were widely covered by the mass media, and so the passage of the Washington initiative was considered an appropriate place to split the dataset for comparison. Also coded was the type of article—news or opinion (with opinion consisting of op-ed pieces and *Times* official blog posts).

Results

As mentioned above, there were a total of 228 articles examined. The range of topics and types of coverage was fairly broad, although the themes were generally consistent within categories (explored more fully below). In table 1, below, the total number of articles by type is presented. The themes and tones identified will be discussed first in total, and then examined in relation to the time before the passage of Washington's recreational marijuana initiative and after.

Overall Themes

There were a number of themes identified across the complete dataset, with several overlapping themes in terms of the news pieces and opinion pieces. In total there were nine themes identified, and they tended to be similar across article types (news or opinion). The themes identified were: athletes/celebrity coverage, marijuana business, federalism/interjurisdictional conflict, marijuana and children, medical marijuana, other (which was used when there was only one article with a theme), policing and marijuana, the politics of marijuana, pot tourism, and the War on Drugs. The complete count of articles by type and theme can be seen in Table 1, on the next page.

By far the most numerous of the themes identified was the politics of marijuana, dominating in terms of numbers in both the news articles and opinion articles. Next most frequent in terms of overall numbers were articles that focused on the business elements of marijuana, though these tended to be more prevalent in news articles rather than opinion pieces. Following business articles was articles on policing and marijuana. These articles tended to be about issues of policing (e.g., sentencing, targeting, profiling) that dealt directly with marijuana enforcement. Next most numerous were articles focused

Table 1. Type, Number, and Dominant Themes of *New York Times* Articles

Article Type	Total Number	Dominant Themes	Number within Theme
News	168	Athletes/Celebrity Coverage	12
		Marijuana Business	27
		Federalism/ Interjurisdictional Conflict	20
		Marijuana and Children	11
		Medical Marijuana	14
		Other	13
		Policing and Marijuana	20
		Politics of Marijuana	43
		Pot Tourism	2
		War on Drugs	5
Opinion	60	Business	3
		Federalism/ Interjurisdictional Conflict	6
		Marijuana and Children	4
		Medical Marijuana	10
		Other	8
		Policing and Marijuana	8
		Politics of Marijuana	18
		War on Drugs	2

on federalism and interjurisdictional conflict. These were generally centered around cities and states challenging federal enforcement efforts, but there were many conflicts reported on regarding municipalities fighting states that had legalized as well. Medical marijuana issues were the next most frequently covered, followed by the other category athletes and celebrity coverage, the War on Drugs (which focused on the overall efforts to deal with drugs, not necessarily police enforcement), and pot tourism.

The breadth of the topics covered in terms of marijuana is rather large, and somewhat interesting in terms of the generality. Much of the political coverage was focused on the campaigns to legalize marijuana in Colorado and Washington, but nearly as much was focused on efforts getting underway in other states, and internecine battles of politicians. Headlines like, "Marijuana Referendum Divides Both Sides," and "A Call to Shift Policy on Marijuana" were common, as was coverage of pronouncements regarding marijuana from politicians from a variety of backgrounds and states. Interesting too was the coverage of the issues of federalism raised by legalization (elsewhere ably covered by Will Oliver in this text).

Overall, the coverage matched well what other observers have documented with many of the categories being observed by others (Vickovic & Fradella, 2011). There were some unique elements in the current dataset (notably the coverage of celebrities regarding marijuana usage) that might be attributed to the method of search (this article examines marijuana in general, previous analyses have focused on medical marijuana), but the general picture painted is one in congress with previous efforts.

Overall Tone

Having examined the topics covered in the overall dataset, it is important to note the tone of the coverage across it, in order to ascertain if it, like the themes, matches previous research. Following Vickovic & Fradella (2011), the tone of articles was assessed using a three-level categorization: positive, neutral, and negative. The complete picture of article tone can be seen in Table 2, below.

Examining the figures in Table 2, we can see that in both news and opinion articles the coverage was largely positive. However, while news pieces had neutral views almost as frequently as positive, the drop is far more substantial

Table 2. Tone Type by Article Type

Article Type	Tone Type	Number of Articles
News	Positive	66
	Neutral	69
	Negative	30
Opinion	Positive	38
	Neutral	10
	Negative	11

in opinion articles. Between neutral and negative, the opposite was true, with news articles demonstrating a much higher drop in terms of numbers and opinion pieces showing neutral and negative articles approximately similar in terms of number of articles. As with the themes, the data above are consistent with Vickovic and Fredella's (2011) findings.

Comparison of Themes Pre- and Post-Initiatives

While overall coverage resembles the findings of previous studies, one question that has not been answered is whether or not the passing of the initiatives in Washington and Colorado had an effect on subsequent media coverage. One way to examine this question is by comparing the type of coverage before and after legalization. In Table 3, below, such a comparison is made.

As can be seen in Table 3, there were some substantial changes in coverage pre- and post-legalization. Coverage regarding celebrity and athlete use of marijuana declined substantially, while articles focusing on the business elements increased to three times their original amount. Additionally, the number of articles examining the effects of legalization and use on children increased, while the articles examining policing and marijuana decreased substantially. Many of the other themes, including federalism/interjurisdictional conflict, medical marijuana, and the War on Drugs, stayed relatively similar in terms of the number of articles which covered those topics.

Table 3. Themes Pre- and Post-Initiatives

Theme	Pre	Post
Athletes/Celebrity Coverage	10	2
Marijuana Business	7	23
Federalism/Interjurisdictional Conflict	12	14
Marijuana and Children	4	11
Medical Marijuana	10	14
Other	9	13
Policing and Marijuana	18	10
Politics of Marijuana	28	33
Pot Tourism	2	0
War on Drugs	3	4

Comparison of Tone Pre- and Post-Initiatives

As with the themes of articles, it is important to examine questions of whether or not the tone of the articles changed substantially after the passage of the initiatives in Washington and Colorado. This comparison is presented in Table 4, below.

Table 4. Tone Pre- and Post-Initiatives

Tone	Pre	Post
Positive	43	61
Neutral	42	38
Negative	24	18

Examining the results shown in Table 4, it is clear that there were some changes, but the overall tone of the conversation covered in the articles remained the same. The substantial increase in the positive coverage after legalization is matched by the decrease in negative coverage. There was also a small decrease in neutral coverage. Overall then, it seems that the coverage tended towards more positive after the passage of the initiatives in Colorado and Washington.

Discussion

The findings presented above provide some interesting questions. While much of the coverage remained the same, there were some substantial changes in terms of both tone and theme. In particular, there seemed to be an increase in some areas that would suggest that the salience of those areas is increasing in terms of public opinion.

Perhaps characteristic of this is the coverage of the business theme. While there was previous coverage of businesses selling marijuana and the issues surrounding them, the substantial increase in that coverage is notable. It is possible that this increase represents an effect of an increase in knowledge, though the fact that the overall coverage did not change in terms of tenor suggests that the knowledge did not present significant detriment. Many of the articles focused on business, especially post-decriminalization, tended to emphasize the amount of profit the businesses would produce, and the tax revenue they would generate for the states involved in legalization. Even when the articles were negative, as with coverage of the problems that banking regulations presented to businesses, they often focused on the ways the businesses had skirted the problem.

Similarly, the increase in coverage regarding marijuana and children is interesting. This is especially so when one considers the fact that within that type of coverage, 60% of the coverage coming after marijuana legalization was negative, with many of the stories focusing on accidental ingestion or perceived increase in risk for usage. The fact that the coverage overall regarding marijuana actually increased in terms of positive coverage when there was a marked increase in stories regarding problems with children and marijuana is particularly perplexing.

One potential reason for this was the relatively small amount of coverage the topic got. Relative to politics, for instance, the number of stories focusing on children and pot were limited, representing a total of 6.6% of the total dataset. This may suggest further, however, that the problems that many of those articles examine are much more limited than anticipated, given that low level of coverage.

Another interesting element is the fact that many of the articles talking about the politics of marijuana use came *after* the passing of the initiatives. The number of articles written regarding politics rose from 28 to 33. While this does not represent a very large increase in terms of the number of articles, it does suggest that there was additional salience in terms of the political coverage. The tone of the political coverage remained substantially similar both before and after the legalization initiatives, but the sub-topics covered in the theme did change, moving from coverage of the races themselves (not just in Colorado and Washington, but elsewhere) to the conversation surrounding post-legalization politics.

Going the opposite direction in terms of amount of coverage, articles focusing on policing and marijuana decreased. This is especially interesting considering the increased discussion within the field of criminology (see Green and Steinmetz, this volume) surrounding issues of marijuana and policing. This is even more surprising when considering that the majority of articles were positive in orientation. The decrease in coverage might be representative of the fact that police were perhaps not yet certain of how the laws would impact them. Moreover, while many of the articles were positive in regards to marijuana (on which they were coded) they were often less positive on the police in terms of both actually policing and police policy (like stop and frisk). This means that the decrease in coverage may be suggestive of an increase in positive perception of the police, though that remains speculative.

One area in which coverage may have changed substantially because of the legalization initiatives is the number of articles covering celebrity or athletes who were caught for marijuana. While this also might simply be a function of fewer being caught, legalization also might be a factor in its newsworthiness. This is because as states legalize recreational use, the topic of marijuana as linked to "drugs" more generally may become less salient.

Overall, there are still significant questions that remain. As the effects of legalization in both Colorado and Washington become more apparent, the tone of the coverage and the topics covered may continue to change. Moreover, as additional states take the steps of legalizing recreational or medical marijuana, the potential impact on society becomes larger, and thus there may be different types of news attention paid to the topic.

Limitations

As with any study, this study presents some significant limitations. First off, it examined a single media source, the *New York Times*. This could be problematic in terms of scope, but is likely more problematic in terms of tone, as the paper is generally considered liberal in orientation. Additionally, the articles themselves sometimes presented difficulties. For instance, an article focusing on the politics of a given jurisdictions struggle with whether to introduce marijuana was difficult to categorize. For purposes of this study, it was categorized where the focus of the article was (politics vs. medical issues), but a dual categorization may have yielded different results.

Finally, there is the time period. While this article covered the two years prior to the initiatives passing in both Colorado and Washington and two years after, the actual implementation of the laws likely delayed some of the impacts legalization had, thus reflecting some possible loss in terms of news coverage.

Conclusion

Given the cultural importance of marijuana over time, how our changing legislation is affecting society is an important question. One way to gauge the change in society is by examining the type and amount of media coverage given to the topic. This is a particularly important method because the media has the ability to affect both policy makers as well as public opinion. Previous work by Hill, Oliver, and Marion (2012) as well as that by Whitford and Yates (2009) suggest that this relationship between actors is complicated when it comes to drugs, but that the media no doubt play a pivotal role.

This study examined the question of how the media has covered marijuana in regards to overall coverage as well as changes in coverage after the successful legalization of recreational marijuana in Washington and Colorado. The analysis included a content analysis of the articles written regarding marijuana in the *New York Times* from 2011–2014. Themes in the articles were identified, for both before and after the initiatives, as was the tone of the articles.

In general, the findings of this brief study support previous literature, though it breaks new ground by examining the impact of specific policies on media coverage. The work of Vickovic and Fredella's (2011) study was largely confirmed in the overall themes and tonality of coverage. However, the changes in the media coverage that presented after the legalization initiatives were passed raise interesting questions for future research. In particular, questions driven by the increasing number of jurisdictions who are legalizing medical and recreational use of pot will become important, as will any action at the federal level regarding marijuana. Moreover, questions about the impact of the laws passed by Washington and Colorado, and recently by Washington, DC, will become more important as increasing numbers of issues, both positive and negative, arise.

References

Ainslinger, H. J., & Cooper, C. R. (1937, July). Marijuana: Assassin of youth. *America Magazine.*

Benavie, A. (2009). *Drugs: America's holy war.* New York, NY: Routledge.

Bertram, E., Blachman, M., Sharpe, K., & Andreas, P. (1996). *Drug war politics: The price of denial.* Berkeley, CA: University of California Press.

Bonnie, R. J., & Whitebread, C. H. (1974). *The marihuana conviction: A history of marihuana prohibition in the United States.* Charlottesville, VA: University Press of Virginia.

Dowd, M. (2014). Don't harsh our mellow, dude. *New York Times.*

Hill, J. B., Oliver, W. M., & Marion, N. E. (2012). Presidential politics and the problem of drugs in America: Assessing the relationship between the president, media, and public opinion. *Criminal Justice Policy Review, 23,* 90–107.

Leon, K., & Weitzer, R. (2014). Legalizing recreational marijuana: Comparing ballot outcomes in four states. *Journal of Qualitative Criminal Justice and Criminology, 2,* 193–218.

Marshall, P. (2005). Marijuana laws: Should state and federal marijuana laws be reformed? *CQ Researcher, 75*(6), 125–148.

Matthew, J. (2009). *How the use of marijuana was criminalized and medicalized, 1906–2004: A Foucaultian history of legislation in America.* London, UK: Edwin Mellen Press.

McArthur, M. (1999). Pushing the drug debate: The media's role in policy reform. *Australian Journal of Social Sciences, 34,* 149–165.

McEwen, W. J., & Hanneman, G. J. (1974). The depiction of drug use in television programming. *Journal of Drug Education, 4,* 281–293.

Musto, D. F. (Ed.) (2002). *Drugs in America: A documentary history.* New York, NY: New York University Press.

Nixon, R. (1973). *Radio address about the State of the Union message on law enforcement and drug abuse prevention.* Online by G. Peters & J. T. Woolley, *The American Presidency Project.* Retrieved from http://www.presidency.ucsb.edu/ws/?pid=4135.

Southworth, K. L. (2004). Reefer in the media: The madness continues. Retrieved from http://breathofstatues.com/uploads/Reefer_in_the_Media.pdf.

Stryker, J. E. (2003). Media and marijuana: A longitudinal analysis of news media effects on adolescents' marijuana use and related outcomes, 1977–1999. *Journal of Health Communication: International Perspectives, 8,* 305–328.

Vickovic, S. G., & Fradella, H. F. (2011). Medical marijuana in the news. *The Southwest Journal of Criminal Justice, 8,* 67–96.

Whitford, A. B., & Yates, J. (2009). *Presidential rhetoric and the public agenda: Constructing the War on Drugs.* Baltimore, MD: Johns Hopkins University Press.

5

Recreational Marijuana Implementation in Colorado and Washington: Referendum v. Initiative

John R. Turner

Introduction

Colorado and Washington were the first two states to legalize recreational marijuana for recreational purposes (Colorado Legislative Council, 2014; Washington State Liquor Control Board, 2014). After citizens in both states voted on this innovative legislation, other states have followed. This is a trend that is likely to continue, especially since the majority of citizens in the United States believe that marijuana should be legal (Pew Research Center, 2013).

For states that decide to legalize marijuana, the key to success will be proper implementation and policy development. Perhaps in the future, how recreational marijuana is implemented will be clear and mistakes made by preceding states will provide valuable lessons. Additionally, uniformity may develop regarding the voting process. The way in which recreational marijuana was proposed to voters and eventually implemented was very different in Colorado and Washington. In Colorado, the legislation reached the ballot through the referendum process, as opposed to the initiative process in Washington (Colorado Department of Revenue, 2013; Washington State Liquor Control Board, 2014).

Marijuana and the Law: A Brief History

Throughout history, the use of marijuana has been a highly controversial issue worldwide (Goode, 1969). Historically, individuals and policymakers have debated whether or not it should be permitted, and if so, then how should it be regulated? Marijuana opponents argue that it could potentially cause individuals to engage in criminal activity or act as a gateway, leading to the use of other drugs that are more debilitating.

According to Marion (2014), marijuana has been used for both recreational and medical purposes by different cultures around the world since ancient times. Marijuana use likely originated in China and then spread to other locations. Historically, individuals have used marijuana to treat many different health related problems and also for recreational purposes (Marion, 2014). Moreover, the legal status of marijuana has been the topic of debate throughout history and this is something that will not likely change anytime soon. However, recently the public support for legalization has grown.

Public Support for Marijuana

A survey that was conducted recently by the Pew Research Center (2013) found that 52% of survey participants believed that marijuana use should be legal (p. 1). Furthermore, 72% of individuals who were surveyed indicated that they believed enforcing marijuana legislation is not worth the expense (Pew Research Center, 2013, p. 3). Additionally, only 32% of American's view the use of marijuana as being immoral. Due to the fact that the majority of citizens are not opposed to the legalization of recreational marijuana, states should look at the pros and cons of legalizing, or at least decriminalizing, recreational marijuana. More individuals are incarcerated for drug crimes in the United States than for all crimes in the United Kingdom, France, Germany, Italy, and Spain combined (Miron, 2004). This coalescing support around legalization is particularly pertinent.

Although the majority of citizens believe that marijuana should be legal, this does not mean that they will vote for it when they get their ballot. Unlike surveys, which allow simple yes and no responses, voters in states where recreational marijuana is on the ballot face a series of questions (Caulkins, Hawken, Kilmer & Kleiman, 2013). For example, the question as to whether or not individuals should be allowed to grow their own marijuana might appear on the ballot. Voters also have to decide on such matters as who can legally possess marijuana, where and how it can be used, and how it should be sold.

Although many members of the general public did not believe that states would ever legalize marijuana, it happened. In November of 2012 citizens of the states of Colorado and Washington voted for measures that would legalize marijuana for recreational, personal use (Colorado Department of Revenue, 2013; Reed, 2011; Washington State Liquor Control Board, 2014). The initiative to legalize recreational marijuana in the state of Washington enacted new legislation, while in Colorado the constitution was amended (Orlando & Adams, 2013). The possession, production, or sale of marijuana continues to be illegal on the federal level (Nadelmann, 2005; Office of National Drug Control Policy, 2010). However, Colorado and Washington have taken a progressive approach on the issue, in opposition to federal drug policy, making it legal for personal recreational use. The federal government has publicly stated that they will not enforce laws against states that elect to legalize recreational marijuana as long as they maintain strict regulatory control (Orlando & Adams, 2013). However, they have also acknowledged that they reserve the right to change their mind at any given time. It is important to note that the implementation of policy in these states has differed greatly. In late 2014, Alaska, Oregon, and the District of Columbia had also legalized recreational marijuana, though this chapter will focus primarily on Colorado and Washington, due to the fact that not much is known about implementation in the other states at this time.

Differences in Implementation

It does not appear that much collaboration has occurred between Colorado and Washington regarding implementation. The system in Colorado is far more advanced in many ways than that of Washington. Unlike the state of Colorado, Washington waited until July of 2014 to begin allowing the cultivation and retail of recreational marijuana. The Washington State Liquor Control Board (WSLCB) issued a timeline for the implementation process; however, no official date was given for allowing recreational marijuana shops to open until the last minute (I-502 Implementation Timeline, 2013). It was a completely different story in Colorado. Marijuana dispensaries opened up to the public in Colorado on January 1, 2014, over 6 months prior to Washington, giving them a head start in many ways. During the first month of open dispensaries in Colorado the state brought in over $1 million from the sale of marijuana (Mundahl, 2014). Although previous projections showed that Colorado would bring in approximately $67 million in annual revenue, it is likely that the original projection will be exceeded. In fact, some experts are convinced that the marijuana tax will generate over $100 million in annual revenue.

One of the reasons that marijuana sales in the state of Washington did not begin until July of 2014 was because policymakers delayed issuing licenses to applicants on two separate occasions. This resulted in businesses being unable to open their doors to the public, even after delays had already been problematic (Lopez, 2014). Although this was economically disadvantageous for all stakeholders involved and frustrating to many citizens of Washington State, these delays were necessary since the state needed to ensure that marijuana would be regulated properly and that implementation would go as planned. As Lopez (2014) suggests, implementation is not something that can just occur in the blink of an eye. It takes careful consideration and planning. Officials in the state of Washington have had to establish a complete framework for a new industry that did not previously exist. Although Colorado had to do this as well, they had a head start.

Why has the implementation process of legalized recreational marijuana been so successful in Colorado, yet slow paced in Washington? The answer could potentially involve the way the legislation was passed. Marijuana was legalized through the referendum process in Colorado, while an initiative was used in the state of Washington (Colorado Department of Revenue, 2013; Washington State Liquor Control Board, 2014). It should be noted that many newspaper articles and documents use the term referendum and initiative interchangeably, and many times erroneously.

Direct Democracy: Defining Initiatives and Referendums

According to Braunstein (2009), initiatives and referendums are similar in that they are both forms of direct democracy that allow the citizens of a particular state to vote directly on legislative issues. However, they are different in many ways. Initiatives, like I-502 in the state of Washington, allow citizens to bypass the legislature and propose statutes (Braunstein, 2009; Matsusaka, 2005). According to Matsusaka (2005) the most powerful form of direct democracy is the initiative. Initiatives begin with ordinary citizens proposing a law. Next, they collect an adequate number of signatures from other citizens in order to qualify their proposed law to be placed on the official ballot. Finally, the proposal is voted into law or rejected through the election process (Matsusaka, 2005).

The initiative is often regarded as the most important advancement associated with direct democracy, because it interrupted the legislature's domination over the statutory agenda (Matsusaka, 2005). In 1898 South Dakota became the first state to adopt the initiative during the progressive movement. Soon thereafter, many states followed. According to Matsusaka (2005), we now have a plethora of empirical support indicating that the initiative process brings significant changes in public policy. Just one example of this is recreational marijuana policy that has been approved in Washington. The legislation in Alaska, Oregon, and Washington, DC, was also placed on the ballot through the initiative process.

Referendums, on the other hand, such as Colorado's Amendment 64, are initiated by the legislature and are then voted on by the public (Braunstein, 2009; Matsusaka, 2005). Although there are several types of referendums, the process in Colorado began through a legislative referendum. According to Matsusaka (2005), legislative referendums occur when the legislature has the responsibility of placing a proposed measure before the voters. This is common with issues that would amend the constitution.

Legalizing recreational marijuana through a referendum with pre-established regulations gave Colorado a major advantage in many ways, such as providing them with a head start. In addition, it opened the door for Colorado to be able to build off of their medical marijuana framework, which helped to simplify the process. Their medical marijuana policies were clearly spelled out and easily interpreted. According to Lopez (2014), although Washington State also allowed medical marijuana during the years preceding the 2012 election legalizing recreational marijuana, the framework and regulations were not defined as clearly. This required policymakers to start from scratch.

General Problems with Implementation

Policymakers in both Colorado and Washington knew that the state would benefit in many ways from recreational marijuana. Economic prosperity, decreased incarceration, and marijuana tourism are just a few of the advantages associated with legalizing recreational marijuana (Healy, 2014; Johnson, 2014). On the other hand, complications such as federal restrictions and impaired driving were just a couple of problems that they knew they would eventually face.

Problems should always be anticipated with any policy implementation. Research has consistently demonstrated that with implementation comes complications. For example, between 1980 and the millennium, state and federal prison incarceration rates quadrupled due to the policy surrounding the War on Drugs (Auerhahn, 2004). In addition to fueling mass incarceration, the

War on Drugs also exacerbated racial inequality (Alexander, 2012). According to Beckett, Nyrop, & Pfingst (2006), between 1990 and 2000, arrest rate for drug offences increased exponentially, which mainly affected minorities and communities of color. It is doubtful that mass incarceration and racial inequality were the intentions of most policymakers. However, creating and implementing policy is never a simple process and problems should always be anticipated, and the implementation of recreational marijuana in Colorado and Washington is no exception.

In Colorado, some counties have decided not to allow the sale or production of recreational marijuana in their jurisdiction, creating problems with the implementation process and decreasing the opportunity for additional tax revenue (Loudenback, 2014). Similar problems exist in Washington State, where some cities have banned marijuana business of any kind.

One of the consequences that Colorado and Washington faced as they were the first states to legalize marijuana for recreational purposes was that both states have had to implement policy that had never existed before in the United States. Creating entirely new public policy can be a challenging task. We often erroneously assume that those who create and implement new policies have the ability to manipulate and predict the outcome, which is simply not accurate (Pressman & Wildavsky, 1984). Knowledge must exist that clearly establishes advantageous results between government choices and favorable views from the public for a program to effectively be created. In cases where this has failed to be established, in Washington and Colorado, for example, the government must then make the decision of whether to go ahead and implement the policy without knowledge and credible data and to proceed as an experiment or to forfeit the idea. According to Pressman & Wildavsky (1984), in these situations individuals who do not learn from experience will become lost. Fortunately, although recreational marijuana was previously illegal, Colorado and Washington can review and analyze policies that they and other states have implemented in regards to medical marijuana (Campoy, 2013). However, it could certainly be argued that in a roundabout way, policy makers in Colorado and Washington have learned from the past. Both policy makers and community members have been seeking alternatives to the prohibition of drugs due to the impact inflicted upon communities by the War on Drugs (Levine & Reinarman, 1991). The idea of decriminalization and the utilization of marijuana for medical reasons have been some of the alternative policies that have been discussed and implemented. According to Levine & Reinarman (1991), one of the reasons policy makers and the public sought these alternatives was because of consequences America had to face during alcohol prohibition.

Washington: The Initiative Process

Washington State initially adopted the initiative and referendum process in 1912, providing citizens a voice in decisions made by the legislature (Reed, 2012). Both systems are still in existence today. Recreational marijuana in the state of Washington was voted into law by an initiative, known as I-502. There are two types of initiatives in the state of Washington, initiatives to the people and initiatives to the legislature. Initiatives to the people occur when an adequate amount of signatures are collected and the initiative is submitted for citizens to vote on. In order for the initiative to become law, the majority of voters must favor the initiative. Any registered voter can introduce legislation to create a new state statute or to amend or repeal existing laws. In order to be placed on the ballot for the general election, initiatives must be filed with the Secretary of State. This is exactly how I-502 found its way to the ballot (Zylstra, 2011).

Supporters of legalized recreational marijuana gathered approximately 350,000 signatures in support of I-502 (Zylstra, 2011). The majority (55.7%) of the population voted in favor of legalizing recreational marijuana at the general election (Orlando & Adams, 2013, p. 2; Martin, 2012). According to Martin (2012), after the legislation was voted on, the state of Washington had one year to develop policy and determine how recreational marijuana would be regulated. Although it took nearly a year and a half after the 2012 election for recreational marijuana retail stores to open to the public in the state of Washington, stores begin opening in Colorado on January 1, 2014 (Healy, 2014).

Colorado: The Referendum Process

When Amendment 64 was placed on the ballot in the 2012 Colorado state election, it was very clear how recreational marijuana was going to be regulated—the goal was to regulate recreational marijuana similar to the way alcohol is regulated. The amendment clearly defined personal use and identified how recreational marijuana would be regulated, cultivated, manufactured, and distributed (Amendment 64, Article 18, Section 16). Therefore, when the amendment was voted into law, these essential factors were already in place.

The referendum process in Colorado was very complex and did not occur overnight. According to Ballotpedia (2012), in order to get the referendum on the 2012 ballot, supporters were required to collect over 85,000 signatures. The measure had failed to gain enough support to get on the ballot 8 times before finally being voted into law. Several hearings and a review by the election board occurred, helping to ensure that the language was appropriate. The initial document had to be changed several times in order to achieve clarity and specificity. By the time the referendum reached the ballot, it was very detailed and had been approved by the state legislature.

On November 6, 2012, over half (55.3%) of the voters in Colorado voted to approve Amendment 64 (Orlando & Adams, 2013, p. 2). The amendment made it legal for individuals over 21 years of age to possess up to one ounce of marijuana and to grow up to six plants (Amendment 64; Orlando & Adams, 2013). The change does not allow the use of marijuana in public areas. Amendment 64 places the responsibility for marijuana regulation and licensing with the Colorado Department of Revenue.

Impact of Initiative and Referendum: After the Election

In the state of Washington, the Washington State Liquor Control Board (WSLCB) regulates the licensing process (2014). I-502 has established three tiers of groups: those who plan to grow, sell, and distribute marijuana, who are producers, processors, and retailers. Individuals who wish to pay two separate licensing fees can apply for both a producer's and a processor's license; however, retailers cannot hold any other licenses regarding marijuana distribution. The state has developed a method to determine how many dispensaries are allowed to operate in each city. After this is established, licenses are issued and retailers are allowed to sell marijuana for recreational use. The dispensaries that are approved are privatized businesses and governed by the WSLCB. They are restricted from erecting establishments in areas near playgrounds and schools where children are likely to assemble. Additionally, they are only allowed to sell marijuana and marijuana related products. The only two options available in the state of Washington for individuals who wish to legally consume recreational marijuana is to purchase it from a licensed state-regulated facility or to obtain a prescription for medical marijuana. Under Washington marijuana law RCW 69.50.401, it is a class C felony for an individual to possess or manufacture marijuana by any other means, including growing one's own.

The implementation and licensing process in Colorado is much different. Although Colorado is ahead of Washington in many regards, they are still crafting the framework for these major policy changes (Campoy, 2013). However, the details that they are focused on are less crucial and can allow the distribution of marijuana to evolve. Issues such as the qualifications necessary to be employed as a lab technician, for example, have yet to be resolved and incorporated into statute.

Possibly one of the reasons that Colorado has surpassed Washington in the area of marijuana retail can be attributed to the fact that the implementation laws and the regulation of recreational marijuana in the state of Colorado appear to be less rigid. For example, in Denver, Colorado, individuals can lawfully smoke marijuana on residential private property even if it is in public view (State of Colorado, 2013). However, it must be noted that regulations such as this are established by individual cities and jurisdictions within the state of Colorado, so this does not apply to the entire state. According to the Colorado Department of Revenue's Marijuana Enforcement Division (2013), interested parties may apply for a license to create a new establishment for the sale of marijuana or, if they are already licensed to sell medical marijuana, they have the option to simply apply to convert their current establishment. One similarity between the two states in regard to the implementation of recreational marijuana policy is that they both require a separate license for the cultivation and the retail of marijuana (Colorado Department of Revenue, 2013; WSLCB, 2014). However, in Colorado, unlike in the state of Washington, a facility can have a shared license to both grow and sell marijuana.

Due to the nature of the business, it is essential for these facilities that manufacture and sell marijuana to be closely regulated to ensure that they are following all of the policies created to keep the public safe. Each state has appointed an agency to oversee these operations (Colorado Department of Revenue, 2013, WSLCB, 2014). Both states have concluded that it is in the best interest of the public for these licensed dispensaries to only sell marijuana, paraphernalia, and other related items. Other areas surrounding the policy of implementing recreational marijuana in which both states are either similar or identical include requiring customers to be at least 21 years of age before they can purchase marijuana, establishing restrictions in regard to the quantity of marijuana that consumers are allowed to purchase, creating legislation making it illegal for individuals to use marijuana in places of public interest, including marijuana retail stores, and implementing a tax code. Although both states have many similar ideals for this policy implementation, they also have a plethora of differences. The licensing of medical marijuana facilities to also sell recreational marijuana is only one of many areas in which the two states differ. Table 1.1 provides a comparison on Colorado and Washington from the time of implementation.

As indicated in Table 1.1, Colorado and Washington went about implementation differently from the start. In the state of Colorado, recreational marijuana was implemented through constitutional change. Washington, on the other hand, voted it in through a general initiative and had to later incorporate changes in statute (Colorado Amendment 64, 2012; I-502, 2012.)

Table 1.1 Key Differences in Colorado and Washington from Time of Implementation

	Colorado	Washington
Law	Referendum—constitutional amendment	Initiative—in statute
Available for Retail	January 2014	July 2014
Production, Processing and Retail	The majority of retailers grow their own product	Retailers are not permitted to grow their own product. Producers, processors, and retailers are separate.
Business Expense	Application: $5,000 Annual: $2,750–$14,000 (Depends on type of license)	Application: $250 Annual: $1,000
Tax	Tax cannot exceed 15%, excluding local tax	25% at each level (producer, processor, retailer, customer)
Personal Growing	Allowed	Not permitted
Retail Stores & Firearms	Armed security permitted	Not permitted
Medical Marijuana Impact	No impact	Goal is to reduce number of patients receiving medical marijuana and to require them to purchase from recreational facilities
Regulation	Colorado Department of Revenue	Washington State Liquor Control Board
Local Authority	Local government is permitted to prohibit recreational marijuana retail stores from operating in their jurisdiction	Local government has the ability to establish ordinances that prohibit recreational marijuana retail stores from operating in their jurisdiction

Note: Information from the Colorado column adapted from *Colorado Amendment 64*. Information from the Washington Column adapted from *Washington I-502*.

By having the amendment prepared prior to the election, Colorado was able to begin allowing licensed citizens to open up their marijuana retail stores on January 1, 2014. The state of Washington did not allow stores to open until July of 2014. Another key difference is that according to Colorado Amendment 64, retailers are permitted to grow their own product. In Washington,

Amendment 502 makes it very clear growers cannot also sell the marijuana that they grow. According to Smith (2014), retailers often do not have enough of a supply to even stay open during many of their business hours. Perhaps if retailers could grow their own marijuana, like in Colorado, this would be less problematic. Although retailers arguably have less freedom and more restrictions in the state of Washington, they do have the upper hand when it comes to the licensing process. Washington applicants are required to pay a $250 application fee, in addition to $1,000 annually if they are approved (Washington State Liquor Control Board, 2014). Applicants in the State of Colorado must pay a $5,000 application fee, in addition to annual fees that range anywhere from $2,750 to $14,000 (Colorado Amendment 64, 2012). Although the retailers are required to pay more in Colorado the citizens save by having less taxation. The tax in Colorado is 15%. In the state of Washington it is 25%, which is charged at every level, grower to processor, processor to retailer, and then the retailer to the customer (Washington State Liquor Control Board, 2014). Furthermore, Washington State forbids firearms to be taken into marijuana stops under any circumstances. In Colorado, retailers are allowed to employ armed guards. Another important difference is that Colorado has incorporated recreational marijuana with medical marijuana, to some degree. In the state of Washington they must be completely separate establishments. One thing that both states have in common is that they have assigned implementation a specific agency. In Colorado, implementation is handled mainly by the Colorado Department of Revenue. The WSLCB is responsible in Washington.

Current Status in Colorado and Washington

It has now been over two years since citizens in Colorado and Washington voted to legalize recreational marijuana. Colorado and Washington were the first two states to oppose federal drug policy and legalize marijuana for recreational use. This has paved the way for other states to do the same. In November of 2014, the legalization of recreational marijuana was on the ballot in Alaska, Oregon, and the District of Columbia, all of which voted in favor of the legislation (Ingraham, 2014). It is likely that this will build momentum and other states will do the same. The key to more states legalizing recreational marijuana is implementation (Rauch, 2014). Administrative and bureaucratic organizations must be created by all states that legalize recreational marijuana in order to oversee growth and distribution, in addition to working with law enforcement to combat the illegal market. According to Rauch (2014), these

Table 1.2 Colorado and Washington Comparison Post Implementation

	Colorado	Washington
Tax Revenue Collected	$18.9 Million	$3 Million
Number of Recreational Shops Open	136	27
Recreational and Medical Permitted in Same Shop	Yes	No

Note: Information from the Colorado column was adapted from *Colorado Department of Revenue* and *Colorado Amendment 64*. Information from the Washington column was adapted from *Washington I-502* and *Washington State Liquor Control Board.*

agencies must carefully establish appropriate taxation in order to deter excessive use, while simultaneously ensuring not to set tax rates so high that it encourages the black market to continue. Government officials should closely monitor outcomes and make adjustments as needed.

Table 1.2 represents a current picture of marijuana legislation in Colorado and Washington. As of July of 2014, the state of Washington reported nearly $12 million in total sales of recreational marijuana, and collected $3 million in tax revenue (Lu, 2014). The Colorado Department of Revenue reported making nearly $18.9 million in tax revenue in July of 2014. Not only is Colorado collecting more tax revenue, they have more recreational shops open. According to the Washington Liquor Control Board (2012), up to 332 retail licenses are available. However, only 27 facilities have opened throughout the state. Colorado, on the other hand, has 136 operational recreational marijuana retail stores (Colorado Department of Revenue, 2014). Additionally, unlike in Washington, Colorado Amendment 64 permits the growth of marijuana for personal use.

Table 1.2 indicates that Colorado is ahead of the game in many ways. They have opened more retail facilities and collected much more tax revenue. One of the reasons for lower than anticipated sales in Washington is due to the fact that retail shops cannot stay supplied (Smith, 2014). The demand is much greater than the available supply. According to Smith (2014), the shortage is due to the fact that Washington State has not issued a sufficient number of licenses to growers and processors. Additionally, many who apply for a license to grow or process marijuana do not meet the required criteria. Furthermore, many applicants that likely do meet the state's requirements are waiting for officials to complete their background checks, which keep getting placed on hold because that the agency is overwhelmed. Although over 2,600 individuals have applied for a license to grow marijuana, only 80 applications have been approved.

Positive Side of the Initiative Process

Although I have consistently made the argument that Colorado has benefited economically to a much greater degree than Washington because of the way the legislation was introduced, I do not want to leave the impression that I am trying to say that Colorado's referendum process was superior. Even though consumers could legally purchase recreational marijuana in the state of Colorado very soon after the election, and the state was able to begin collecting taxes and licensing almost immediately, sometimes the best practice is to be patient, not to rush. The market is currently much more limited in Washington than in Colorado, especially regarding nontraditional recreational marijuana, such as edibles. Although Washington State officials want new products to become available to consumers over time, they want to roll them out slowly to ensure the safety of citizens.

USA Today reported that shortly after recreational marijuana legislation was passed in Colorado, two individuals died as the result of a THC overdose from edibles (Hughes, 2014). They report that edible forms of marijuana are absorbed in the stomach as opposed to the lungs, which causes it to take longer for individuals to notice the effects. Overdosing by consuming edibles can lead to psychosis, death, and other serious health problems. Prior to these fatalities, the idea of anyone overdosing on THC was often laughed at—but now it is a reality.

Current Status of Other "Legal" States

One advantage that other states have over Colorado and Washington is that they have examples to follow and relate to. The ability to learn from the mistakes of others provides states that follow Colorado and Washington with a significant advantage if they are careful during the implementation process. Although Oregon will not begin allowing the possession or use of recreational marijuana until July 1, 2015, they appear to be taking the implementation process seriously. According to Measure 91, the Oregon Liquor Control Commission will be responsible for tax, licensing, and regulation of recreational marijuana. Measure 91 is similar to Washington State's I-502 in that both were passed through the initiative process and both established timelines for when the producing and retail of recreational marijuana would begin. Although it is too early to determine whether or not Oregon will follow their timeline, if they do it would be a dramatic improvement. It seems as though Oregon has modeled their recreational marijuana policy using a combination of what has worked in both Colorado and Washington. For example, as in Colorado, Oregon citizens will be allowed to grow enough marijuana for personal use. The state has also decided to do a few things differently than the other two states, for example, in addition to issuing licenses for producing, processing, and retail, they are allowing individuals to apply for a wholesale license. According to Measure 91, those who possess a wholesale license will be able to purchase marijuana from producers in large quantities and then distribute it to retail stores.

Alaska has also taken a unique approach to the implementation of recreational marijuana policy after residents voted in favor of Measure 2, which is an initiative also allowing the use and sale of marijuana for recreational purposes (Ferner, 2014). Although the legislation passed in November 2014, making Alaska the fourth state to legalize recreational marijuana, it was not the first time that this issue has been on the ballot. Citizens voted against it in 2000 and in 2004. Although parts of Measure 2 concerning possession will go in effect in late February 2015, those who want to apply for a recreational license cannot begin applying until February 2016. According to Alaska's Alcoholic Beverage Control Board (2015), as of now, nothing has changed and selling or purchasing marijuana remains illegal. Most implementation issues such as licensing, cultivating, and other key matters have not been determined.

While the implementation process in Alaska has yet to get off of the ground, it is looking even more grim for Washington, DC. Although approximately 70% of citizens voted in favor of the Initiative 71, Congress has stopped the implementation of the legislation from moving forward (Davis, 2015). One Republican Congressman has indicated that moving forward with Initiative 71 will result in the District of Columbia being held in violation of Congress. While President Obama recently passed a budget that would allow DC to pursue the implementation of recreational marijuana and remove restrictions imposed by Congress, it has yet to be approved and will likely be challenged by conservative lawmakers.

The Future of Recreational Marijuana

Growth of the medical marijuana industry was accurately predicted by scholars throughout the United States. According to Marion (2014):

> There could be significant growth opportunities for businesses dealing in product safety controls, trafficking, commerce software, digital marketing, social media, data mining, and patient education, among other areas (p. 210).

Not only have more states opened their doors for medical marijuana and decriminalization, but the District of Columbia, in addition to the states of Alaska, Colorado, Oregon, and Washington, has legalized marijuana for recreational use. Until the elections in Washington State and Colorado in 2012, no advanced jurisdictions or nations, including the Netherlands, had permitted the commercial production and retail of marijuana for non-medical purposes (Pacula et al., 2014). Now that four states and the District of Columbia have paved the way for recreational purposes, other states and nations will inevitably follow.

It is widely believed that California will be the next state to legalize recreational marijuana in 2016, even though the legislation was voted down in 2010 (Wisckol, 2015). Polls in the state indicate the viewpoints of citizens has shifted and now the majority favor legalizing recreational marijuana. Although many of the state's residents support the policy change, opponents of the legislation have a financial advantage. In 2010 opponents of recreational marijuana legislation had a very large monetary advantage.

Conclusion

Marijuana implementation has been challenging in Colorado and Washington, essentially because it is something that had never before been attempted in the United States. Although an idea may sound good, many policies that sound appealing have turned out to be quite difficult when applied in real-world scenarios (Pressman & Wildavsky, 1984). Pressman & Wildavsky (1984) argue that policy must be measured in how practical implementation will be, as opposed to its attractiveness (Rothman, 1980). Although some argue that marijuana implementation is not practical and should not occur, others are very strongly in favor of legalizing it. Both states went about the election and implementation process differently and both states have faced numerous problems. However, overall, the implementation process has not been as problematic as some originally suggested. As issues have developed in both states, policymakers have tried to address and resolve them. There are still unresolved issues and it is only logical that more problems will develop over time. As long as these issues are appropriately addressed states will likely see the black market dramatically reduced or eliminated, economic prosperity, and a reduction in incarceration rates.

References

Alexander, M. (2012). *The new Jim Crow: Mass incarceration in the age of colorblindness.* New York: The New York Press.

Answers to frequently asked questions about marijuana. (2010). Office of Nation Drug Control Policy. Retrieved from http://www.whitehouse.gov/ondcp/marijuana.

Auerhahn, K. (2004). California's incarcerated drug offender population, yesterday, today, and tomorrow: Evaluating the War on Drugs and Proposition 36. *Journal of Drug Issues, 34*(1), 95–120.

Beckett, K., Nyrop, K., & Pfingst, L. (2006). Race, drugs, and policing: Understanding disparities in drug delivery arrests. *Criminology, 44*(1), 105–137.

Braunstein, R. (2004). *Initiative and referendum voting: Governing through direct democracy in the United States.* New York, NY: LFB Scholarly Publishing.

Campoy, A. (2013, August 19). States wrestle with how to label pot; States legalizing recreational marijuana wrestle with best way to test potency. *Wall Street Journal*, pp. 1–3.

Caulkins, J. P., Hawken, A., Kilmer, B., & Kleiman, M. K. (2012). *Marijuana legalization: What everyone needs to know.* Oxford, NY: Oxford University Press.

Colorado Amendment 64, Article 18, Section 16.

Colorado Legislative Council. (2014). *Focus Colorado: Economic and revenue forecast* (pp. 1–90). Retrieved from http://www.colorado.gov/cs/Satellite?blobcol=urldata&blobheader=application/pdf&blobkey=id&blobtable=MungoBlobs&blobwhere=1251999888405&ssbinary=true.

Colorado Marijuana Legalization Initiative, Amendment 64. (2012). In *Ballotpedia: An interactive almanac of US politics.* Retrieved from http://ballotpedia.org/Colorado_Marijuana_Legalization_Initiative,_Amendment_64_(2012)#Path_to_the_ballot.

Davis, A. C. (2015, February 2). Obama budget would clear path for legal sales of recreational marijuana in DC. *Washington Post.* Retrieved from http://www.washingtonpost.com/local/dc-politics/obama-budget-would-allow-recreational-pot-use-in-dc/2015/02/02/93461e52-ab06-11e4-ad71-7b9eba0f87d6_story.html.

FAQ's on I-502. (2014). Washington State Liquor Control Board. Retrieved from http://liq.wa.gov/print/5600.

Ferner, M. (2014, November 5). Alaska becomes fourth state to legalize recreational marijuana. *Huffington Post.* Retrieved from http://www.huffingtonpost.com/2014/11/05/alaska-marijuana-legalization_n_5947516.html.

Goode, E. (1969). *Marijuana.* New York, NY: Atherton Press, Inc.

Healy, Jack (2014, January 1). Colorado stores throw open their doors to pot buyers. *New York Times.* Retrieved from http://www.nytimes.com/2014/01/02/us/colorado-stores-throw-open-their-doors-to-pot-buyers.html.

Hughes, T. (2014, May 8). Marijuana "edibles" pack a wallop. *USA Today.*

I-502 implementation timeline (2013). Washington State Liquor Control Board.

Information for consumers. (2014). Colorado Department of Revenue. Retrieved from http://www.colorado.gov/cs/satellite/Revenue.

Ingraham, C. (2014, November 14). Analysis: What four crucial votes mean for US legalization momentum. *The Washington Post.* Retrieved from http://www.thecannabist.co/2014/11/04/marijuana-oregon-florida-dc-alaska-legalization/22427/.

Johnson, E. M. (2014, July 8). Shortage looms as Washington rolls out retail pot sales. *Chicago Tribune.* Retrieved from http://www.chicagotribune.com/news/nationworld/chi-washington-marijuana-shortage-20140706-story.html.

Levine, H. G., & Reinarman, C. (1991). From prohibition to regulation: Lessons from alcohol policy for drug policy. *The Milbank Quarterly, 69*(3), 461–494.

Liccardo Pacula, R., Kilmer, B., Wagenaar, A. C., Chaloupka, F. J., & Caulkins, J. P. (2014). Developing public health regulations for marijuana: Lessons from alcohol and tobacco. *American Journal of Public Health, 104*(6), 1021–1028.

License approval or denial. (2014). Washington State Liquor Control Board. Retrieved from http://liq.wa.gov/print/5600.

Lopez, G. (2014, June 4). Why Washington is taking so long to get recreational pot in stores. *VOX Media.* Retrieved from http://www.vox.com/2014/6/4/5763262/why-washington-is-taking-so-long-to-get-recreational-pot-in-stores.

Loudenback, J. (2014). New marijuana law face implementation challenges. University of Southern California. Retrieved from http://bedrosian.usc.edu/new-marijuana-laws-face-implementation-challenges/.

Lu, A. (2014, September 14). States weighing legal pot look to tax revenues in Colorado, Washington. *Huffington Post.* Retrieved from http://www.huffingtonpost.com/2014/09/16/marijuana-tax-revenue_n_5829922.html.

Majority now supports legalizing marijuana. (2013, April 4). Pew Research Center. Retrieved from http://www.people-press.org/2013/04/04/majority-now-supports-legalizing-marijuana.

Marijuana Initiative FAQs. (2015). State of Alaska Alcoholic Beverage Control Board. Retrieved from http://commerce.state.ak.us/dnn/abc/Resources/MarijuanaInitiativeFAQs.aspx.

Marion, N. E. (2014). *The medical marijuana maze: Policy and politics.* Durham, NC: Carolina Academic Press.

Martin, J. (2012, November 6). Voters agree to legalize pot. *Seattle Times*. Retrieved from http://blogs.seattletimes.com/politicsnorthwest/2012/11/06/marijuana-legalization-takes-commanding-lead/.

Matsusaka, J. G. (2005). The eclipse of legislatures: Direct democracy in the 21st century. *Public Choice, 124*(1/2), 157–177.

Measure 91 frequently asked questions. (2014). State of Oregon. Retrieved from http://www.oregon.gov/olcc/marijuana/Documents/Measure91_FAQ.pdf.

Miron, J. A. (2004). *Drug war crimes: The consequences of prohibition*. Oakland, CA: The Independent Institute.

Mundahl, K. (2014, February 1). Colorado weed has already brought in $1.2M in taxes. *WSB-TV*. Retrieved from http://www.whio.com/news/news/national/colo-weed-has-already-brought-12m-taxes/ndB6g/.

Nadelmann, E. A. (1995). Drug prohibition in the United States: Costs, consequences, and alternatives. In *The American drug scene: An anthology* (pp. 322–335). Los Angeles, CA: Roxbury Publishing Company.

Orlando, J., & Adams, T. (2013). *Marijuana legalization* (No. 2013-R-0422) (pp. 1–5). Connecticut: Office of Legislative Research.

Pressman, J. L., & Wildavsky, A. (1984). *Implementation* (3rd ed.). Berkeley, CA: University of California Press.

Rauch, J. (2014, May). It's all in the implementation: Why cannabis legalization is less like marriage equality and more like health care reform. *Washington Monthly*. Retrieved from http://www.washingtonmonthly.com/magazine/march_april_may_2014/features/its_all_in_the_implementation049294.php?page=all.

Reed, S.; Washington State Secretary of State. (2011). *Initiative No. 502 proposal to the legislature*.

Reed, S. (2012). Filing initiatives and referenda in Washington State. Washington State Elections Division.

Wisckol, M. (2015, January 2). State's pot activists prep for 2016. *Orange County Register*. Retrieved from http://www.ocregister.com/articles/marijuana-645900-california-state.html.

Zylstra, Brian. (2011). *Marijuana measure petitions roll in*. Retrieved from http://blogs.sos.wa.gov/FromOurCorner/index.php/2011/12/marijuana-measure-petitions-roll-in/.

6

Marijuana Legalization: Comparing Recent Ballot Initiatives*

Kenneth Leon and Ronald Weitzer

Introduction

The US government criminalizes cultivation, distribution, and possession of marijuana and labels it a Schedule I drug (i.e., one with no medical value and a high potential for abuse). Twenty-three states and the District of Columbia, however, now permit access to medical marijuana and ballot measures to legalize recreational marijuana have gained some traction as well. The measures failed in Alaska in 2000 and 2004, Colorado and Nevada in 2006, California in 2010, and Oregon in 2012. They succeeded in Colorado and Washington in 2012 and in Alaska, Oregon, and Washington, DC, in 2014.

The national context is important. Over half the population (52%) has used marijuana according to one recent poll (CNN, 2014), and a growing number of Americans support legalization for recreational use. Public support for this rose from 12% in 1969 to 25% in 1980 to 31% in 2000 (Gallup, 2014), and has now passed the halfway mark, hovering between 55 and 58% (CNN, 2014; Gallup, 2014). Whereas 70% considered smoking marijuana "morally wrong" in 1987, only half as many (35%) took this view in 2014 (CNN, 2014). The growing tolerance regarding recreational marijuana is partly a byproduct of the medical marijuana movement, with the latter paving a path for the decrimi-

---

* Revised and updated version of an article published in *Journal of Qualitative Criminal Justice and Criminology*, v.2, no.2 (October 2014): 193–218.

nalization of recreational possession. Almost half of the states now have practical experience with regulation of a substance that may be transferred from the medical to recreational sphere rather than embarking on an enterprise completely *de novo*. Earlier attempts to legalize marijuana possession—in Alaska in 2000 and 2004, and Nevada and Colorado in 2006—arguably failed in part because there was not, at that time, a critical mass of medical marijuana states with a significant record of regulating the drug to serve as a precedent for recreational legalization.[1]

This essay examines four recent campaigns to legalize recreational marijuana in California, Colorado, Oregon, and Washington. We identify similarities and differences in the provisions of the ballot measures, key proponents and opponents in each state, and the arguments they made in defense of their position. Because our analysis compares four cases, we cannot provide either an in-depth examination of any one case or a comprehensive account (in one essay) of all the factors that influence the success or failure of such ballot initiatives. But our research does allow for the identification of (a) major similarities and differences among the four cases and (b) some tentative explanations for ballot failure in California and Oregon and success in Colorado and Washington—explanations that can be tested in future research on other states with recreational marijuana ballot initiatives.

Background

Prohibitory drug laws have been liberalized in the past. Scheerer (1978) compared the reform of drug laws in Germany and the Netherlands in the 1970s, with Germany increasing sanctions against cannabis possession and distribution, while the Netherlands relaxed penalties for possession and inaugurated a limited kind of regulation. Both reforms were top-down legislative decisions, not driven by popular pressure. In fact, Scheerer argued, both the German and Dutch populations were, at the time, "adamantly punitive" toward drugs. But in the Dutch case, legislators took the initiative in advocating a more tolerant approach, whereas their German counterparts took the opposite position. Scheerer assumed that elite opinion largely determines public policy in the area of vice: "Decriminalization normally occurs in spite of a

1. Medical marijuana had been approved in only five states prior to Alaska's vote on recreational marijuana in 2000, and eleven states had approved it by the time of Colorado and Nevada's 2006 vote on recreational marijuana.

punitive and repressive public, and not because it is welcomed by a community of liberal eggheads" (Scheerer, 1978, p. 590).

Reform was also top-down in the United States in the 1970s. At the national level, the Comprehensive Drug Abuse Act of 1970 eliminated mandatory-minimum penalties, reduced maximum sentences, eliminated a provision preventing convicted offenders from being eligible for suspended sentences or probation, and provided treatment for first-time offenders arrested for drug possession (Peterson, 1985). A key reason for this reform was the perception among members of Congress that young middle- and upper-class white drug users were victims of iconic drug traffickers (Peterson, 1985). Between 1973 and 1978, eleven state legislatures reduced punishment for possession of small amounts of marijuana (penalties consisted of a small fine). The eleven states were diverse and included all regions of the country. DiChiara and Galliher (1994) argued that a window of opportunity opened in the 1970s as a result of increasing arrests of middle- and upper-class youths coupled with the interests of law enforcement agencies, seeking more efficient use of limited resources. Like Peterson (1985), DiChiara and Galliher found that politicians are more likely to revisit the rules when high-status white youth become subject to punishment for victimless crimes. Decriminalization is a way of resolving a situation of "moral dissonance," where violators are seen as having high social status but low moral status (as offenders) (Lempert, 1974, p. 6). The 1970s experiment with decriminalization ended in the following decade: states that had previously decreased penalties for marijuana possession increased sanctions during the 1980s in the context of the Reagan administration's robust drug war.

More recent examples of top-down reform are Portugal's decriminalization of all illegal drugs in 2001 and Uruguay's legalization of cannabis in 2013. Both resulted from legislative action, following recommendations of a 1998 government-appointed commission in Portugal and a presidential proposal in Uruguay in 2013. The top-down nature of Uruguay's reform contrasts with a deficit of popular support for the measure—58% to 68% opposed it in recent polls (*The Economist*, 2013).

Despite these cases of state-driven reform and Scheerer's (1978) assumption that the public is not a major player in the reform of vice laws, history shows that top-down liberalization is not the only trajectory. By legislative action, Italy decriminalized possession and non-profit distribution of all drugs in 1975; recriminalized possession in 1990 following a spike in drug-related overdoses; and then re-decriminalized possession by popular referendum in 1993, with 55% of Italians voting for decriminalization (MacCoun & Reuter, 2001, pp. 231–233). In the United States, recent marijuana law reform has resulted from legislative action in some states, but was driven by popular ballot initiatives elsewhere; 12 of the 23 state medical marijuana laws resulted from ballot initiatives rather than legislative action.

The trend toward liberalization has not been linear. In 2012, for example, Arkansas voters rejected a medical marijuana measure and Oregon voters rejected a recreational marijuana initiative. Federal government intervention remains a possibility in states where marijuana possession is now legal, especially if a more conservative administration takes office after the 2016 national election. In the sphere of victimless crime, legal reforms often take the form of what Dombrink and Hillyard (2007) call *problematic normalization*, where initial progress toward normativity is contested or diluted or stymied altogether. This dynamic has been evident in conflicts over same-sex marriage, doctor-assisted suicide, abortion, and prostitution (Dombrink & Hillyard, 2007; Sharp, 2005; Weitzer, 2012). Regarding medical marijuana, problematic normalization in the form of post-enactment conflicts and implementation problems have occurred in several states, including disagreements over (a) commercialization: business involvement in medical marijuana; (b) health and public safety: perceived and actual risks; (c) proliferation: growing usage or the surge in dispensaries in some areas; and (d) eligibility: consumers who enter the system without genuine medical needs (Geluardi, 2010; Regan, 2011). Similar challenges are likely in the implementation of recreational marijuana systems (e.g., Fisher, 2014). Moreover, the medical and recreational sectors may have conflicting interests. Medical marijuana forces have tried to block some recreational proposals, or specific aspects of them, because they compete economically with the medical sector. And the stakes are high: sales from medical marijuana in California are estimated to be as high as $1.3 billion annually, with sales tax revenue as high as $105 million (California State Board of Equalization, 2014). In the first half year of recreational legalization in Colorado and Washington, tax and license revenue is estimated at $22 to $25 million (Elinson, 2014).

This paper examines four recent cases of attempted legalization. Table 1 lists each ballot initiative, its outcome, previous decriminalization (i.e., formal reduction of penalties), and the date medical marijuana was approved. Table 1 includes three additional states that voted on ballot initiatives in 2014; the recency of these cases prevented inclusion in this chapter.

Table 1. Ballot Initiatives in Seven States

State	Year	Initiative	Outcome	Medical Marijuana Approved	Previous Decriminalization
California	2010	Proposition 19	NO (53.5%)	1996	1975, 2000, 2010
Oregon	2012	Measure 80	NO (53.4%)	1998	1973, 1995
Colorado	2012	Amendment 64	YES (55.3%)	2000	1975
Washington	2012	Initiative 502	YES (55.7%)	1998	2003
Alaska	2014	Measure 2	YES (52.1%)	1998	1975
Oregon	2014	Measure 91	YES (55.6%)	1998	1973, 1995
Washington, DC	2014	Initiative 71	YES (69.5%)	1998	2014

Note: *Previous decriminalization* here refers to *de jure* reduction in criminal penalties or substitution of civil penalties, not removal of all penalties.

Predictors of Vice Legalization

Campaigns to decriminalize vice (such as prostitution, gambling, or drugs) raise issues that are less salient in debates over more mundane issues. Vice-related ballot measures are highly susceptible to emotional appeals (e.g., addictive gambling, victimization of women), moral panic (e.g., impact on youths, proliferation of the vice, organized crime), and social justice and civil rights claims (e.g., same-sex marriage) (Dombrink & Hillyard, 2007; Sharp, 2005; Skolnick, 1988).

Scholars have identified a set of factors that enhance the odds that a particular vice will be decriminalized (Lenton, 2004; Skolnick, 1988; Weitzer, 2012), and we consider these factors relevant to our analysis of marijuana legalization. These analysts argue that the greater the number of such factors in any given case, the higher the chances of decriminalization or legalization:

1. Significant numbers of people engage in the vice, and they have conventional lifestyles; the vice is not concentrated in the lower-class or in a fringe subculture;

2. There is evidence that legalization will produce less harm than criminalization; e.g., the vice does not create dependency or interfere with one's ability to fulfill obligations and does not endanger public health more generally;
3. Production and distribution of the vice can be controlled by the authorities;
4. There is support for decriminalization from law enforcement, leading politicians, and/or business elites;
5. Young people can be shielded from the vice; involvement of minors will remain prohibited;
6. Adults who wish to avoid the vice can be shielded from it (e.g., restrictions on public use, advertising marijuana products);
7. The vice can be confined to the private sphere;
8. Legalization can produce revenue for the government;
9. Business owners can be vetted to eliminate those with previous felony convictions or ties to organized crime;
10. The regulatory regime can be subjected to periodic review, and modification if necessary; any oversight body will be independent of the purveyors of the vice.

Some of these preconditions are met across our four cases; we know, for example, that a significant number of Americans have used marijuana and that most of them have conventional lifestyles, crossing virtually all demographics. All four ballot measures prohibit minors from accessing legal marijuana, and all limit use to the private sphere.[2] Beyond this, our analysis will determine, to the extent that our data permit, whether and how some of the other preconditions were addressed in the four ballot measures and the regulatory regimes stipulated in each measure.

However, the success of a marijuana ballot initiative depends on other variables as well—including the status of leading advocates and opponents, the nature of media coverage and editorializing, timing (national or mid-term election), youth turnout, and whether the federal government was intervening or threatening to intervene if the measure passed.

We hypothesize that if a ballot initiative and its corresponding campaign outspend the interest group(s) that opposed it, it should be a substantive pre-

2. A recent *Huffington Post*/YouGov (2014) poll reported that two-thirds of Americans favored allowing people to smoke marijuana in a private residence and a majority in a members-only marijuana club, but only a small minority thought that people should be allowed to smoke marijuana on a public sidewalk (15%), park (18%), or in a bar (25%).

dictor of ballot initiative success. Conversely, should opponents outspend proponents, the initiative would be less likely to succeed at the polls. Funding is a variable of interest due to the correlation between fundraising and successful election outcomes; laws tend to pass and candidates elected when they have significantly more funding than their opponents.

Political climate is another variable of interest. First, is there an observable difference in outcomes during a national election year (2012) versus a midterm election year (2010)? Second, do federal authorities play a role in shaping outcomes (e.g., Justice Department, Office of National Drug Control Policy)? We expect that opposition from the federal government will impede the success of a ballot initiative. Third, what is the stance of state or prominent local officials and candidates (e.g., governor or mayors)? We expect that if the latter publicly endorse a recreational marijuana ballot initiative, it will be associated with higher support among the electorate and therefore more likely to pass at the polls (Tesler, 2014).

The media are obviously important. Newspapers and television newscasts influence public perceptions of ballot measures through editorials or the content of news reporting. We hypothesize that endorsement of a ballot initiative from a state's major newspapers increases the odds of passage.

Establishing all necessary and sufficient conditions of ballot success is a lofty goal for a qualitative examination of four cases. However, our analysis does allow for the identification of certain key variables and consideration of some tentative explanations for the success and failure of ballot measures that can be tested in future research on other cases.

Methods

The cases examined were California, Colorado, Oregon, and Washington. California's ballot initiative took place in 2010, the other three in 2012 (see Table 1). Data were derived from three main sources. First, we content-analyzed two major newspapers in each of the states: the *Los Angeles Times* (N=50) and *San Francisco Chronicle* (30) in California; the *Denver Post* (35) and *The Gazette* (20) in Colorado; *The Oregonian* (29) and *Statesmen Journal* (8) in Oregon; and the *Seattle Times* (90) and *Tacoma News Tribune* (17) in Washington. All articles that were available via the source website were included from the beginning of coverage of the ballot measure until the voting date—for a total of 279 articles. For each major state newspaper, we selected all articles that included the name of the ballot initiative or that included the keywords "marijuana" and "legalization." We also examined editorials regarding each measure in secondary newspapers in each state.

Using a grounded theory approach, we coded for items that appeared to have influenced whether a measure passed or failed. Primary coding categories included: prominent individuals and organizations that took a position regarding the ballot initiative; sources of campaign funding; general framing; specific arguments in favor and against the initiative; role of the state's medical marijuana sector; and key areas of concern as expressed or reported in leading newspapers. The frequencies of specific themes and arguments in newspaper articles and editorials were documented to establish which factors seemed to be the most relevant in each state. All articles were open-coded and recoded after specific themes and variables of interest became apparent. Themes and the way in which ballot initiatives were framed were drawn largely from editorials and the substantive arguments present in state news reporting. For ex-

Table 2. Interviewees

State	Name	Date Interviewed	Professional Affiliation
California	Nate Bradley	May 3, 2013	Private Investigator. Former law enforcement officer
	Dale Gieringer	April 24, 2013	State Director, National Organization for the Reform of Marijuana Laws
Colorado	Mason Tvert	May 8, 2013	Director of Communications, Marijuana Policy Project
	Brian Vicente	May 10, 2013	Co-author of Amendment 64. Co-director of Campaign to Regulate Marijuana Like Alcohol
Oregon	Rep. Peter Buckley (D)	June 25, 2013	Co-chair of Joint Committee on Ways & Means, Oregon House of Representatives
	Paul Stanford	May 8, 2013	Primary author of Measure 80
Washington	Jonathan Martin	May 3, 2013	Reporter, *Seattle Times*
	Roger Roffman	April 20, 2013	Professor and consultant for I-502

ample, if racially disparate criminal justice outcomes were referenced more than the expected tax revenue from legalizing cannabis, then the frame of social justice would be stronger than the frame of fiscal benefits. On the opposition side, the dominant frames might vary from state to state: e.g., fear of increased use among minors; predicting federal intervention to block implementation; concern that passage would only exacerbate existing problems associated with the medical marijuana system (allegedly "out of control" in some states).

Second, newspaper data were cross-checked and expanded upon via interviews with two activists or experts in each state, most of whom played an active role in either formulating the initiative or contributing to the debate (see Table 2). Ethics approval for the human subjects aspect of the study was granted by the university's IRB, and interviewees gave informed consent to be interviewed and identified in the study. And third, we content-analyzed key themes and messages in a small selection of television advertisements, recorded debates, and town hall meetings involving the ballot measures.

Findings

The four ballot measures were similar in some respects: Possession is restricted to persons over age 21, public use is outlawed, tax revenue can be produced (if marijuana is purchased at a store), drugged driving is prohibited, and employers may prohibit use at the workplace and/or off-work via drug testing. The prohibitions on youth involvement, public use, and drugged driving and the provision for tax revenue satisfy four of the ten preconditions for vice legalization previously listed. Our four cases differ, however, in other significant respects.

California

2010 was not California's first attempt at marijuana legalization. A 1972 ballot initiative (also called Proposition 19) would have decriminalized possession, cultivation, processing, and transporting marijuana for persons aged 18 and older, and it would have prohibited persons under the influence from "engaging in conduct that endangers others." No other regulations were stipulated. The measure mustered only 33.5% support among voters.

California's second Proposition 19, in 2010, won more approval (46.5%) than its 1972 predecessor, but failed, despite the $4.5 million spent in support of it versus the $420,000 spent by opponents (NIMSP, 2014). The provisions included:

- Adults 21 and older may possess, cultivate, or transport marijuana for personal use;
- Possession and cultivation must be solely for personal consumption, not for sale to others; individuals may cultivate on private property in an area up to 25 square feet;
- Local governments may authorize, license, regulate, and tax the retail sale of marijuana and the location of businesses;
- Possession is prohibited on school grounds, as is adult use with minors present and providing marijuana to anyone under 21;
- Consumption is permitted only in a residence or other private space, except that marijuana may be consumed in licensed establishments if allowed by local laws;
- Current prohibitions against driving while impaired are retained;
- The measure does not specifically permit employers to drug test employees, but the measure states that it does not affect existing laws prohibiting use of drugs in the workplace.

Major backers included the ACLU, Marijuana Policy Project, Drug Policy Alliance, United Food and Commercial Workers Union, National Black Police Association, NAACP's California branch, Law Enforcement Against Prohibition (LEAP), and progressive financier George Soros. Arguments in favor of the measure included anticipated tax revenue; the potential for job growth; reducing racial disparities in drug arrests; and the argument that the state's medical marijuana system was allowing many ineligible users to obtain marijuana, thus necessitating a broader legalization remedy.

Opposing forces included the Chamber of Commerce, the state's four leading newspapers, and various organizations (e.g., Police Chief's Association, Public Safety First). Fear of increased use among youth was particularly strong in California, as well as the concern that roads, workplaces, and communities would be less safe. The Drug Free American Foundation (2010) released television ads warning voters that use by minors would skyrocket and that intoxicated drivers would create dangers on the roadways. One of the most prominent arguments against the initiative was that it would not generate tax revenue because it allowed for personal cultivation and contained only a local option of creating taxable retail outlets. Opponents also warned that thousands of acres of farmland would be allocated toward marijuana cultivation (Drug Free America Foundation, 2010). Additionally, opponents criticized the provision that allowed counties and municipalities to devise their own regulations or ban retail sales outright, which they argued would create a hodgepodge of policies throughout the state.

Opposition was voiced across the state's political spectrum: by Gov. Arnold Schwarzenegger (R), both candidates for governor and state attorney general, California's two US Senators (Barbara Boxer [D] and Dianne Feinstein [D]), and House Speaker Nancy Pelosi (D). The opposition of all top Democratic politicians has been identified as a major impediment to popular support for the measure (Tesler, 2014). Moreover, national officials took a strong stand against the measure. The current and five former national drug czars and the US Attorney General publicly opposed Proposition 19, which may have fueled public concern about possible legal battles if the measure passed. A few weeks before the election, Attorney General Eric Holder announced that federal authorities would "vigorously enforce" federal marijuana laws in California regardless of whether Proposition 19 passed; he stated that the Justice Department "strongly opposes" the measure and that passage would be to "the detriment of our citizens" (quoted in Hoeffel, 2010b). As one of our interviewees, the director of NORML's California branch, stated, "Towards the end of the Prop. 19 campaign, the Attorney General and the administration came out rather strongly against the initiative and I think that may have given people second thoughts as to whether the whole thing was feasible" (Gieringer interview). Nate Bradley of LEAP agreed that when the Attorney General "said they were going to vigorously enforce the law, that took even more momentum away" (Bradley interview).[3] Such federal opposition in 2010 was not replicated in the three states with ballot initiatives in 2012, and we consider this a significant variable contributing to the successful outcomes in Colorado and Washington (cf. Kamin, 2012). Subsequent to these victories, in August 2013, the Justice Department announced that it would allow Colorado and Washington to implement the measures provided that mechanisms were established to prevent distribution to minors, involvement of criminal organizations, transportation to states where possession remains illegal, and other conditions (Cole, 2013).

It is noteworthy that the organization representing the state's medical marijuana sector, the California Cannabis Association, opposed Proposition 19; they feared that the provision allowing local jurisdictions to ban dispensaries would lead to closure of existing medical marijuana stores in some areas. One

3. It is also possible that legislation in mid-2010 took some of the steam out of the legalization campaign. A bill, signed by Gov. Schwarzenegger, downgraded the penalty for possession of up to one ounce of marijuana from a criminal misdemeanor to a civil infraction with a maximum $100 fine.

of the strongest criticisms of the measure centered on the proliferation of medical marijuana stores in the state, and the corollary claim that the medical sector was "out of control," which recreational availability would only aggravate. The rapid spread of medical dispensaries was especially controversial in Los Angeles. Just a few months before the election, the Los Angeles City Council ordered the closure, by June 7, 2010, of 439 medical marijuana dispensaries in the L.A. area, allowing another 130 to remain (Hoeffel, 2010a). Many of the stores had opened in violation of a moratorium on new dispensaries and had been the target of complaints from nearby residents (Hoeffel, 2010a). The surge in under-regulated medical marijuana stores—in Los Angeles and some other parts of the state—may have influenced some voters' decisions to vote against Proposition 19. A statewide poll found that 38% of California's registered voters opposed allowing marijuana dispensaries to operate in their city or town—39% in Los Angeles and 30% in the liberal San Francisco Bay area (Field Research Corporation, 2013).

Other contentious issues included the ballot provision allowing local jurisdictions to decide how to regulate marijuana: "The local-option framing of it, where you'd have a different law in every city and county of California, sets up a chaotic system, which I think scared off a lot of people" (Gieringer interview). In addition, the "wording that limited the right of employers to do drug testing ... was enough to set off fire alarms at the Chamber of Commerce, and so the Chamber of Commerce and other business interests became galvanized in opposing the initiative" (Gieringer interview). (As noted, the measure did not mention drug testing but did allow employers to prohibit drug use at work.) An op-ed in the *Los Angeles Times* by six former national drug czars cited a host of other anticipated problems: Usage would increase; tax revenues would be meager because users could grow their own supply and thus be free of taxes; and the number of intoxicated drivers on the roads would skyrocket, leading to more accidents and fatalities (Kerlikowske et al., 2010). And a September 2010 editorial in the *Los Angeles Times* labeled the measure "an invitation to chaos":

> It would permit each of California's 478 cities and 58 counties to create local regulations regarding the cultivation, possession, and distribution of marijuana.... The proposition would have merited more serious consideration had it created a statewide regulatory framework for local governments, residents, and businesses. But it still would have contained a fatal flaw: Californians cannot legalize marijuana. Regardless of how the vote goes on Nov. 2, under federal law marijuana will remain a Schedule I drug, whose use for any reason is proscribed by Congress. Sure, California could go it alone, but that would set up an inevitable

> conflict with the federal government that might not end well for the state. That experiment has been tried with medical marijuana, and the outcome has not inspired confidence (*Los Angeles Times*, 2010).

These objections were echoed in the state's three other leading newspapers. The *San Diego Union-Tribune* (2010) published an editorial entitled "No to Ganja Madness," again predicting that "chaos" would result from the patchwork of regulations among jurisdictions, that the current "explosion" of medical dispensaries in the state would skyrocket under recreational legalization, and that the measure would create a "collision course" with the federal government. Similar arguments were made by the *San Jose Mercury News* (2010) and the *San Francisco Chronicle* (2010), which called the medical marijuana system a "nightmare for many communities" that would only be magnified by Proposition 19 because of the lack of "state controls over distribution and product standards." The *Chronicle* also worried about the "stench" of 25 square-foot outdoor marijuana gardens in residential areas.

Even some of those who supported the principle of legalization considered Proposition 19 poorly framed. Television ads funded by Public Safety First and the No-on-19 campaign called the measure "a jumbled, legal nightmare." It was

> riddled with drafting errors that instead of raising revenue could jeopardize more than $9.4 billion in federal funding for California schools. And by making it impossible for employers to enforce drug-free workplace rules [an incorrect claim], Prop 19 could even allow school bus drivers to smoke marijuana right before they climb into the driver's seat (No On Prop 19 ad, 2010).

In sum, the major reasons for Proposition 19's failure included opposition of newspapers representing the four largest cities, alleged flaws in the state's existing medical marijuana regime, and strong opposition from state politicians and federal officials.

Oregon

Two years later, Oregon's ballot measure was rejected by the same margin as California's: 53.4 % voted against it. Measure 80 would have:

- Allowed adults to grow and possess any amount of marijuana;
- Permitted sales and cultivation, with regulations to be provided by a new Cannabis Commission;

- Mandated a drug education program for youth arrested for possession;
- Created a seven-member Cannabis Commission, five of whom would represent growers and processors; the commission would oversee zoning and licensing and would be mandated "to promote Oregon cannabis products in all legal national and international markets," in the words of the ballot measure;
- Required Oregon's attorney general to defend the new law and actively advocate for similar laws nationally and internationally.[4]

The most popular arguments in favor of the measure were that it would regulate an existing illegal market, raise substantial public revenue, and increase public safety. Supporters estimated that a potential $140 million would be gained in tax revenue, while $60 million would be saved in reduced law enforcement costs (KATU News, 2011). Some advocates also packaged the measure as being consistent with the culture of the Pacific Northwest, a culture that combines progressive and libertarian values. Indeed, Oregon was the first state to allow doctor-assisted suicide, to allow voting by mail, and to decriminalize marijuana in the 1970s (a violation punishable by a maximum $100 fine). This legacy was depicted as a cultural context that was favorable to drug legalization.

The rationales inscribed in the ballot measure were unique in some respects. The Preamble to Measure 80 invokes George Washington, Thomas Jefferson, and the book of Genesis to support legalization. It proclaims that "George Washington grew cannabis for more than 30 years" and that Thomas Jefferson invented a device to process hemp. Part of the Preamble offers a rather awkward and convoluted justification:

> cannabis prohibition is a sumptuary law of a nature repugnant to our constitution's framers and which is so unreasonable and liberticidal as to ... unnecessarily proscribe consumption of a "herb bearing seed" given to humanity in Genesis 1:29, thereby violating their unqualified religious rights under Article 1, Section 3 and their Natural Rights under Article 1, Section 33 of the Oregon Constitution [and] violates the individual's right to privacy and numerous other Natural and Constitutional Rights.

---

4. According to the text of Measure 80, Oregon's Attorney General would be required to defend the law against any federal challenges and prosecutions and also to "propose a federal and/or international act to remove impediments to this chapter, deliver the proposed act to each member of Congress and/or international organization, and urge adoption of the proposed federal and/or international act through all legal and appropriate means."

Paul Stanford, the chief proponent of Measure 80, later reflected:

> The Preamble talked about some historical and scientific facts about marijuana and cannabis, and *The Oregonian's* editorials and commentary painted that negatively as a manifesto for cannabis and belittled it, even though the facts cited therein were incontrovertible. The Preamble turned out to be a liability, politically, and was used against it (Stanford interview).

The original draft of Measure 80 would have created an oversight commission whose members would be appointed by the governor. This was changed in the final draft to a grower-dominated commission (5 of its 7 members), which fueled concern that oversight would be hollow or biased toward the industry. The state's leading newspaper, *The Oregonian* (2012), called this "equivalent to putting Philip Morris in charge of state tobacco policy," and even the measure's top advocate considered this a blunder:

> Several advocates in the cannabis community ... said that we shouldn't give the governor that much leeway [appointing commission members]. So we made that [change to grower-dominated].... In retrospect, that was a mistake. We should not have had people in the industry compose five out of seven members of the commission (Stanford interview).

The Oregonian (2012) branded the measure "comical" and "surreal" and stated, "Voters should reject this initiative and ask state and federal leaders for more coherent drug policies." This editorial compared Oregon's measure unfavorably to Colorado and Washington's because the latter impose limits on possession and on the number of retail outlets and give oversight responsibility to a government agency rather than a grower-dominated commission.

The newspaper of the state capitol, Salem, focused on other dangers. It claimed that marijuana was both "addictive" and a "gateway drug" leading users to experiment with other illegal substances, and argued that passage would inevitably make marijuana more available to minors. In addition, persistent use "leads to a decline in brain functioning" (*Statesman Journal*, 2012). The main newspaper in liberal Eugene, Oregon, derided the measure's romanticized depiction of cannabis use: in addition to noting the measure's clash with federal marijuana law, *The Register-Guard* (2012) denounced it as an attempt to create a "cannabis culture" in Oregon:

> Measure 80 is not an attempt to accommodate the reality of widespread and mostly harmless marijuana use. Instead, it aims to cre-

> ate a new reality, making Oregon into a state where the recreational use and commercial development of marijuana is not simply tolerated but celebrated.... It is not just anti-prohibition—it's overtly pro-pot.

The latter is a reference to the provision requiring state authorities to advocate legalization in other states. The newspaper also belittled the "sponsor's evangelistic attitude" in invoking Genesis and the Founding Fathers.

Finally, in a public debate on the measure, District Attorney Josh Marquis used the novel argument (against the measure) that there was no need for it because possession was already sufficiently decriminalized: Measure 80 was a "solution searching for a problem" because, he claimed, possession of less than one ounce is currently treated leniently in Oregon (City Club, 2012).

The pro-legalization camp had a deficit of elite backing. Supporting the measure were the Oregon chapter of the National Association of Criminal Defense Lawyers, the medical marijuana sector, some local politicians, and the NAACP's regional branch. But strongly opposing the measure were the state's three largest newspapers, Gov. John Kitzhaber (D), the Sheriff's Association, and the District Attorney's Association.

The measure's radical provisions, lack of elite sponsors, dubious justifications (historical, religious, and natural-law), and strident opposition from the state's three largest newspapers were major impediments to the measure's success. But even against these odds, it is noteworthy that fully 47% of voters supported the initiative, perhaps because proponents outspent opponents $531,000 to $71,000 (NIMSP, 2014).

Colorado

Colorado voters rejected a recreational marijuana initiative in 2006, with 58% voting against it. Six years later, a new measure (Amendment 64) passed by 55.3%. Its provisions include:

- Possession of up to one ounce is allowed for persons 21 years of age and older;
- A resident can cultivate up to six plants in an enclosed, locked space;
- Both state residents and non-residents can purchase marijuana;
- Oversight and licensing of cultivation facilities, product manufacturing sites, and retail stores by the Department of Revenue, which also regulates alcohol and tobacco;

- Local authorities will determine the location and number of marijuana stores in their jurisdictions; local officials may prohibit cultivation and manufacturing facilities as well as retail stores in their jurisdiction;
- Marijuana stores are subject to state and local sales taxes;
- A DUI/DWI provision may be established by the governor and Department of Revenue. It was not mandated in Amendment 64, but a statute signed into law in May 2013 established limits on marijuana blood levels while driving.

The organization Smart Colorado led the opposition campaign and raised $433,000 to fight the measure (half of which came from the Florida group, Save Our Society from Drugs). Other vocal opponents included the Denver Chamber of Commerce, the *Denver Post*, Focus on the Family, Citizen Link, Visit Denver, Downtown Denver Partnership, Gov. John Hickenlooper (D), Denver Mayor Michael Hancock (D), state Attorney General John Suthers (R), the Colorado Education Association, and law enforcement organizations. Law enforcement groups either opposed or abstained from taking a position (e.g., opposition came from the Colorado Drug Investigator's Association, a trade group for drug enforcement officers). Given the wide variety of sectors represented by these actors, their reasons for opposing the amendment were multifaceted.

Arguments against the amendment included: (a) the standard claim that marijuana would become more available to youths, (b) an expected battle with the federal government over marijuana policy, (c) a concern that non-residents would flock to Colorado for the purpose of "marijuana tourism", and (d) a concern in the business community that legal cannabis would harm the state's reputation and make it harder to recruit new businesses to the state. A *Denver Post* (2012) editorial echoed some of these points while rejecting others. It began by declaring that possession should be legalized—at the national, not state, level. Rejecting the idea that legalization would put youth at risk, the editorial drew a parallel with the underage ban on alcohol purchases. What worried the *Denver Post*'s writers was the anticipated clash with the federal government and the fear that Colorado would become a magnet for out-of-state buyers, growers, and distributors. The opposition argument in California that delegating regulatory decisions to local authorities would create an unworkable patchwork and that a single, statewide model was preferable was not a major opposition argument in Colorado, nor was California's claim that the medical marijuana sector was already out of control echoed in the Colorado debate.

The Chamber of Commerce's opposition was based on several concerns. While proponents favored the potential revenue that would result from taxing marijuana distributors, big business countered that becoming a marijuana-friendly state would damage the state's image and perhaps deter new investment. They also feared that passage would result in businesses having to modify their drug-free policies, perhaps allowing marijuana use by employees. The latter concern was unfounded: under the regulations effective January 1, 2014, employers retain the right to fire workers who are intoxicated at work.

Economic justifications for Amendment 64 included the claim that passage would create at least 350 jobs and that substantial new tax revenue would be generated. Indeed, some businesses liked the possibility that Colorado might become a hub for marijuana tourism, generating demand for hotels, restaurants, rental cars, and other services.

Advocates outspent opponents 5 to 1: $3.5 million vs. $707,000 (NIMSP, 2014). Fundraisers included the Campaign to Regulate Marijuana Like Alcohol (raising $1.3 million) and the Marijuana Policy Project ($830,000). The two largest individual donors were Scott Banister, a San Francisco Internet entrepreneur, and Peter Lewis, chairman of Progressive Insurance Company. Other supporters include former Republican congressman Tom Tancredo, the Colorado branch of the NAACP, a coalition of more than 300 physicians, the United Food and Commercial Workers Union (Colorado's largest union), and the Colorado Center on Law and Policy. Having bipartisan support from a well-known right-wing politician, Rep. Tom Tancredo, as well as the Colorado Democratic Party, may have contributed to the measure's success (Tvert interview). More importantly, unlike in California, the medical marijuana community was largely supportive of the measure, evidenced by a petition drive in which more than 150 medical marijuana-related businesses allowed volunteers to collect signatures inside their stores. Colorado's medical sector supported Amendment 64 partly because the provisions of the new law gave preferential status and other benefits to existing medical marijuana businesses (indeed, as of January 2014, the only dispensaries where recreational users could obtain the drug were existing medical marijuana stores). The unified stance of the medical and recreational sectors differed from the situation in the other states.

Washington

Washington legalized recreational marijuana by the same margin as Colorado, with 55.7% voting for it. A poll of voters one day after the election found that support was strongest among Democrats, liberals, moderates, those with higher education, and families with $100,000+ income; opposition came from older age groups, conservatives, Republicans, the highly religious, and the less educated (Associated Press, 2012). Initiative 502 provided for the following:

- Designates the Washington State Liquor Control Board as the regulating authority; tightly regulates and licenses distribution, similar to the control of alcohol;
- Taxes marijuana sales and earmarks marijuana-related revenues; imposes an tax of 25% at each point of transfer between manufacturers, processors, and retailers;
- Prohibits growing marijuana in private residences, allowing only medical marijuana patients to do so;
- Prohibits marijuana stores near schools, daycare and youth centers, parks, and libraries;
- Outlaws public use or display;
- Establishes a blood-test limit for driving under the influence;
- Allows employers to dismiss employees who test positive for THC.

After the ballot passed, the number of recreational marijuana stores was capped at 334, the same number as alcohol stores in the state (only 70 such stores were operating by the end of 2014). A jurisdiction may not prohibit a store, although some have recently tried to ban them from their area.

Key opponents included medical marijuana entrepreneurs, law enforcement officials, substance abuse staff, and Gov. Christine Gregoire (D), whose opposition was mainly based on concerns over federal government intervention if the measure passed. In addition, the two candidates for governor in the 2012 election both opposed I-502 due to their concerns about the impact on the medical marijuana sector. Representatives of the drug prevention and law enforcement sectors tended to focus on marijuana's harms, such as the risks to young people from early-onset use and the risk of mental health problems for adults who use the substance frequently.

As in California, the medical marijuana sector was a vocal opponent: "They showed up at most hearings and public meetings, and were loud and noisy.... They would get up and yell and interrupt meetings. People were influenced, so I think they were actually effective" (Martin interview). Sensible Washington, a medical marijuana association, offered several reasons for rejecting Initiative 502. They opposed the DUI provision, claiming that it had no scientific basis, and they argued that the measure was too restrictive, because it would effectively criminalize medical patients who needed the drug because their chronic use would make many of them test positive while driving a car. Sensible Washington also thought that individuals aged 16 to 20 should be eligible if their medical condition warranted consumption. So, in this case, the medical marijuana sector opposed the measure not because it would interfere with their own profits but instead because they considered the regulations too restrictive.

In a public debate with a proponent (Alison Holcomb of the ACLU), John Toker of Sensible Washington cited additional problems with I-502: First, he called it "pseudo-legalization" because it limits possession to only one ounce. Second, he advocated a system with fewer restrictions than the measure's elaborate set of regulations (Working People Unite, 2012). And third, Sensible Washington opposed the measure's prohibition on cultivation for personal use, which would harm medical marijuana users who may need a personal source of the drug (Elliot, 2012). Responding to this critique, proponents pointed out that I-502 prohibits personal growing marijuana for recreational use, but registered medical patients are permitted to continue growing limited amounts on their private property and can possess a 60-day supply of marijuana (New Approach Washington, 2012).

Unlike the pro campaigns in the other three states, Washington's advocates highlighted a set of criminal justice problems to support legalization, an issue covered extensively by the *Seattle Times* and the *Tacoma News Tribune.* The argument centered on the harms of the law's overreach, enforcement costs, racialized law enforcement, and involvement of the criminal underworld in the marijuana trade—while failing to reduce usage. The campaign emphasized that over 241,000 state residents had been arrested for marijuana possession since 1986 and claimed that this cost of this enforcement was $306 million—with blacks and Latinos arrested disproportionately (Marijuana Arrest Research Project, 2012). Social justice and harm-reduction framing was therefore quite prominent during this state's debate on the measure. One of our interviewees elaborated on this issue:

> Efforts to prevent access to marijuana are largely ineffective, and these efforts come with great costs. Not only financial costs for the operation of the law enforcement and criminal justice system, but also with major social justice inequities in how the laws are actually implemented ... in terms of people of color being arrested far more than whites even though the epidemiological data make it clear that people of color use marijuana at a somewhat lower level. The campaign was also emphasizing that the tax revenues that this [new] legal market could generate could be put to good use in terms of public health and public safety (Roffman interview).

Along with some other newspapers, such as *The Olympian* (Olympia, the state capitol) and *The Spokesman-Review* (Spokane), the measure won support from the *Seattle Times* (2012) editorial board:

> For several years, recreational marijuana has effectively been decriminalized in Seattle, and there has been no upsurge in crime or road deaths from it. But even in Seattle, recreational marijuana is still supplied by criminals—by definition.... Initiative 502 aims to take the marijuana business out of the hands of gangs. That is what legalizing alcohol did in the 1930s.

The proponents of I-502 greatly outspent the opposition, spending $6.2 million in comparison to their opponents' miniscule $16,000 (NIMSP, 2014). For the pro side, a substantial part of the funding came from Peter Lewis of the Progressive Insurance Company and business magnate George Soros.

The campaign gained legitimacy and credibility when a former US Attorney, John McKay, became a sponsor and published an op-ed in the *Seattle Times* calling for legalization. The ranks of supporters included 16 state legislators, the former head of Seattle's FBI office, Charles Mandigo, Seattle City Attorney Pete Holmes, and television evangelist Pat Robertson. Another influence on Washington voters may have been Rick Steves, a well-known travel writer who frequently appears on PBS channel travel shows. Reporter Jonathan Martin from the *Seattle Times* noted that Rick Steves is a "beloved figure in the Seattle area because he has a travel company that has been here a long time. He's a regular radio show. He's just a super folksy, easygoing guy. He was just a great face for the campaign" (Martin interview). Steves' support of I-502 added credence to the initiative.

Advocates for I-502 were effective in framing the initiative in terms of social justice and harm-reduction benefits; legalization would reduce criminal justice inequities and reallocate law enforcement resources to more important matters.

Discussion

Scheerer's (1978) state-centric, top-down model of drug legalization is clearly obsolete. The US experience since 1996 with both medical and recreational marijuana measures demonstrates a citizen-driven alternative to the legislative model. The decriminalization of possession in eleven states in the 1970s was done entirely within the halls of state legislatures, but of the 23 jurisdictions that now allow medical marijuana, 12 resulted from popular ballot initiatives.

With only four cases in the present study, it is difficult to say with certainty that any particular variable is more important than others in predicting whether a recreational ballot measure will succeed or fail. Moreover, the factors of interest cannot be subjected to quantitative analysis. Other limitations of this study include the lack of certain kinds of data (e.g., records of how campaign funds were used), the modest number of interviewees, and the fact that the latter discussed the ballot process in hindsight. But we have attempted to identify factors that appear to be important influences on ballot outcomes. Specific provisions within a measure can certainly shape the vote, especially if they attract (straight or sensationalized) media coverage and television and radio ads. But what also matters is how the measure is generally *framed* in the public square. California's measure was framed by opponents as a recipe for conflict with the federal government, at a time of an escalating federal crackdown in the state, and as lacking in statewide regulatory norms that would only exacerbate existing problems with the state's medical marijuana system. Oregon's measure was derided as "too radical," with no limits on possession or the number of cannabis stores and a regulatory commission that was dominated by the marijuana industry. In Colorado, more than the other states, the overarching framing was that marijuana was less harmful than and should be regulated like alcohol. And the dominant framing of Washington's measure was that legalization would help to promote social justice because it would remove marijuana from the criminal justice system and reduce racially disparate outcomes. In none of the three 2012 debates did the opposition emphasize the California argument that the medical marijuana system was out of control and that adding recreational marijuana to the mix would only make things worse.

In both Colorado and Washington, legalization was also framed as a public health and safety issue—less as a danger to public health and more as a way of advancing it. In Washington, legalization was presented as a way to further drug education, treatment, and controlled use. In Colorado, a key campaign message was that marijuana is objectively less harmful to health than alcohol, thus seemingly justifying Amendment 64. Challenging the argument that usage and dependency would increase, proponents argued instead that legalization was consistent with a harm-minimization orientation that places education, health, and treatment, and not criminal justice, at the core of marijuana policy.

The role of the federal government is important. All four states had a preexisting medical marijuana sector, yet California's experience with federal action against medical marijuana establishments appears to have diluted support for Prop. 19. Federal intervention fueled concerns regarding how the government might respond to recreational legalization. Just two years later, the policy window opened as the Obama administration largely stayed silent during the November 2012 election, perhaps because this was a national election and the president wanted to avoid alienating supporters in the three states.[5] California was the only state that, at the time of the vote, experienced significant intervention from the Justice Department, which appears to have diminished the amount of support for its legalization measure. Intervention by the judiciary is another possibility. The Attorneys General of Nebraska and Omaha recently filed a federal lawsuit, asking the US Supreme Court to declare Colorado's law unconstitutional because it allegedly increases the amount of marijuana flowing into neighboring states—an example of how the federal government may yet intervene in at least one recreational marijuana state (Healy 2014). In the area of drug reform, the role of the federal government is clearly an important factor in state-level legal change.

One question is whether funding for vice-legalization campaigns matters. It is perhaps no surprise that Oregon's radical measure was the least funded of the three 2012 ballot initiatives. Advocates raised only $531,000, which pales in comparison to the $6.2 million in Washington and $3.5 million in Colorado in support of the measures. As noted above, financial support for the Washington and Colorado measures far eclipsed the amounts raised by opponents, so it does appear that funding was a predictor in both states. But funding alone does not ensure success. California's failed measure received $4.5 million from supporters, ten times more than the opposition's $420,000. And despite the significant variations in funding, voter support for the two failed ballot initiatives was identical (California 46.5%, Oregon's 46.6%) as was support for the two successful measures (Colorado 55.3%, Washington 55.7%). In other words, while generous funding can help to sway voters on vice issues, other factors can outweigh campaign financing.

The age distribution of voters matters significantly. Two recent polls (Gallup 2014; CNN 2014) both reported that 67% of young adults endorse legaliza-

5. A November 2012 Gallup poll and a March 2013 Pew Research poll reported that 64% and 60% of Americans, respectively, felt that the federal government should not intervene to enforce federal marijuana laws in states that currently allow marijuana possession. In May 2014, the US House of Representatives voted (219–189) for a measure that would prevent federal government interference in states that allow cultivation, sale, and possession of medical marijuana. It remains to be seen whether the Senate will follow suit and whether the president will sign the bill. Since 2003, six similar measures had failed to pass the House.

tion of marijuana for recreational use. If a similar majority of youth in any given state support legalization, it can be argued that youth turnout may have a decisive effect on the outcome of marijuana ballot measures. The youth turnout figures in our four cases lend some support to this hypothesis. In California, the percentage of voters in the 18–29 age group declined by half between the 2008 general election (20% of the vote) and 2010 midterm election (10% of the vote) (Bacon, 2010). Had this age group turned out in the same numbers in 2010 as they did in 2008, it is possible that Proposition 19 would have won (Hoeffel, 2010c). In the other three states, youth turnout increased between 2008 and 2012: from 12 to 17% of voters in Oregon, 14 to 20% in Colorado, and 10 to 22% in Washington (Atlas Project, 2013). The substantial rise in the youth vote may help to explain ballot success in Colorado and Washington. A Colorado poll taken in early October 2012 found that 56% of likely voters aged 18–34 supported the ballot measure, compared to 48% of all likely voters (SurveyUSA, 2012), and a poll of registered voters in Washington conducted right before the election (in late October) found that fully 75% of those aged 18–29 supported Washington's ballot initiative (KCTS, 2012).

The liberal political culture of the Pacific Northwest (e.g., only Oregon and Washington allow doctor-assisted suicide) may have had a positive impact in Washington but could not overcome the perceived deficiencies of Oregon's measure. History shows that a state's political culture does not need to be progressive for the decriminalization of vice to occur; some conservative states decriminalized marijuana possession in the 1970s, whereas some vice-tolerant states like Nevada passed harsh laws (DiChiara & Galliher, 1994; Galliher & Cross, 1983). For this reason, we do not consider a state's historical political culture a robust predictor, although it may have some impact. Coupled with whatever influence the Northwest political culture may have had on the outcome in Oregon and Washington in 2012, Washington's initiative also had other pillars of support: substantial financial backing and support from a wide variety of actors. Having former federal law enforcement officials and the legal community publicly endorse the initiative gave tremendous gravitas to the campaign. However, the stance of candidates running for office or the incumbent governor was found to have limited impact on ballot outcomes: there was wide variation on this measure among the cases.

Washington and Colorado's ballot measures satisfy many of the preconditions that Lenton (2004), Skolnick (1998) and Weitzer (2012) outline as important factors for vice decriminalization, presented earlier in this chapter. Since there have been only seven attempts to legalize recreational marijuana in recent years (2010–2014), it difficult to identify a "best practices" formula for drug liberalization. Yet it does appear that meeting most, if not all, of the preconditions listed above will improve the chances that a vice-related ballot measure will succeed in any given state. Also critically important is the *dynamic process* in which opposing forces and media outlets frame the ballot initiative generally and highlight its specific benefits or problems. Our analysis suggests that support from political leaders, law enforcement officials, the medical marijuana sector, public health community, and young voters are important—as is the central framing of the issue. However, as evidenced by the failures of California and Oregon's initiatives, even if some of these conditions are met, they do not ensure success. A "triggering event" can also play a role, such as the Attorney General's threat of federal intervention if California had passed its ballot measure in 2010 (Galliher & Cross, 1983).

Nationwide, support for legalization jumped a remarkable 10 percentage points in the year following the 2012 Colorado and Washington victories from 48% in late November 2012 to 58% in October 2013 (Gallup, 2014). Three jurisdictions voted on recreational legalization measures in November 2014: Alaska, Oregon, and Washington, DC. Federal authorities remained silent during the debate on these ballot measures, but there was robust opposition to them within Alaska and Oregon—where exit polls showed that only 31% and 22% of Republicans, respectively, voted in favor, while 78% and 79% of Democrats did so (Tesler 2014). All three measures passed.[6]

Oregon's Measure 91 garnered 55.6% support. It avoided the bizarre justifications of its 2012 counterpart, benefitted from the legalization of recreational marijuana across the border in Washington, and gives regulatory power to the state's Liquor Control Commission rather than the industry-dominated commission proposed in 2012. Supporters of the measure spent $7 million on the campaign (far more than the amount in 2012, $531,000) and eclipsed the opposition's $128,000. *The Oregonian* (2014) endorsed Measure 91, reversing its sharp opposition to Measure 80 in 2012.

In Alaska, despite a huge turnout of conservative voters and Republican political victories, 52.1% of voters endorsed legalization (Measure 2). The state's major newspapers offered a mix of opinions,[7] and proponents outspent opponents ($1,131,000 vs. $151,000).

Despite the leading newspaper's two editorials opposing Initiative 71 (*Washington Post*, 2014a, 2014b) and the fact that very little money was spent promot-

6. According to an exit poll, only 56% of Democrats voted in favor of California's 2010 measure, along with 30% of Republicans (Tesler, 2014).

7. The *Juneau Empire* supported and the *Daily News Miner* opposed Measure 2. The other major newspapers took no position but printed op-eds pro and con, including opposition from Senator Lisa Murkowski (R) and Fairbanks Police Chief Keith Mallard.

ing the measure, it attracted 70% support in Washington, DC—high because the city is populated largely by Democrats and because it is a city rather than a state (the latter having rural or suburban areas that tend to be more conservative than large cities). Washington, DC's, measure departs from the others in several ways:

(1) it is a form of decriminalization, not legalization, because it lacks regulatory elements;
(2) implementation is contingent on congressional approval (mandated for such measures in DC);
(3) it allows individuals 21 years of age and older to "possess, use, purchase, or transport," but not sell, up to two ounces of marijuana, to grow up to six plants, and to "transfer" to another person up to one ounce of marijuana "without remuneration"; the anomaly here is that one can *purchase but not sell* marijuana or cannabis plants;
(4) it does not prohibit possession or use in public places, except on federal property.

After the November 2014 vote, Congress passed legislation that prevented the city from spending money to implement the measure, but city officials responded by instructing police not to arrest people who grow or possess marijuana as long as they are in compliance with the new law.

Research on future ballot outcomes will help to confirm whether the factors identified in this study are corroborated as important in other contexts and thus have more general salience.

References

Associated Press. (2012, November 7). Washington voters legalize recreational pot use. *The Spokesman-Review.*

Atlas Project. (2013). *Marijuana ballot measures and youth turnout.* Retrieved from http://atlasproject.net/daily-blog/marijuana-ballot-measures-and-youth-turnout/.

Bacon, P. (2010, November 3). Low turnout by young voters hurts Democrats in midterm elections. *Washington Post.*

California State Board of Equalization. (2014). *Medical marijuana/Legalization of marijuana.* Retrieved from http://www.boe.ca.gov/news/marijuana.htm.

City Club of Portland. (2012). Measure 80 debate. Retrieved from *YouTube.* http://www.youtube.com/watch?v=b1LanOUiYPk.

CNN. (2014). Poll, January 3–5. CNN/ORC International poll, N=1,010.

Cole, J. (2013, August 29). Memorandum: Guidance regarding marijuana enforcement. US Department of Justice.

Denver Post. (2012, October 14). Amendment 64 is the wrong way to legalize marijuana. Editorial.

DiChiara, A., & Galliher, J. (1994). Dissonance and contradictions in the origins of marihuana decriminalization. *Law & Society Review, 28*, 41–78.

Dombrink, J., & Hillyard, D. (2007). *Sin no more*. New York: NYU Press.

Drug Free America Foundation. (2010). No to Prop 19. Retrieved from http://www.youtube.com/watch?v=IDudTp-NOi8.

The Economist. (2013, December 11). Uruguay's cannabis law: Weed all about it.

Elinson, Z. (2014, October 24). Oregon initiative seeks lower pot taxes than cities want. *Wall Street Journal*.

Elliott, S. (2012). Sensible Washington: Here's why we oppose I-502 "legalization." *Toke of the Town*. Retrieved from http://www.tokeofthetown.com/2012/10/sensible_washington_heres_why_we_oppose_i-502_lega.php.

Field Research Corporation. (2013). The Field Poll, no. 2442, February 5–17. N=834 registered voters.

Fisher, M. (2014, July 27). A dividing line. *Washington Post*.

Galliher, J., & Cross, J. (1983). *Morals legislation without morality*. New Brunswick: Rutgers University Press.

Gallup Poll. (2014). Illegal drugs (1969–2013 polls). Retrieved from http://www.gallup.com/poll/1657/illegal-drugs.aspx.

Geluardi, J. (2010). *Cannabiz: The explosive rise of the medical marijuana industry*. Sausalito, CA: PoliPoint Press.

Healy, J. (2014, December 19). 2 neighbors of Colorado sue over marijuana law. *New York Times*.

Hoeffel, J. (2010a, May 5). L.A. orders 439 medical marijuana dispensaries to close. *Los Angeles Times*.

Hoeffel, J. (2010b, October 16). Holder vows fight over Prop. 19. *Los Angeles Times*.

Hoeffel, J. (2010c, November 3). Youth vote falters, Prop. 19 falls short. *Los Angeles Times*.

Huffington Post/YouGov poll. (2014). July 28–31. N=1,000 adults.

Kamin, S. (2012). Medical marijuana in Colorado and the future of marijuana regulation in the United States. *McGeorge Law Review, 43*, 147–167.

KATU News. (2011, March 28). Push to sell marijuana in Oregon kicks off. Retrieved from http://www.katu.com/news/local/118824839.html.

KCTS. (2012, October 18–31). *KTCS 9 Washington Poll*, N=722 registered voters. Retrieved from http://www.washingtonpoll.org/results/kcts9wapoll_oct31.pdf.

Kerlikowske, G., Walters, J., McCaffrey, B., Brown, L., Martinez, B., & Bennett, W. (2010, August 25). Why California should just say no to Prop. 19. *Los Angeles Times.*

Lempert, R. (1974). Toward a theory of decriminalization. University of Michigan Public Law Working Paper, No. 209.

Lenton, S. (2004). Pot, politics, and the press: Reflections on cannabis law reform in Western Australia. *Drug and Alcohol Review, 23*, 223–233.

Los Angeles Times. (2010, September 24). Snuff out pot measure. Editorial.

MacCoun, R., & Reuter, P. (2001). *Drug war heresies.* New York: Cambridge University Press.

Marijuana Arrest Research Project. (2013). 240,000 marijuana arrests: Costs, consequences, and racial disparities of possession arrests in Washington, 1986–2010. Retrieved from http://www.marijuana-arrests.com/docs/240,000-Marijuana-Arrests-In-Washington.pdf.

NIMSP (National Institute on Money in State Politics). (2014). *2011–2012 Ballot measure overview.* Retrieved from http://classic.followthemoney.org/press/ReportView.phtml?r=504&ext=7#Recreational Marijuana Measures, 201.

New Approach Washington. (2012). Backgrounder: I-502 and medical marijuana. *Yes on I-502—New Approach Washington.* Retrieved from http://www.newapproachwa.org/sites/newapproachwa.org/files/I-502%20Backgrounder%20-%20Medical%20Marijuana%20-%20073012.pdf.

No on Prop 19. (2010). No on Proposition 19 Radio Ad. Retrieved from *YouTube.* Retrieved from http://www.youtube.com/watch?v=vM7PHxBVMbw.

The Oregonian. (2012, September 22). Vote no on Measure 80, Oregon's marijuana manifesto. Editorial.

The Oregonian. (2014, August 23). It's time to legalize recreational marijuana. Editorial.

Peterson, R. (1985). Discriminatory decision making at the legislative level: An analysis of the Comprehensive Drug Abuse Prevention and Control Act of 1970. *Law and Human Behavior, 9*, 243–269.

Regan, T. (2011). *Joint ventures: Inside America's almost legal marijuana industry*. Hoboken, NJ: Wiley.

Register-Guard. (2012, October 3). Marijuana legalization: No. Measure 80 overreaches, underregulates. Editorial.

San Diego Union-Tribune. (2010, October 18). No to ganja madness. Editorial.

San Francisco Chronicle. (2010, September 16). Proposition 19: Vote no. Editorial.

San Jose Mercury News. (2010, October 13). No on Proposition 19: Legalizing marijuana is inevitable, but this is the wrong way. Editorial.

Scheerer, S. (1978). The new Dutch and German drug laws: Social and political conditions for criminalization and decriminalization. *Law & Society Review, 12*, 585–606.

Seattle Times. (2012, September 22). Approve Initiative 502—It's time to legalize, regulate, and tax marijuana. Editorial.

Sharp, E. (2005). *Morality politics in American cities*. Lawrence: University of Kansas Press.

Skolnick, J. (1988). The Social Transformation of Vice. *Law and Contemporary Problems, 51*, 9–29.

State of Colorado. (2013). Office of the Governor and Department of Revenue. *Task Force report on the implementation of Amendment 64*. Retrieved from http://www.colorado. gov/cms/forms/dor-tax/A64TaskForceFinal Report.pdf.

Statesman Journal. (2012, November 1). Marijuana legalization deserves a "no" vote. Editorial.

SurveyUSA. (2012). *Results of Survey 19856*. October 9–10, poll of likely voters. N=614. Retrieved from http://www.surveyusa.com/client/PollReport.aspx?g=c33f6e0a-00b5-4764-8ee2-525a01ca58b0.

Tesler, M. (2014, November 10). How Democrats derailed marijuana legalization in California. *Washington Post*.

Washington Post. (2014a, September 14). DC voters should reject the rush to legalize marijuana. Editorial.

Washington Post. (2014b, October 21). On marijuana legalization plans, the district should slow down. Editorial.

Weitzer, R. (2012). *Legalizing prostitution: From illicit vice to lawful business*. New York: NYU Press.

Working People Unite. (2012). I-502 Debate: Marijuana legalization in Washington state. Retrieved from http://www.youtube.com/watch?v=KbXzCLnHA1s.

7

No Tokes over the Line: Marijuana Decriminalization, Medicalization and Legalization As It Affects Decarceration*

Mary K. Stohr and Cheyenne Foster

Introduction

Relatively recent efforts to decriminalize and medicalize, and since 2012, to legalize, marijuana at the state level are turning the drug war orthodoxy on its head. No longer does the old "no tolerance" hold and people in many states, but particularly in Colorado, Washington State, and as of November 4, 2014, Alaska, Oregon, and the District of Columbia, are saying "hell yes" rather than "just say no" to marijuana. In December 2014 the United States Department of Justice even gave the go ahead to the growth and sale of recreational marijuana on Indian Reservations, should tribes elect to do so (Barnard & Wozniacka, 2014). There are in effect no tokes "over the line" in these states and potentially on reservations, as there is no line left; that was obliterated when the War on Drugs, at least as it concerns marijuana, was abandoned.

Given these realities, one would expect that corrections will be greatly affected by legalization: fewer people will be arrested for illegal drug use so there will be fewer people on probation, incarcerated in jails and prisons, and ultimately paroled. Treatment programs for correctional populations will be filled with subscribers to "harder," and still illegal, drugs and with alcoholics and ad-

---

* The first part of this chapter title is derived from the song title by the folk rock duo of the 1960s and 1970s, Mike Brewer and Tom Shipley, "One Toke Over the Line."

dicts who commit their crimes when drunk or high. Moreover, although still illegal at the federal level, one might reasonably expect that federal enforcement of drug laws, at least as it is related to marijuana use in the states, and particularly in the states where use is now legal, might decrease too. Although these are changes one might assume would take place given the changes in drug laws, it has yet to be determined if this is, or will be, what is happening.

In this chapter we briefly explore the history of marijuana use and its criminalization during the twentieth century and subsequent decriminalization, medicalization, and legalization in the twenty-first century. We touch on the purported medicinal benefits of marijuana and the challenges that have prevented the full-fledged research on it. Decriminalization, medicalization, and legalization of marijuana, and reduced sanctions for other drug offenses, have vastly changed the criminal justice landscape and are likely to stall the seemingly relentless march to incarcerate in the United States. It is our contention that there will be repercussions for correctional populations based on these statutory changes and those will come in the form of increased decarceration, an effect we may already be witnessing in jails.

The Evolving History of the "Evil Weed": Marijuana

Marijuana has a long, tangled, and tragic history. Records suggest that marijuana use most likely originated in China (Booth, 2003; Marion, 2014). Even in early civilizations, spanning as far back as 2,900 BC, it was used both recreationally and medicinally (Booth, 2003; Marion, 2014; Mosher & Akins, 2014; ProCon.org, 2014b). Although the intoxicating and psychoactive effects are noted in the historical records, medical use was highly valued in many regions, such as ancient Greece, ancient Egypt, and ancient China. During these periods, marijuana was used for a myriad of medical purposes, with the common theme being pain relief for ailments such as aches, gout, and inflammation (Marion, 2014). Eventually, marijuana made its way west. In colonial America and up until a little over century ago (the 1910s), it was regarded as a relatively benign substance. In 1914 the Harrison Act was signed into law, which regulated and restricted the distribution of opiates and coca products. This law also made non-medical marijuana illegal, although medical marijuana was still technically legal (Harrison Narcotics Tax Act of 1914).

The Harrison Act did not end the medical use and distribution of marijuana; in fact, it became more popular after alcohol consumption was restricted with Prohibition (Marion, 2014). However, Harry Anslinger, the first commissioner of the US Treasury Department's Federal Bureau of Narcotics, made it his mission to rid the streets of the "evil weed" and portrayed the substance as a volatile drug that causes insanity in youths and drives them to suicide and murder (Anslinger & Cooper, 1937). In the classic anti-marijuana movie, which epitomizes the Anslinger and later societal angst about the deleterious effect of the evil weed, *Reefer Madness* (1936), marijuana is depicted as causing young people, as embodied by the "Bill" and "Mary" of the film, to engage in "drug crazed abandon" (authors' warning: these are some of the oldest teenagers, most stilted actors, and worst dancers you might encounter on film). According to the script provided before the movie begins, Marihuana—this was the Mexican spelling of the drug—is a "ghastly menace" and the "real public enemy number one" as it leads to uncontrollable violence (*Reefer Madness*, 2003). In a foreshadowing of the drug war we have come to know and 35 years before President Nixon declared a War on Drugs in 1971, the term "war on drugs" is featured as a newspaper front page heading in the movie.

Spoiler alert: In the film Mary is shot and killed by a drug pusher, Jack, after almost being raped by another high teenager, Ralph, who is made insane from smoking too many reefers. Then Bill is framed for Mary's murder (after getting high and having intimate relations with another teenager—not Mary) and convicted, and then released when the truth comes out. The truth of Bill's innocence is revealed only after another murder, this time of Jack (who had murdered Mary, accidentally), committed by Ralph, and the suicide of a female witness (who spilled the goods on Jack)—the same one who had the intimate relations with Bill (it is not just the *history* of marijuana which is tangled). And all of this after Bill and Mary enjoy just one joint! Talk about one toke over the line!

White women especially, according to testimony before Congress, in the Ways and Means Committee, by Anslinger, might be tempted after usage of this evil weed to involve themselves promiscuously with devilish men (who not coincidentally are darker skinned than they are) and the concomitant "sin, degradation, vice, and insanity" (*Reefer Madness*, 2003, originally distributed in 1936; Anslinger, 1937).

Included in Commissioner Anslinger's (1937) testimony was a request for assistance with enforcement from the city editor of the *Alamosa Daily Courier* (September 4, 1936) to the Bureau of Narcotics, including the following excerpts about crimes committed by those who were high on marijuana:

> Gentlemen: Two weeks ago a sex-mad degenerate, named Lee Fernandez, brutally attacked a young Alamosa girl. He was convicted of assault with intent to rape and sentenced to 10 to 14 years in the state

> penitentiary. Police officers here know definitely that Fernandez was under the influence of marihuana.
> I wish I could show you what a small marihuana cigarette can do to one of our degenerate Spanish-speaking residents. That's why our problem is so great; the greatest percentage of our population is composed of Spanish-speaking persons, most of who are low mentally, because of social and racial conditions.

In a report by a commissioner of public safety and an assistant city chemist (also as part of Anslinger's testimony):

> [W]e find then that Colorado reports that the Mexican population there cultivates on an average of 2 to 3 tons of the weed annually. This the Mexicans make into cigarettes, which they sell at two for 25 cents, mostly to white high school students.

Anslinger's advocacy before Congress resulted in the Marihuana Tax Act, which was signed into law in 1937, one year after *Reefer Madness* was distributed. At the time of his testimony in 1937, Mr. Anslinger claimed that every state had adopted a uniform narcotic law (which had been promoted by Anslinger) and which regulated the traffic in marijuana. The federal act gave teeth to the efforts to control marijuana use across the states, but the movie helped spread the "moral panic" about it (Goode & Ben-Yehuda, 1994). Stanley Cohen coined the term "moral panic" to mean:

> A condition, episode, person or group of persons emerges to become defined as a threat to societal values and interest; its nature is presented in a stylized and stereotypical fashion by the mass media; the moral barricades are manned by editors, bishops, politicians, and other right-thinking people (Cohen, 1972, p. 9).

It should come as no surprise that with Anslinger as its crusader, and people of color identified as the threat, the marijuana moral panic quickly erupted. A series of propaganda missives were subsequently issued through the media resulting in restrictive legislation that featured Mexican Americans as the villains of their stories and targets of their legislation (Goode & Ben-Yehuda, 1994). In order to save society from such a "menace," the Marihuana Tax Act seemed the only logical conclusion.

This statute imposed a tax that made it illegal to grow, buy, and sell marijuana products without registering with the federal government. In order to register the marijuana, growers, buyers, and sellers would need to obtain a stamp from the US Treasury Department. By giving the government regulatory power over marijuana, the perceived threat should have been alleviated. However, the new law created a ripple effect in other institutions. With the passing of the law, physicians then experienced extreme difficulty prescribing marijuana to their patients. Going through the process of registering medical marijuana made the prescribing of it much more difficult than prescribing another form of medication to patients, which essentially resulted in the cessation of medical marijuana prescriptions (Inciardi & McElrath, 2011). Of course, the de jure legal process, but de facto criminalization, created by the new law affected more than just the medical field.

Despite the requirement to register marijuana, the Treasury Department was not issuing any stamps (Marion, 2014). Thus, it quickly became a legitimized method of criminalizing those who were in possession. Because of this, there was no real way to legally distribute or obtain marijuana, which fundamentally criminalized the substance. Clearly, the discussion of the Marijuana Tax Act was racially charged and it was enacted at least in part to preserve the sanctity of white youth (Inciardi & McElrath, 2011). Regardless of the seemingly racially neutral law, the Marijuana Tax Act was the result of marijuana being perceived as a threat to white society because of its "un-American origins" and visibility in African American and Mexican culture (Inciardi & McElrath, 2011, p. 140). During his crusade, Anslinger also connected marijuana use to Mexican immigrants, thus sparking the notion of foreign danger (Marion, 2014). Anslinger and Cooper (1937) even reference a hypothetical distributor of marijuana cigarettes as a "hot tamale vendor" as opposed to a "food vendor." Making marijuana foreign, or non-white, spurred the moral panic and helped rally support for its prohibition. This is not a new concept for American drug policies. The Harrison Narcotics Tax Act was essentially the result of white society blaming Chinese immigrants for an increase in opium and cocaine addictions. Much like the Harrison Act targeting Asian populations, the Marijuana Tax Act targeted Hispanics in the 1930s.

It was in 1969 that the Marijuana Tax Act was ruled unconstitutional by the Supreme Court. Despite this seemingly progressive step, in the following year the Comprehensive Drug Abuse Prevention and Control Act was passed. This law categorized all substances into five classes based on their medical value and potential for abuse. It established mandatory minimum sentences for possession, possession with intent to sell, sale, and sale to a minor for each category. Marijuana was placed under Schedule I, which essentially marks it as having no medical benefit and as a drug with a high risk for abuse. In 1972, the National Organization for Reform of Marijuana Laws (NORML) petitioned the Drug Enforcement Agency to reclassify marijuana as a Schedule II drug to allow for medical use. Over a decade later, in 1989, the Director of the DEA finally made a decision and responded by not reclassifying marijuana; leaving it classified as a Schedule I drug (Marion, 2014). However, in only a few years, states had begun to pass their own medical marijuana laws regardless of its classification.

In 1991, San Francisco set the stage by passing the first medical marijuana initiative. The entire state of California was soon to follow in 1996 and became the first state to legalize medical marijuana. It wasn't long before other states began to pass medical marijuana legislation of their own, allowing patients and caregivers to grow and cultivate marijuana for the treatment of certain diseases as well as to protect physicians from punishment for recommending it. Currently, twenty-three states and the District of Columbia have passed medical marijuana legislation (ProCon.org, 2014a). However, because medical marijuana is still federally illegal, debates on how to enforce these laws are prevalent. The war on medical marijuana is ongoing. Regardless of the wave of states passing medical marijuana legislation, it remains a Schedule I drug, meaning it has no medical value according to federal law (Marion, 2014).

Medicinal Challenges and the Reported Benefits of Marijuana

Even though the use of medical and recreational marijuana is federally illegal, it is allegedly the most commonly used illegal drug in the United States (Inciardi & McElrath, 2011; Marion, 2014; Mosher & Akins, 2014). Some researchers have argued that recreational marijuana use can have several adverse health effects including lower educational attainment, psychoses and cardiovascular disease in adulthood, decrease in cellular immunity, and increase in risk of dependence and accidents (i.e., car accidents) (Hall, 2014; Hollister, 1986; Ryan, 2011). However, other researchers identify the limitations of such studies and note that these relationships may not be causal, but may be the result of other risk factors (Hall, 2014; Mosher & Akins, 2014). Although some negative effects of marijuana use are likely to be uncovered, more research is needed to isolate its exact adverse effects.

On the other end of the spectrum, some researchers argue that regardless of its classification as a Schedule I drug, there is little risk associated with using marijuana (Mosher & Akins, 2014; Grinspoon, 1999; Hollister, 1986). Tests have shown that it poses health and safety risks, but that these are no greater risks than those of other licit drugs, such as caffeine, alcohol, and tobacco (Hollister, 1986). This directly contradicts the Schedule I classification that defines marijuana as having a high risk of abuse. But because marijuana is still classified as a Schedule I drug at the federal level, it is also deemed to have no medical benefit. However, marijuana and cannabinoids are purported to have many medical purposes and benefits, which include relief of pain and inflammation, relief of nausea caused by chemotherapy, relief of muscle spasms associated with multiple sclerosis, lowering intraocular pressure in glaucoma, and possibly assisting in immunosuppression, which may be regarded also as an adverse effect, but can be useful in aiding in organ and tissue transplants (Hollister, 1986; Iversen, 1993; Marion, 2014). It is these potential benefits that have encouraged organizations and legislators to push for more lenient regulations.

Legislators and NORML are currently agitating for the reclassification of marijuana to a Schedule II to at least allow for medical testing (Marion, 2014; NORML, 2014). Reclassifying marijuana could help legitimize medical testing, although the current conventional route for medical legitimacy may create other issues when testing marijuana (Grinspoon, 1999). Some researchers argue that the legislation for medical testing is too restrictive and can actually impede our full understanding of the benefits marijuana has to offer (Grinspoon, 1999; NORML, 2014). Rather than assessing the value in case reports, expert opinions, and clinical expertise, the Food and Drug Administration requires evidence from a double-blind study which may not be possible for testing marijuana. The studies that do exist produce many inconclusive results, largely due to the difficulty in isolating the effects of marijuana because of testing restrictions (Grinspoon, 1999; Hall, 2014; Hollister, 1986; Iversen, 1993; Ryan, 2010). Even when potential benefits are found, the psychoactive properties deter opponents of the drug from accepting its uses. Although it is possible to isolate certain effects from the psychoactive effects, relying on that process only creates more obstacles (Iversen, 1993). However, despite the barriers that regulations and adversarial pushback present, some medical health professionals have recognized the potential benefits of marijuana as a viable option for patients facing certain medical conditions (Grinspoon, 1999; Mosher & Akins, 2014).

Decriminalization and Legalization: A Recognition of Failed Policy

Such pragmatism as to its medical usefulness and the sense that marijuana use is likely to be no more dangerous than other socially acceptable drugs (i.e., tobacco and alcohol), coupled with the realization of the daunting costs of corrections, has likely spurred the movement to begin a "drug war détente" as noted by the Vera Institute (Subramanian & Moreno, 2014). In a review of state-level drug laws from 2009 to 2013, the researchers at the Vera Institute found that since 2009 over 30 states have reformed their drug laws affecting mandatory penalties, sentencing, early release, community sanctions, and related effects. According to Subramanian and Moreno (2014, p. 14–17). These changes in sentencing laws have included:

- Eleven states from all regions of the country have repealed or reduced the sentence length of mandatory sentences;
- Eleven states have also restricted the use of sentence enhancements;
- Ten states have increased judicial discretion to be more lenient in their sentencing;
- Ten states have engaged in "redefining or reclassifying drug offenses";
- Five states have changed the sentence presumptions to reduce the involvement of drug offenders in the corrections system;
- Three states have increased the ability to release drug offenders; and
- Five states have altered their marijuana laws, moving to outright legalization of the sale of and the possession of small amounts of marijuana (i.e., Colorado, Washington State, Alaska, Oregon, and Washington, DC).

Additional statute reforms across several states that affect drug offenders include the increased use of community-based sanctions (over prisons), intensified incentives for programming, and a sharp escalation in the use of drug courts and drug treatment generally.

At the federal level there has been less statutory activity beyond the unanimous passage of the Fair Sentencing Act by Congress in 2010 which reduced the disparity in sentencing for crack cocaine versus powder cocaine from 100 to 1 to 18 to 1. In addition to this legislation, however, the US Sentencing Commission has issued guidelines which reduce sentences for many types of drug offenses and Attorney General Eric Holder has indicated his support of such reforms (Subramanian & Moreno, 2014). Furthermore, in 2014 a number of bills related to reduced sentences for offenders and increased use of community sanctions or alternatives to prison are before Congress and the support for the "War on Drugs" has so weakened that some of these bills may well pass with widespread bipartisan support. As the Vera Institute researchers aptly remark, "Have we entered a new era of fairer and more cost-effective responses to drug-involved offenders? With state reforms well-established and the federal government following suit, indications are that there is reason to believe that we may be" (Subramanian & Moreno, 2014, p. 24).

The intent expressed in these statutes and changes in policies is to decrease the use of prisons, but also jails, for drug offenders, particularly small-time users and marijuana consumers. Therefore, it is not too much of a risk for us to contend here that the collective effect of these statutory changes at the state and federal level has and will be to decrease the use of incarceration. As many of these laws are relatively new, the effects are only now being felt in the states and localities. But if the California example tells us anything, it is that a sea change in policy can very quickly result in a major shift in practice. At this juncture the landscape and sentiments regarding the now-latent drug war are shifting so that we are likely to see much more decarceration of such offenders in the near future.

Decarceration: Marijuana Convictions No Longer Provide a Gateway to Prison (or Jails)

It has often been argued that marijuana is a "gateway" drug leading to the use of other "harder" drugs such as methamphetamines, cocaine, or heroin (DeSimone, 1998; Golub and Johnson, 1994: Hall, 2014). Though the research on this point is far from definitive, it is really immaterial for our purposes here, as we are concerned with whether arrests and convictions for marijuana offenses will continue to serve as a "gateway" to future jail and prison stays as they have in the past. Naturally we would expect that the efforts to decriminalize, medicalize, and legalize marijuana in the states are likely to lead to the opposite effect, or decarceration. "Decarceration" is defined by Hogan and her colleagues (2014, p. 3) as "a decrease in numbers or rates of correctional clients placed in institutional environments (i.e., prisons and jails) and/or as a movement of correctional clients from more secure (such as a prison or jail) to less secure (such as parole or probation) modes of correctional control."

How much decarceration has occurred across the country in community corrections, jails, and prison populations is documented and varies widely by jurisdiction and state (Greene & Mauer, 2010). The Bureau of Justice Statistics (BJS) data indicates that at year-end 2012 and mid-year 2013 for jails we saw a fourth year of decreases in correctional populations (Glaze & Herberman, 2013; Minton & Golinelli, 2014). The overall number of adults under probation or parole supervision or incarcerated in jails and prisons by 2012 was 1 in 35 adults in the United States or the same rate as 1997, down from a high of 1 in 31 in both 2006 and 2007 (see Figure 1; Glaze & Herberman, 2013, p. 1). Meanwhile, the rate of persons under community supervision per 100,000 United States residents in 2012 and in state prisons dropped, but the number in jails or incarcerated in federal prisons increased slightly. By 2013 we were seeing another drop in jail populations too, the fourth straight drop in five years (Minton & Golinelli, 2014). Admittedly, much of this decrease in prison populations (for 2012 anyway, which saw the smallest percentage decrease in populations of the four consecutive years of decrease—a mere drop of 51,000 persons nationwide) was due to a court-ordered decrease in California prisons, which had the subsequent effect of increasing jail populations in that state as some of those inmates were realigned out of prisons to jails or community corrections (see also California's Public Safety Realignment Act of 2011; Glaze & Herberman, 2013, p. 2–3). By 2013 there was even a slight decrease in federal prison populations, the first year-to-year decrease in recent memory (Carson, 2014, p. 17).

By 2014, the Sentencing Project was reporting that BJS's newest figures for 2013 indicated that prison populations were increasing in a majority of states, albeit with a modest increase in prison populations of 4,300 inmates over 2012 figures (Sentencing Project, 2014, p.1). As Marc Mauer, longtime Executive Director of The Sentencing Project cautioned, "These figures challenge premature and overly optimistic forecasts of the end of mass incarceration. Tackling the prison juggernaut will require broader reforms to reduce prison admissions and sentence lengths."

Having said this, decarceration has become a nationwide phenomena with up to 25 states experiencing a decrease in their rate of imprisonment in 2009 and 2010 (Guerino et al., 2011; West et al., 2010); declines which continued through 2012 and which had not been seen in the United States for forty years. Three states—New York, New Jersey, and Maryland—had multi-year declines in admissions to their prisons from 2000 to 2009 and other states had anemic growth rates before they experienced declines (i.e., Illinois, Michigan, Delaware, and Texas) (West et al., 2010). Though incarceration rates in jails stalled or increased slightly in 2012, 111 of the 170 largest jails with populations of 1,000 or more inmates experienced decarceration by 2010 (Minton, 2011, pp. 1–2) and by mid-year 2013 the overall figures for the jail populations in the country were down again, by as much as 55,000 since 2008 (Minton & Golinelli, 2014, p. 6). The rated capacity of jails actually decreased in 2013, which was the first decline in capacity since the Annual Survey of Jails began in 1982 (Minton and Golinelli, 2014, p.3). And the percentage of rated capacity in jails in 2013 (84%), or the amount of bed space occupied, was lower than it had been in 1984 (86%) (Minton and Golinelli, 2014, p. 3). It also appears that the slight increase in jail populations in 2012 (by 8,000), before they decreased again in 2013 was due almost entirely to the shift of about 8,000 inmates from prisons to jails in California after the *Plata* decision and the subsequent realignment legislation (see the following discussion of this decision). If not for this shift, it is likely that we would have five straight years of declines in jail populations in the United States.

Moreover, by 2013, several states and localities closed 20-plus different correctional facilities, spurred by and/or resulting from decreased funding or the number of admissions (The Sentencing Project, 2013, p. 1; Hogan et al., 2014; Kyckelbahn, 2013; Petersilia & Cullen, 2014). And support for increases in the use of incarceration have faltered as conservatives have joined liberals in localities, the states, and at the federal level in their distrust in the value of incarceration, particularly for low-level offenders (Petersilia & Cullen, 2014).

In a recent survey by the PEW Research Center on American attitudes about the drug war, the researchers found that there was a definite shift towards support for treatment over incarceration for drug offenders, even for those using more "hard" drugs such as heroin and cocaine. They found that 67% of those surveyed supported treatment as opposed to 26% who favored prosecution for illegal drug users, with 7% indicating they did not know how they should respond (The Pew Research Center, 2014). In an earlier survey the researchers found that a majority of Americans supported the legalization of marijuana (The Pew Research Center, 2013).

So if there is evidence that the use of incarceration has decreased recently and the political stomach for supporting mass incarceration is no longer there, then the question becomes: is the decriminalization, medicalization, and legalization of marijuana responsible for at least some of these decreases? Petersilia & Cullen (2014, p. 21) make a cogent case that much of the overall decrease in incarceration numbers in the last few years can be attributed to enormous reductions in prison inmates in California in response to the US Supreme Court 2011 decision, *Brown v. Plata,* which mandated that the prison population be reduced by 25% in two years. In response, California's Governor Jerry Brown signed the Public Safety Realignment Act which shifted responsibility for a large number of convicted felons from the state to the counties. In just four years the state's prison population has declined by 24% and is at the lowest level it has been at in 17 years (Petersilia & Cullen, 2014, p. 23). Not surprisingly, however, the numbers of inmates in jails has risen steeply in some California counties and some of those low-level offenders are doing relatively long sentences (of more than a year and sometimes several years) in facilities which are ill equipped to provide for the needs and services that long-term inmates require.

Of course, and as Petersilia and Cullen (2014) acknowledge, there are other forces at work that are or may have the salutatory effect of reducing incarceration beyond the realignment of the California system. According to the authors (2014, pp. 18–20) and as mentioned by Hogan et al. (2014), these factors include a lack of support for mass incarceration, better science regarding assessment that is more likely to result in more effective decarceration, a greater emphasis on evidence-based correctional programming, the fact that several states and localities are willing to close correctional facilities, and the recognition that surveys show that the American public is more pragmatic about incarceration (its value and its reduced use) than has been true for some time.

At the time of this writing (November 2014) the implementation of the Colorado and Washington legalization laws is less than a year old in both states, which means that not enough time has passed to affect incarceration rates in prisons, though the implementation of the laws might already be affecting jail populations. Unfortunately, the collective data on jail incarceration promulgated by the Bureau of Justice Statistics is usually at least half a year to a year behind and not always state specific. And if there are recent decreases in jail populations, and as we indicate in the foregoing there are—reductions in overall populations in four of the last five years—it is possible that these are also affected by decriminalization and medicalization of marijuana as much or more than legalization, which has not had as much time to take effect.

Although we would note that legalization itself, ahead of implementation, may have an *anticipatory effect* on correctional populations, by signaling to criminal justice actors—police, prosecutors, judges—after legalization has become the law of the land, but before that law has been implemented, that less attention should be paid to minor marijuana offenders given that their behavior would be legal within the year. Among those four-out-of-five-year declines in jail populations we see some evidence that decriminalization, medicalization, and anticipatory legalization may be having some effects. The number of adult males incarcerated in jails is markedly down for much of the last decade, and at least from 2005 through 2013, by as much as 57,000, though the number of whites incarcerated in jails is at an all-time high (Minton & Golinelli, 2014, p. 6). This means these decreases appear to be in the numbers of African-American men (down about 45,000 since 2008, which appears to be the peak of jail incarceration) and Hispanic men (down about 20,000 since 2008) incarcerated in jails, since the number of women incarcerated in jails is up overall for 2000 through 2013 (Minton & Golinelli, 2014, p. 6). As we know the drug war had a disparate impact on minority-group men and women, particularly African-American and Hispanic men and women, we would expect the easing of that war to also affect them (Alexander, 2010). It is difficult to tell from the BJS figures if minority group women are also affected as the number of women incarcerated in jails, as we mentioned, is up; it might be that since the number of whites incarcerated in jails is also up that these increases are all or mostly in the number of white women. If true, this would mean that decarceration among minority group women is also occurring in jails, perhaps as a result of an easing of the drug war too. Unfortunately, this latest BJS report on jail populations does not include any information about state-by-state decreases in jail populations or whether those decreases were in numbers of those incarcerated for marijuana offenses, nor does it include race/ethnicity, gender *and* marijuana offenses, and offenders matched in tandem.

Conclusions

Correctional populations have increased for forty years, peaking in 2008, which in hindsight may turn out to be the very apogee of the drug-war effect. In four out of the last five years for jails, and three out of the last four years for state prisons, and one year for federal prisons, using 2013 as the end data point, we have witnessed a startling occurrence: the relatively slight, but steady, decrease in the use of incarceration (Carson, 2014). Whether these decreases were related to drug law changes is not yet clear, but in view of the breadth of those changes, it is likely they serve as a partial explanation for it. As marijuana legalization spreads across the states, and even to American Indian reservations, we can expect, and hope, that there will be nowhere for correctional populations to go but down. A collateral and beneficial effect is likely to be decreased incarceration of minority group men and women for minor drug offenses, individuals who were previously caught up on the drug war battlefield and over the long history of versions of this war, were demonized as enemy combatants.

In order to determine if the decriminalization, medicalization, and legalization has had a significant effect on incarceration, scholars need data from localities, states, and the federal government about who is under correctional supervision or incarcerated and what offenses they have been charged with and/or convicted of. Without such information, or with only incomplete information, as it is published by the Bureau of Justice Statistics, it is impossible to know how much the abating of the drug war is reducing incarceration and who is the more likely beneficiary of that monumental shift in policy. For our part, and assuming the legalization of marijuana continues in states and localities and is not hampered by federal interference, we expect that decarceration will continue in all areas of corrections.

References

Alexander, M. (2010). *The new Jim Crow: Mass incarceration in the age of color blindness.* New York, NY: The New Press.

Anslinger, H. J. (1937). Congressional Hearings on HR 6385 (April/May). Retrieved from http://www.druglibrary.org/schaffer/hemp/taxact/t10a.htm.

Anslinger, H. J., & Cooper, C. R. (1937, July). Marijuana: Assassin of youth. *American Magazine.*

Barnard, J., & Wozniacka, G. (2014, December 12). US Department of Justice says Indian tribes can grow and sell marijuana. *Moscow-Pullman Daily News*, 4A.

Carson, A. E. (2014). Prisoners in 2013. Washington, DC: US Department of Justice, Bureau of Justice Statistics.

Cohen, S. (1972). *Folk devils and moral panics: The creation of mods and rockers.* Oxford: Blackwell.

DeSimone, J. (1998). Is marijuana a gateway drug? *Eastern Economic Journal, 24*(2), 149–164.

Glaze, L. E., & Herberman, E. J. Correctional populations in the United States, 2012. Bureau of Justice Statistics, Office of Justice Programs, US Department of Justice. Retrieved from http://www.bjs.gov.

Golub, A., & Johnson, B. D. (1994). The shifting importance of alcohol and marijuana as gateway substances among serious drug abusers. *Journal of Studies on Alcohol and Drugs, 55*(5), 607–614.

Goode, E., & Ben-Yehuda, N. (1994). Moral panics: Culture, politics, and social construction. *Annual Review of Sociology, 20,* 149–171.

Greene, J., & Mauer, M. (2010). Downscaling prisons: Lessons from four states. New York: Sentencing Project.

Grinspoon, L. (1999). Medical marihuana in a time of prohibition. *International Journal of Drug Policy, 10,* 145–156.

Guerino, P., Harrison, P., & Sabol, W. (2011). Prisoners in 2010. Washington, DC: US Department of Justice, Bureau of Justice Statistics.

Hall, W. (2014). What has research over the past two decades revealed about the adverse health effects of recreational cannabis use? *Addiction.* doi: 10.1111/add.12703.

Hogan, N., Garland, B., Wodahl, E., Hass, A., Stohr, M. K., & Lambert, E. (2014). Closing the iron bar inn: The issue of decarceration and its possible effects on inmates, staff and communities. Forthcoming in *Punishment and Society, 16*(4).

Hollister, L. E. (1986). Health aspects of cannabis. *Pharmacological Reviews, 38*(1), 1–20.

Inciardi, J., & McElrath, K. (2011). *The American drug scene: An anthology* (6th ed.). New York: Oxford University Press.

Iversen, L. L. (1993). Medical uses of marijuana? *Nature, 365,* 12–13.

Kyckelhahn, T. (2013). State Corrections Expenditures FY 1982–2010. Washington DC: Bureau of Justice Statistics, US Department of Justice.

Minton, T. (2011). Jail inmates at midyear 2011—statistical tables. Washington, DC: US Department of Justice, Bureau of Justice Statistics.

Minton, T., & Golinelli, D. (2014). Jail inmates at midyear 2013—statistical tables. Washington, DC: US Department of Justice, Bureau of Justice Statistics.

Mosher, C. J., & Akins, S. M. (2014). *Drugs and drug policy: The control of consciousness alteration* (2nd ed.). Los Angeles: Sage Publications, Inc.

NORML. (2014). *Medical necessity defense.* NORML. Retrieved from http://norml.org/marijuana/medical/item/medical-necessity-defense?category_id=733.

Petersilia, J., & Cullen, F. T. (2015). Liberal but not stupid: Meeting the promise of downsizing prisons. Forthcoming in *Stanford Journal of Criminal Law and Policy.*

Pew Research Center (2014). *America's new drug policy landscape.* The Pew Research Center. Retrieved from http://www.people-press.org/2014/04/02/americas-new-drug-policy-landscape/.

Pew Research Center (2013). *Majority now supports legalizing marijuana.* The Pew Research Center. Retrieved from http://www.people-press.org/2013/04/04/majority-now-supports-legalizing-marijuana/.

ProCon.org. (2014a). *23 legal medical marijuana states and DC.* Retrieved from http://medicalmarijuana.procon.org/view.resource.php?resourceID=000881.

ProCon.org. (2014b). *Historical timeline: History of marijuana as medicine—2,900 BC to present.* http://medicalmarijuana.procon.org/view.timeline.php?timelineID=000026.

Reefer Madness (2003, originally distributed in 1936). Narberth, PA: Alpha Video Distributors.

Ryan, A. K. (2010). Marijuana use effects: The lasting effects of marijuana use on educational attainment in midlife. *Substance Use & Misuse, 45*(4), 554–597.

Sentencing Project (2014). Prison population reductions stalled in 2013. *The Sentencing Project News.* Retrieved from http://www.sentencingproject.org.

Subramanian, R., & Moreno, R. (2014). *Drug war détente? A review of state-level drug law reform, 2009–2013.* Vera Institute of Justice. Retrieved from http://www.vera.org/sites/default/files/resources/downloads/state-drug-law-reform-review-2009-2013-v6.pdf.

West, H., Sabol, W., & Greenman, S. (2010). *Prisoners in 2009.* Washington, DC: US Department of Justice, Office of Justice Programs, Bureau of Justice Statistics.

Relevant Laws

Comprehensive Drug Abuse Prevention and Control Act of 1970, Pub. L. No. 91-513, 84 Stat. 1236, 1292 (Oct. 27, 1970)
Harrison Narcotics Tax Act (Ch. 1, 38 Stat. 785)
Marijuana Tax Act of 1937, Pub. 238, 75th Congress, 50 Stat. 551 (Aug. 2, 1937)

8

Cannabis-Impaired Driving: The Extent of the Problem and Countermeasures Being Taken Now and to Be Taken in the Future

Nicholas Lovrich, Ericka Christensen, and Douglas Routh

Introduction

One major consequence of the legalization of marijuana, either for medicinal use or for recreational purposes, is that the incidence of cannabis-impaired driving will increase substantially. Even before the dramatic voter-approved changes in drug laws in Colorado and Washington in 2012 permitting the state-regulated production and retail sale of marijuana to adults, the problem of "drugged driving" (i.e., impaired driving caused by one or more drugs not including alcohol) was growing as a significant challenge for law enforcement and traffic safety advocates. The problem is widespread in our country; the Office of National Drug Control Policy in the Executive Office of the President set out as one of its 2014 national drug control strategy goals for improving the public health and public safety of the American people the reduction of "the prevalence of drugged driving by 10%" (ONDCP, 2014, p. 4). Similarly, the countries of the European Union have experienced very much the same problem of the progressive displacement of alcohol by drugs among impaired drivers. Both illicit (controlled substances) and prescription drugs are involved, and—just as we are doing in our country—our European counterparts have studied varying approaches to this major public health and safety challenge. They have reported recently on findings derived from a comprehensive review of the available research conducted by European scientists to better understand and manage the ever-worsening problem on their respective national and collective roadways (DRUID, 2012).

This chapter will provide an overview on the problem of cannabis-impaired driving in the US, and tangentially other countries, and examine the yet spotty literature on the known effects of cannabis use on driving behavior and behind-the-wheel decision-making. This literature is yet in its infancy in the United States given the extreme difficulty American university-based scientists have had in doing research with marijuana on nearly all US college campuses. In comparison to the wealth of studies on the effects of alcohol on driving accumulated over the course of three decades or more, the American cannabis-impairment dosage and effects studies are relatively few in number compared to the more numerous studies done in Europe and the Commonwealth countries. Those scientific studies which have been published are a bit diverse in their findings reported and in their conclusions drawn. The chapter discusses this literature in brief overview, and moves on to detail the law enforcement response to addressing the dangers of drugged driving in general, and of cannabis-impaired driving in particular. The DRE (Drug Recognition Expert) and ARIDE (Advanced Roadside Impaired Driving Enforcement) programs are both discussed in this regard, and the Washington State Patrol, which houses the coordinator of the state's DRE program, helped to construct an account of the various steps taken by the state's law enforcement and traffic safety communities to prepare for the legalization of recreational marijuana as of July 1, 2014. These observations are intended to be instructive for both the law enforcement and traffic safety communities of Oregon, Alaska, and Washington, DC, where marijuana legalization was enacted in 2014, and in the additional US states, such as Arizona, California, Connecticut, Massachusetts, New Mexico, Rhode Island, and Vermont, that are likely to join in for this ongoing social experiment, permitted under the ever-watchful eye of a suspicious federal government. These states are likely to either enact legislation or place the question of legalization of recreational use on the ballot, despite the fact that the federal government maintains marijuana on the list of "Schedule 1" (most dangerous) illicit drugs (Garvey and Yeh, 2014).

This account is likewise instructive for the criminal justice and the criminology academic community as it develops its own perspective on how to present drugged driving issues in textbooks and teaching curricula, and how to direct future academic research to be undertaken in this area. It is clear from this depiction of the many challenges faced by law enforcement that many difficulties are associated with enforcing impaired driving laws, difficulties occasioned by being required to combine the testimony of skilled and well-trained officers capable of making well-informed judgments concerning impairment *and* securing blood evidence collected in a timely manner, documenting presence of either a *per se* level of THC or measureable presence ("zero tolerance") at the time of arrest. It is likely that this type of hybrid process of impairment judgment based upon both a systematic field assessment *and* physical blood evidence on record, collected upon the issuance of a judicial search warrant, will be legally required to satisfy the demands of due process of law in prosecuting drugged driving in most of the US states where legalization of the recreational use of marijuana is probable.

After this hopefully informative discussion, the chapter presents some empirical findings on how difficult it has been for police officers on patrol—even those with highly specialized training, working under ongoing oversight and supervision, receiving periodic update training, and possessing considerable field experience—to correctly determine the presence and influence of the psychoactive element in cannabis—9-tetrahydrocannabinol (THC)—in their actual field interactions with drug-impaired drivers. The coordinators of the DRE programs of the states of Washington and New Mexico provided raw data, in the form of field-generated DRE officer assessments and associated toxicological reports, to criminal justice researchers (faculty and doctoral students) at the Division of Governmental Studies and Services at Washington State University for coding and digitization for ultimate analysis. The results of those analyses are reported here. It is indeed clear from these empirical findings that cannabis impairment is often difficult to document, and that new field diagnostic tools in the hands of law enforcement, school and workplace safety personnel, and emergency medical personnel and others who must deal with drugged driving and related activities would likely be very helpful for the promotion of public health and public safety in the years ahead.

The final section of the chapter provides a brief overview of the types of research being carried out across the country and in Europe to address the challenges of cannabis-impaired driving. This section concludes with a discussion of how this work on THC detection is building a foundation for expanding the ability of law enforcement officers and others needing to detect additional impairing drugs beyond THC in drivers who are detained for suspicion of impaired driving.

Extent of the Problem

An Associated Press story prepared by veteran reporter Joan Lowry received wide distribution in American newspapers on February 6, 2015, under the banner "Federal Report: Fewer Drivers Drinking; More Using Drugs" (Lowry,

2015). That story noted that the US National Highway Traffic Safety Administration in the US Department of Transportation has conducted a series of anonymous surveys of large numbers of randomly selected drivers five times over the past 40 years. That research was carried out periodically following largely the same research protocol, most recently by the highly regarded Pacific Institute for Research and Evaluation (PIRE) of Calverton, Maryland. The survey entails a careful process of random selection of drivers from the normal traffic stream in dozens of locations across the country, with each person recruited for participation being interviewed and tested for the presence of impairing drugs. The surveys are carried out at three separate periods of the day on Fridays and Saturdays. Roadside signage for voluntary and compensated participation in the survey is placed on display in high traffic volume areas featuring access to a suitable parking lot where highly trained and richly experienced PIRE survey crews conduct their data collection on Friday afternoon (1:30–3:30pm), Friday evening (10:00pm to midnight), and in the early hours of Saturday morning (1:00–3:00am). The second day of data collection occurs Saturday afternoon, Saturday early evening, and in the early hours of Sunday morning.

The locations for the data collection are held in strict confidence by all concerned until the very latest possible moment to minimize the problem of self-selection of volunteers, and survey participants are told to desist from contacting their friends and/or relatives to take part in the survey; filter questions are used in the survey to weed out all potential volunteers who may have been contacted through social media. Local law enforcement agencies are involved in site selection and planning, and they provide security support backup for the survey crew; however, law enforcement is not in visible presence among the PIRE crew collecting survey data, securing saliva swabs, collecting breath samples for alcohol detection, and obtaining blood samples for laboratory analysis and documentation of drugs present. The local news media and press in each location are given advanced notice of the survey, and news media leaders are asked to cooperate faithfully with the important goal of maintaining anonymity to survey participants by not recording any images of faces, of distinguishing images of human bodies, or license plate numbers in their news coverage of the survey.

The drivers who decide to pull over and participate in the roadside survey process are guaranteed no adverse law enforcement action, even if they are found to be impaired. In such cases of apparent impairment these persons and their vehicles are taken safely to their original destination and no police contact or driving record notation is made; at no point in the process are names or drivers' license information or license plates recorded in the PIRE anonymous survey process. The study participants are asked to complete a short questionnaire administered by PIRE staff featuring demographic background and some attitudes about drugs and driving habits, they blow into a Portable Breath Test device to measure breath alcohol content level (BrAC), they provide a saliva sample which is safely stored and coded to the participant's study ID number, and a professional phlebotomist extracts a blood sample. Study participants receive a cash payment (of about $50–60) and proceed on their way unless they are suspected of being impaired, in which case arrangements are made to get them and their vehicles safely to their destination at PIRE's expense. The saliva and blood samples are sent to a forensic laboratory for analysis.

The findings from the latest roadside survey conducted (2013–2014) indicated that among US weekend nighttime drivers the prevalence of alcohol-involved drivers was down by about 30% from the previous survey administered in 2007, and down by 75% since the first roadside survey conducted in 1973. *However*, more than 15% of drivers volunteering for the survey tested positive for at least one illegal drug, a figure up from the 12% documented in 2007. The percentage of nighttime drivers with marijuana in their blood stream grew by nearly 50% over that time period—8.6% in 2007 as compared to 12.6% in 2014. It is noteworthy that the drug demonstrating the largest increase over time in weekend nighttime prevalence was THC. In the national roadside survey conducted in 2007 a total of 8.6% of the drivers participating in the study tested positive for THC, but in the 2013–2014 iteration of the survey 12.6% tested positive, an increase of 48%. These estimates of prevalence are conservative of course; many drivers who were knowingly high from cannabis consumption at the time of the survey would not be likely to volunteer for the roadside survey for fear of arrest or being detained. Even though such outcomes would not occur given the procedures in place for protecting the rights and interests of human subjects built in to the study protocol, people in the general driving public are not aware of those protections.

These same types of prevalence figures reported for the United States have been documented in Europe. The DRUID study (a loose acronym for Driving While Under Influence of Drugs, Alcohol and Medicines), funded by the European Commission for the European Union and its member states, represents the most ambitious study of impaired driving ever done, and featured data collection on a grand scale and two meta-analyses featuring virtually all available drug-impaired driving research done by European scientists. The DRUID project took 5 years to complete (2006–2011), and its findings were published in 2012. Sound data on the prevalence of psychoactive substances among European drivers were generated from many roadside surveys conducted between January of 2007 and July of 2009. All of these surveys were of similar design to that described above for the PIRE surveys done in the United States; they were carried out in those thirteen European countries that agreed to follow a uniform study design template. Body fluids (saliva and blood) taken from nearly 50,000 randomly selected drivers were analyzed from those surveys. With regard to cannabis, the authors of the report noted the following:

> Cannabis seemed to be a weekend drug mainly used by young male drivers. There was a significant difference in the prevalence of cannabis in different time periods, most prevalent in weekend days and least prevalent in weekend mornings. However, cannabis was found during all days and hours of the week in most countries (DRUID, p. 22).

The cut-off levels used for the documentation of a positive TCH concentration were 1.0 ng/mL in blood and 27 ng/mL in saliva. The highest drug prevalence noted among illicit drugs was that of THC, followed by cocaine and amphetamines in rather distant second and third positions, respectively. Overall, for all nations combined and considered separately, alcohol was found in 3.48% of the drivers, illicit drugs in 1.90%, medicinal impairing drugs in 1.36%, and combinations of two or more drugs and drugs consumed in combination with alcohol in another .67% of randomly selected drivers (DRUID, p. 17).

The extent of the problem of cannabis consumption and driving impairment is estimated from prevalence documented in roadside surveys; this is one important form of evidence to be sure. However, a second type of evidence is also very important in forming an appreciation of the scale of the drugged driving problem. That second type of evidence comes in the form of accident and fatal injury archival record data analysis. In the United States the FARS (Fatality Analysis Reporting System) data are constructed and maintained by each of the fifty states in conformity with federal standards of reporting; the ever-growing FARS dataset provides an accurate longitudinal record of alcohol and drug involvement in fatal accidents in the United States. The standards in question are set by the National Highway Traffic Safety Administration, and reports for the nation are developed and disseminated periodically by the Federal Highway Administration, which is also responsible for determining the vehicle miles traveled (VMT) each year to serve as a base for the calculation of comparable fatalities/VMT ratios over time. All official reports emanating from the FARS data archive are prepared by the NHTSA National Center for Statistics and Analysis. These periodic reports provide a rather sobering account of the steady increase in the incidence of drug-involved fatal accidents in the United States, particularly with respect to novice drivers and young adult male drivers (National Center for Statistics and Analysis, 2015, January).

Not surprisingly, the DRUID study's European public health and public safety researchers documented the same unfortunate pattern of disproportionate youth and young adult drug-impaired involvement in their review of research on motor vehicle crashes involving motorist hospitalizations and/or fatalities. For persons hospitalized and killed in traffic crashes in the thirteen European countries taking part in the DRUID study, persons 25–34 (predominantly males) were most likely to test positive for impairing drugs, and among those drugs cannabis is the most often detected controlled substance (2012, p. 23).

Limited Success of Youth Desistance Messaging

For many years there was a concerted, nationwide effort to dissuade American youth from indulging in cannabis consumption. Marijuana was broadly seen as representing the major "gateway drug" to serious drug dependence and leading to likely movement on to more harmful banned substances. This campaign to dissuade youth from use is perhaps best described as a classic "losing battle" phenomenon, despite some solid evidence that cannabis use in adolescence is associated with higher risk of driving accidents, drug dependence and adverse psychosocial outcomes and mental health problems in adulthood (Hall, 2014). The many D.A.R.E. (Drug Abuse Resistance Education) and related school-based programs in the United States (and replicated to some extent in 54 other countries) specifically designed to discourage youth from involvement with drugs have been submitted to many short-term and long-term outcome assessments alike. Meta-analyses carried out on those many program evaluation studies uniformly conclude that little to no beneficial effect can be attributed to this type of formal instructional intervention by specially trained police officers with either primary or secondary school students (see the research summarized in West and O'Neal, 2004, and Pan and Bai, 2009). While an estimated 80% of public school districts across the country continue to operate the D.A.R.E. programs and similar cops-in-schools initiatives they implemented in the early days of the program despite this compelling absence of evidence of documented beneficial outcomes, the reasons they tend to give for maintaining their programs are worthy of note. The reasons offered for program continuation have much more to do with building better relations between schools and the police and between the police and youth in their respective communities than any putative beneficial impact on the likelihood of drug experimentation in high school and early adulthood (Miller, 2001; Birkeland et al., 2005).

An even more direct source of evidence of lack of overall impact of this approach to dissuading youth from a very strong inclination to experiment with "grown up" behaviors and activities is found in the series of annual surveys conducted by the Survey Research Center at the University of Michigan for the longstanding Monitoring the Future program. These national surveys involve random sampling of 8th, 10th, and 12th grade students (approximate weighted Ns ranging between 2,000 and 3,600 for each grade level) over the period 1975 to 2014. The micro data (de-identified individual-level data) from these annual surveys are publicly available through the widely respected and long-established Interuniversity Consortium for Political and Social Research (ICPSR) and are generated under the federally supported National Addiction & HIV Data Archive Program (NAHDAP). The survey items featured in the lengthy questionnaire cover a broad range of controlled substances, including the drugs LSD, cocaine, ecstasy, crack, heroin, amphetamines, crystal methamphetamines (i.e., "ice"), synthetic stimulants (i.e., "bath salts"), the pain medications most often used recreationally (e.g., OxyContin, Percocet), and marijuana. In the survey US middle school and high school students are asked about their customary patterns of drug use—with response options ranging from yearly use to monthly use to daily use. Responses to these items permit a careful monitoring of increases and decreases in the rates of reported use of each of the drug categories over a long span of time. Equally valuable, additionally, are the questions relating to the perception of harm resulting from use of these controlled substances. The students are asked the following question in this regard:

> **How much do you think people are harming themselves (physically or in other ways), if they ...**
>
> For each of the categories of controlled substances included in the survey students are asked how much harm they ascribe to trying the drug "once or twice," to making "occasional use" of the drug, and to making "regular use" of the substance. The figure on the next page sets forth findings for 12th-grade students on perception of harm resulting from smoking marijuana regularly.

Two observations are in order before characterizing the trend in annual US youth assessments of the potential harm of regular use of marijuana. First, the pattern of ascribed harm depicted in Figure 1 for 12th-grade students is substantially the same for 8th- and 10th-grade students. Secondly, with respect to patterns of reported use the same can be said—the patterns over time for 8th-grade students and 10th grade students are very similar to those of 12th-grade students. With respect to reported daily use, the frequency has remained between 2% and 8% on a consistent basis for entire run of the surveys for 12th-grade students. Monthly use among these students has likewise remained nearly constant, fluctuating between just under and just over 20%. Finally, lifetime

Figure 1. Declining Rates of Ascription of Harm to Regular Use of Marijuana, 1985–2014

Year of *Monitoring the Future* Survey	Percent 10 20 30 40 50 60 70 80 90 100%
1985	70.4%
1987	73.5%
1989	77.5%
1991	78.6%
1993	72.5%
1995	60.8%
1997	58.1%
1999	57.4%
2001	57.4%
2003	54.9%
2005	58.0%
2007	54.8%
2009	52.4%
2010	46.8%
2011	45.7%
2012	44.1%
2013	39.5%
2014	36.1%

Percent 12th-Grade Students Indicating *Great Harm* from Regular Use of Marijuana

use for 12th-grade students has held steady in the 45% range over the entire course of annual Monitoring the Future series. This evidence of failure to "move the needle" on reported use in the middle and high school student population contributed mightily to the ultimate dictum on the part of criminal justice and criminology researchers that the D.A.R.E. program was not able to achieve the rates of desistence from drug experimentation among youth hoped for by its Los Angeles Police Department originators (Rosenbaum and Hanson, 1998). A good many community groups and police departments which worked with their local schools to make D.A.R.E. instruction available to the children in their community have continued to support the program for good reasons relating to police–community relations and youth outreach and school resource officer-related benefits; the hoped for benefit of reducing the incidence of drug experimentation through the high school years has not, unfortunately, been among the most desired and broadly expected benefits of the program.

Many of the supporters of D.A.R.E are hopeful that the new "keepin' it real" course content which replaces the abstinence theme of the past and the substitution of problem-based learning exercises for drug-fact laden lectures will produce more favorable outcomes (Nordrum, 2014).

It is clear from the survey results displayed in Figure 1 that over the course of the past two decades high school seniors have become decidedly less likely to ascribe harmful effects to the regular use of marijuana. The "gateway drug" label pinned to marijuana may have rung somewhat true for the youth of the 1980s and early 1990s, but clearly after 2005 there has been a steady decline in the ascription of harm to regular use of marijuana among American youth entering young adulthood. The strong abstinence message that once characterized D.A.R.E. was quite apparently landing on deaf ears in more recent years. In their analysis of the Monitoring the Future data collected over the period 2001–2011, researchers O'Malley and Johnson (2013) show how this declining "perception of harm" ascribed to marijuana translates directly into high-risk driving behavior on the part of youth. These researchers duly note that high school seniors in the US are reporting increasingly lower levels of likelihood of driving after drinking over this time period, but higher likelihood of driving after using marijuana. O'Malley and Johnson opine that stronger efforts are needed to combat adolescent driving under the influence of illicit drugs; it might be added that these efforts are particularly important in those states having or potentially moving toward the legalization of recreational marijuana where no persons under 21 are allowed to possess or use marijuana (legal or illicit), let alone drive after doing so.

Evidence on the Effect of Cannabis Use on Driving

There is considerable disagreement among researchers on just how impairing marijuana is on one's ability to drive safely. Much of the early research on cannabis and driving performance was carried out in laboratory settings and involved driving simulator studies. These studies consistently documented adverse effects at increased doses, and indicated that cannabis impairs the psychomotor skills necessary for safe driving (see summaries of studies set forth in Ramaekers et al., 2004; Iversen, 2003). However, studies done outside of the laboratory and simulator context in "naturalistic" settings (i.e., with people on the road) have not produced such clear findings of cannabis-impaired driving. Three types of such naturalistic studies are found in the published research grant-supported report literature—namely, cross sectional studies, cohort studies, and case-control studies.

Cross-sectional studies involve the analysis of archival data on injured drivers and fatally injured drivers. In these types of studies cannabis is consistently shown to be one of the most often documented psychoactive substances present (though always second to alcohol), and it is well established that individuals who drive within two hours of using marijuana have raised rates of collision (Asbridge, Poulin, and Donato, 2005). Based on a comprehensive meta-analysis recently published by Elvik (2013), it can be concluded that the same dose response relationship demonstrated in the laboratory with driving simulators is found in the naturalistic setting offered by archival data on injury and fatal crashes. Likewise, the driving impairment impact of THC consumption is in some evidence, although the impact is far less than is evident for alcohol consumption. Very comparable findings with respect to dose response were reported in the DRUID meta-analysis based on European epidemiological studies (p. 31).

Fewer studies have been reported of the cohort and case-control (e.g., culpability studies such as Longo et al., 2000) variety where more controlled comparisons are possible, but in the few studies available up to this point the findings are decidedly mixed—some report an impairing consequence to marijuana use (e.g., Mann et al., 2007), some find little to no effect (e.g., Lachenmeier and Rehm, 2015), and some even report a beneficial effect (Ronen et al., 2008). In virtually every case of a direct comparison of impairing consequences in such studies, however, alcohol is uniformly found to be more seriously impairing than cannabis. This is equally the case in US-based studies and the research done in Europe and summarized in the meta-analyses conducted for the DRUID study (Asbridge et al., 2012).

Some research has been reported even suggesting that the liberalization of marijuana laws has actually benefitted society and improved public safety by reducing the occurrence of fatal accidents. The argument advanced is that as drivers consume less alcohol and substitute marijuana for getting high during their recreation, the likelihood of seriously impaired driving actually declines. In support of this line of argument researchers Anderson, Hansen, and Rees (2013) present evidence from a longitudinal study of traffic fatalities in the seventeen states which enacted medical marijuana laws. They document an 8–11% decrease in traffic fatalities in those states in a comparison of pre- and post-liberalization years; no comparable decrease took place in states not permitting the medicinal use of marijuana. In support of their argument the three economists note that other researchers have reported that frequent users of cannabis quite commonly believe that they can self-monitor and exert control over their driving performance in ways that alcoholics normally cannot do (McGuire et al., 2011).

Whatever might be the actual risk to impairment present from the consumption of cannabis, it is noteworthy that the research literature appears to be rock solid on adverse interaction effects occurring between cannabis and alcohol. When cannabis and alcohol are used concurrently whatever putative beneficial effects might attain for cannabis over alcohol, such as driving more slowly and being more deliberate in decisions while behind the wheel, these benefit effects are not at play and the driving impairment is commonly severe (Marks and MacAvoy, 1989; Terry-McElrath, O'Malley and Johnson, 2014). Unfortunately, the incidence of mixing alcohol and marijuana is all too commonplace in the United States, and likewise in the European Union nations where the highest prevalence of mixing the two was found among the 25–34 young adult age group (DRUID, p. 22). The same youth and young adult-concentrated incidence of conjoint use of cannabis and alcohol is present in the United States (Bingham, Shope and Zhu, 2008). In this regard, Logan, Mohr, and Talpins conclude their study of oral fluids testing approaches with this pertinent observation: "... the data confirm reports in other related populations with respect to prevalence of combined alcohol and drug use on the impaired driving population. Policies that exclude drivers with blood or BrAC concentrations above the alcohol *per se* limit are missing substantial numbers of drivers with co-morbid drug and alcohol problems—in this cohort as high as 53% of all drug using drivers" (2014, p. 6).

The Call to Arms for Traffic Enforcement

As the prospects for continued liberalization of marijuana laws appeared to be looming large for law enforcement, the leaders of the International Association of Chiefs of Police (IACP) placed the topic of drug-impaired driving on their agenda for the 119th annual conference held in San Diego, California, in October 2012. Upon ample discussion and due consideration of the organization's membership, and upon recognition of the imminent passage of state-level legislation permitting either medical marijuana and/or recreational marijuana to be sold to adults, the following resolution drafted by the IACP's Narcotics and Dangerous Drugs Committee was duly adopted.

Combating the Dramatic Increase in Drug-Impaired Driving Offenses

October 3, 2012

WHEREAS, the International Association of Chiefs of Police ("IACP") recognizes that drug-impaired driving constitutes a significant law enforcement and societal problem; and
WHEREAS, according to the "Drugged Driving Research: A White Paper," prepared for the National Institute of Drug Abuse by the Institute for Behavior and Health, Inc., within the United States drugs other than alcohol are involved in approximately 18 percent of motor vehicle driver deaths; and
WHEREAS, the 2012 National Drug Control Strategy outlined a policy focus for a 10 percent reduction in drugged driving by 2015; and
WHEREAS, an estimated $59.9 billion in costs are attributable to drugged driving; and
WHEREAS, according to the National Highway Traffic Safety Administration marijuana accounted for 70 percent of illicit drugs used by drivers; and
WHEREAS, studies by the US Department of Transportation and the Dutch Ministry of Transport concluded that the effects of THC, the active ingredient in marijuana, significantly impairs drivers and makes them more likely to fall asleep at the wheel; and
WHEREAS, preventing citizens from operating motor vehicles while under the influence of drugs is critical to public safety; however, there is no consistent method of identifying drug impairment and the presence of drugs in the body; and
WHEREAS, drug-impaired drivers are less frequently detected, prosecuted, or referred to treatment than drunk drivers because few police officers are trained to detect drug impairment and prosecutors lack a clear legal standard under which to prove drugged driving cases; and
WHEREAS, the "Policy Focus Reducing Drugged Driving" section of the 2012 National Drug Control Strategy recommends five strategies to address this growing problem: 1) encourage states to apply the per se standard used for commercial drivers to drivers impaired by illegal drugs and the impairment standard used for intoxicated drivers to other drug-impaired drivers; 2) collect further data through more consistent use of the Fatality Analysis Reporting System ("FARS") and

> more frequently conducted National Roadside Surveys; 3) educating communities and professionals—particularly new drivers, drivers on prescription drugs, and medical professionals—about drugged driving risks and legal consequences; 4) implementing the Drug Evaluation and Classification ("DRE") program across jurisdictions so that law enforcement is uniformly trained to detect drugged drivers; and 5) developing standard laboratory methodologies and further researching oral fluid testing to determine if it constitutes a reliable and widely available roadside test; now, therefore, be it
> RESOLVED, that the IACP recommends adopting the strategies outlined in the 2012 National Drug Control Strategy to address this significant public safety issue (emphasis added).

Because the law enforcement community of Washington State faced the direct challenge arising from the passage of Initiative 502 in November of 2012, with implementation date of July 1, 2014, set as the first day of legal retail sales out of state-licensed dispensaries, a depiction of their plan of action provides valuable insight into the prospects and challenges of meeting the call to arms issued in the IACP's resolution. It should be recalled, of course, that vigorous enforcement and prosecution of impaired driving under the influence of marijuana was explicitly included in the list of conditions which must be observed to avoid federal intervention (pre-emption) under the Controlled Substances Act of 1971. Attorney General Holder announced on August 29, 2013, that in those states adopting laws permitting recreational and medical marijuana the absolute ban against driving while impaired by marijuana must be observed.

The socio-political setting for Washington State's law enforcement community response to this explicit call to arms in the war against drug-impaired driving was that the citizens of the state had turned out in record numbers (81% turnout) to vote in the election of November 2012, and a clear majority (55.7%) of those citizens voted to pass Initiative 502, providing for the legal production, processing, and sale of recreational marijuana by private businesses licensed to operate under strict regulation by the Washington State Liquor Control Board (WSLCB). The initiative was drafted by Alison Holcomb of the Washington Chapter of the American Civil Liberties Union (ACLU) with the assistance of John McKay, former US Attorney for Western Washington and then (and currently) a professor of law at the Seattle University School of Law. This pairing of the liberal Democrat ACLU attorney and the popular Republican "crime fighter" (McKay's father was the chair of the Bush 2004 Presidential Campaign for Washington) into a team advocating "smart reform" of the state's drug laws on marijuana proved to be a powerful force for further change in the state that had enacted a medical marijuana law by the initiative process (I 692) in 1998.

This bipartisan coalition of forceful and respected figures was blessed with substantial funding for their initiative campaign from many diverse sources, including that of the longtime advocate of drug law reform, George Soros. John McKay was not only a forceful speaker and advocate for such reform, but he was a veritable household name in the state because of his celebrity as being among the group of US Attorneys summarily dismissed by former US Attorney General Alberto Gonzales in December 2006. That entire episode degenerated into a virtual scandal over the politicization of a heretofore merit-driven process within the US Department of Justice, ultimately resulting in Gonzales' resignation on August 27th of 2007. McKay and his counterparts in other states who were dismissed succeeded in getting rid of the US Attorney General—no mean feat, indeed! In the process of leading that fight against a broadly sensed injustice John McKay became a sort of folk hero in Washington State, among moderate Republicans and Democrats of virtually all stripes (Toobin, 2007).

The initiative crafted by Holcomb with the assistance of McKay was promoted as a "drug law reform" designed to at once deprive organized crime of a lucrative source of income, and at the same time transform the marijuana market into a source of substantial income through taxation at the point of production, point of processing, and again at the point of sales. Moreover, a portion of the revenue generated from legal cannabis sales would be used to document and then address any cost to public health and public safety that might arise. To assuage the law enforcement community the authors of Initiative 502 included a per se level of THC of 5 nanograms/milliliter of blood (5ng/ml) as advocated in the ICAP resolution with respect to preferred public policies. To stem opposition from the substantially unregulated, anxious, and well-established medical marijuana community in the state the authors of the initiative did not bring medical marijuana under the scope of WSLCB regulation, and they expressly excluded the use of THC-COOH or carboxy-THC (a principal metabolite of THC) in the specification of *per se* limits for impaired driving. The thought in mind here was one of protecting medical marijuana users, persons who would be somewhat likely to have carboxy-THC in their bloodstream after medicinal use; this provision of the initiative would shield them from arrest and prosecution for drug-impaired driving. Among such persons carboxy-THC would be present in the blood long after any consumption of marijuana would have occurred, given the absorption of cannabis into the fatty tissues and its slow, prolonged release into the bloodstream. While there is some controversy over how impairing THC is on driving (Ingraham, 2014) and what levels are impairing (Jones, Holmgren and Kugelberg, 2008; Grotenhermen et al., 2007), there is absolute agreement among researchers that carboxy-THC is not associated with driving impairment.

In the decidedly liberal setting of Washington State the authors of Initiative 502 built into the initiative dedicated revenue streams for the two research universities based on a percentage of revenues collected, and explicitly identified a revenue source for the Washington State Institute for Public Policy (WSIPP) to conduct periodic benefit-cost analyses for legislative and public review of positive and negative outcomes arising from Initiative 502. WSIPP is a nonpartisan entity established in 1994 which reports to the state legislature, and whose research agenda and operations are overseen by a bipartisan supervisory board featuring active participation by university-based researchers and an equal number of Democratic and Republican legislators (Watson, 2011). The initiative directs WSIPP to generate its benefit-cost analyses on a timely basis so that proponents and opponents of I 502 have equal, open access to how the analysis is done and what the results observed suggest for maintaining, modifying, or repealing the initiative (Wallach, 2014).

Given this sustainable source of state revenue to support research related to the legalization of recreational marijuana it is likely that the law enforcement and traffic safety communities of Washington will turn to the state's research universities, the University of Washington and Washington State University, to address the many issues which will arise surrounding such matters as the "political" *per se* standard of 5 ng/ml THC. In 30+ years of research that underlies our current *per se* presumptive (though refutable) impairment limits of .08 BAC for adults, and lower limits for commercial vehicle operators and drivers under 21 years of age, remains to be undertaken and reported for amount of THC normally causing driving impairment.

In advance of this research, however, the traffic safety forces of Washington State followed the recommendation of the IACP resolution to implement "the Drug Evaluation and Classification ("DRE") program across jurisdictions so that law enforcement is uniformly trained to detect drugged drivers ..." Among the nation's law enforcement agencies the Washington State Patrol (WSP) has been viewed as a clear leader, maintaining an exacting high standard for excellence as exemplified by the sustaining of its CALEA (Commission on Accreditation of Law Enforcement Agencies, Inc.) accreditation through budgetary lows and highs alike. In the area of traffic safety the agency has taken on its customary leadership role for the entire state, serving as the host agency for the state's DRE program in its Impaired Drivers Unit (Mosher et al. 2008).

The WSP hosted its first DRE training in 1996, with the first class and each succeeding class having roughly an equal number of trainee slots for WSP and for municipal and county law enforcement agencies. A notable participant in the first DRE class was Lieutenant Lowell Porter, who subsequently rose through the ranks to become chief of the Washington State Patrol, and upon retirement was appointed director of the Washington Traffic Safety Commission by the governor. The agency is currently involved in instructing its 29th DRE training school. The DRE program strives to maintain approximately 200 certified officers, and endeavors to recruit and train between 20 and 35 new trainees every year depending on retirements, reassignments, promotion in rank, and other developments among the DRE cadre.

These DRE officers can be considered the "first line of defense" against drug-impaired driving. The program was originally designed to address a problem of occasional occurrence wherein a driver is detained for suspicion of impaired driving and a portable breath test reveals that there is no alcohol present to account for the observed signs of impairment. The officer responsible for the initial contact with such a suspect then requests that a DRE-trained officer come to the location of the traffic stop to conduct a detailed, 12-step drug influence evaluation. That field assessment entails a considerably enhanced standard field sobriety test, featuring a series of pulse rate notations, pupil size estimation, vertical nystagmous assessment, stimulus tracking, eye convergence, eyelid droopiness notation, the Rhomberg balance test, a walk and turn test, a one-legged stand test, internal clock test, nose touch, a hippus test, rebound dilation, reaction to light, blood pressure, and temperature. The DRE 12-step assessment is sanctioned by the joint action of the IACP and NHTSA, and provides the basis of expertise-based testimony in contested cases of drug-impaired driving. In *State v. Beaty* (2002) Division II of the Washington State Court of Appeals ruled that Washington trial courts must accept a DRE's opinion as to impairment of an accused person contesting arrest *if* the 12-step process was followed in its entirety.

In addition to conducting this evaluation, the DRE officer must designate which drug category (or categories) they presume to be the cause of the impairment from the following list:

1. Central nervous system depressant
2. Central nervous system stimulant
3. Hallucinogen
4. PCP
5. Narcotic analgesic
6. Inhalant
7. Cannabis

Under current law the DRE must, if they feel they have probable cause to suspect impairment, request a judicial search warrant for the taking of blood evidence. If the request is granted the DRE completes a narrative report on the matter and sends the blood evidence through the chain of custody to the Washington State Crime Lab for testing and the generation of a toxicology report. That report is subsequently attached to the field assessment and the DRE program coordinator is responsible for monitoring officer performance. DRE officers in good standing must conduct a minimum number of assessments each year, and they must demonstrate a 70% "hit rate"—that is, in at least 7 in 10 evaluations they must have identified a drug category that produced a positive verification in the associated toxicology report.

It should be noted that the DRE assessment process in Washington State had relied upon the premise of an implied consent to extract blood from drivers suspected of drug-impaired driving as a condition of enjoying the privilege of driving in Washington. However, the US Supreme Court issued its judgment in *Missouri v. McNeely* (2013) holding that the implied consent premise long-established in impaired driving enforcement was no longer permissible. In clearly rejecting the legal argument made that the requirement of judicial warrants for blood draws in impaired driving and other cases raises a high risk of lost evidence—as is the case in the metabolizing of cannabis and loss of THC evidence—the court ruled in favor of privacy rights and raised the barrier to routine swift collection of blood evidence in marijuana-impaired driving cases.

Once the threshold of marijuana legalization was crossed with the passage of I 502 it was clear to the Washington State Patrol, the Washington Traffic Safety Commission, and the Washington Association of Sheriffs and Police Chiefs that the state's cadre of about 200 DRE officers (about 100 in New Mexico) was not going to provide sufficient coverage for drug-impaired driving in the state. It was decided to enhance law enforcement readiness for the pending challenge by carrying out training in the ARIDE (Advanced Roadside Impaired Driving Enforcement) program on an emergency action schedule. The course resulted from the recognition by the IACP and NHTSA of the rising problem of drug-impaired driving across the nation and the need for many patrol officers—not just DRE specialists—to be aware of the issue and capable of dealing with drug-impaired motorists. Nationally, over 8,500 officers are certified as graduates of ARIDE training (Bill O'Leary, NHTSA, USDOT via personal communication, 02/04/2014).

In Washington, virtually all of the commissioned officers of the WSP have received ARIDE training. In addition, the WSP Academy has incorporated the ARIDE curriculum in its training and features an entire week of instruction dedicated to impaired driving, including explaining how the DRE officers interface with patrol officers in drug-impaired driving cases. Similarly, the ARIDE curriculum has been incorporated into the state's Basic Law Enforcement Academy (BLEA) operated by the Washington State Criminal Justice Training Center (CJTC). In that training the consistency of ARIDE and DRE themes and standard practices are emphasized for consistency and shared understandings. Statewide, a total of 108 ARIDE classes have been held and 1,462 police officers have received classroom instruction and been certified in this timely subject of statewide concern.

The Track Record on DRE Assessments in Cannabis Cases

Given the centrality of the DRE program as the "first line of defense" and as the spearhead of training for patrol officers, what can be said about their documented ability to spot cannabis-impaired driving and successfully demonstrate that ability with blood evidence? Fortunately, the DRE Program Coordinators of the states of Washington and New Mexico shared their archival records (in hard copy) of DRE field assessments and associated toxicology reports so that an empirical assessment could be made of the relative ease or difficulty of documenting cannabis-impairment in blood evidence. The authors of this chapter are indebted to the series of three Washington State DRE program coordinators (Courtney Stewart, Rob Sharpe, and Mark Crandall) who provided these records for five years of Washington DRE assessments (2006–2010), and to Detective Christine Frank of the Albuquerque Police Department, who did likewise for her state's program. These hard copy files were coded, digitized, and analyzed at Washington State University and provide an important insight into the difficulties associated with THC-impairment recognition and documentation in the DRE process. The coding process entailed multiple coders (graduate students in the Department of Criminal Justice and Criminology) going through a process of attending DRE officer training sessions to understand the 12-step process and seeing it carried out in a training setting with impaired persons. They conducted test coding of field evaluation reports and toxicology reports to compare coding results, and then developed a coding guide which allowed a high rate of inter-coder reliability to be achieved (96%) on a sample of over 1,300 cases drawn from over 6,000 cases for Washington. In the case of New Mexico, all 350+ cases were coded and digitized.

In the cases where cannabis was designated as a suspected cause (sometimes along with another impairing drug), Table 1 displays the figures for "false positives" (that is, the selected category was not confirmed in the toxicology report) in the Washington and in New Mexico DRE data.

Table 1. False Positives for Cannabis-Suspected Cases

WASHINGTON Number of Cases = 458	
Cases confirmed by THC found in the blood sample	= 263 (57%)
Cases with no THC, but Carboxy-THC present	= 33 (7%)
Cases with no confirmation of cannabis consumption	= 162 (35%)
NEW MEXICO Number of Cases = 216	
Cases confirmed by THC found in the blood sample	= 54 (25%)
Cases with no THC, but Carboxy-THC present	= 16 (7%)
Cases with no confirmation of cannabis present	= 146 (68%)

One type of error is the failure to confirm a suspected source of impairment coming from the consumption of marijuana. It is clear from the figures in Table 1 that it is difficult indeed to diagnose cannabis impairment; it is a suspected cause of demonstrable impairment at the time of arrest, but there is no blood evidence to confirm that suspicion in nearly half the cases in Washington and in three-in-four cases in New Mexico. It must be reiterated that in many of these cases impairment was present and documented in the toxicology report for some impairing drug or drugs—but THC was not present in the blood sample associated with that case.

Another assessment of accuracy moves in the opposite direction—that is, in those cases where THC is found in the blood sample, how often was cannabis checked by the DRE officer as a source of impairment? Table 2 sets forth evidence on the "false negative" rate documented in the Washington and New Mexico archival DRE data.

It is clear that there is less error moving from the blood evidence back to the DRE's suspicion of the probable cause of the observed impairment as indicated by the DRE 12-step process. However, it remains the case that between one-in-five and one-in-three DRE cases the presence of THC in the blood sam-

Table 2. False Negatives for Cannabis-Present in Blood Sample Cases

WASHINGTON Number of Cases = 324	
Cases in which DRE officer marked cannabis as a cause of impairment	= 263 (81%)
Cases in DRE officer did not check cannabis as a cause of impairment	= 61 (19%)
NEW MEXICO Number of Cases = 263	
Cases in which DRE officer marked cannabis as a cause of impairment	= 178 (68%)
Cases in DRE officer did not check cannabis as a cause of impairment	= 85 (32%)

ple did not generate a cannabis suspicion on the part of the DRE-trained officer. It is important to note that in many of the false negatives multiple drugs were present in addition to THC, hence the probable cause of impairment was indeed a reflection of the presence of some impairing substance.

Research Being Done to Aid Drugged Driving Enforcement

The difficulty in detecting and documenting cannabis-impaired driving is apparent even for the well-trained and experienced DRE officers, let alone the officers prepared only with ARIDE training, as useful as that likely is for managing the increased volume of cannabis-involved cases. Added to this scenario of difficulty of assessment are the limitations placed upon police arising from the ruling of the US Supreme Court in the *Missouri v. McNeely* (2013) case with respect to the requirement of a judicial search warrant for routine police blood draws and in the process setting aside the implied consent presumption commonly employed in the past; this court holding adds further to the urgent need for "point-of-contact" collection of biological samples. As noted, this type of evidence collection "is important for detecting rapidly metabolized drugs and being able to relate observed driving performance to a toxicological result" (Logan, Mohr and Talpins, 2014: 1).

In this important area of research a number of researchers in the United States and Europe alike are focusing on the collection and on-site analysis of oral fluids. The report prepared for the American Academy of Forensic Sciences by Maggitti, Logan, and McMullin describes in excellent outline form the work being done with oral fluids for the detection of THC in particular (2012). Field testing is ongoing of four such devices in a study being done by PIRE for NHTSA in jail settings in California as this chapter is being written. Similarly, comparable work is being reported on studies being conducted in the European countries represented in the DRUID study (Chu et al., 2012).

While this work is indeed important, serious concerns have been raised by bioethicists and privacy rights advocates worried about the ever-expanding reach of the state in regard to DNA profiles (Rosen, 2003). Oral fluids carry human DNA information along with potential evidence of drug consumption, and groups such as the ACLU are very much opposed to the collection and retention of DNA profiles for persons who have not been convicted of any crime (Maschke, 2008). Similar concerns for privacy have been raised in both the United Kingdom and in the European Community (Shellberg, 2003). In 2008 the European Court for Human Rights in Strasbourg ruled that the maintenance of DNA records of persons innocent of any crimes is a violation of Article Eight of the U.N. Human Rights Convention with regard to the right to respect for private and family life. In the United States, the California ACLU has challenged California's Proposition 69 (2004) which was voted into law by a wide margin permitting the expansion of "DNA Fingerprinting" databases to include arrestees, not just certain categories of convicted persons. Similarly, working with funding provided by the National Human Genome Research Institute of the National Institutes of Health, attorneys Simoncelli and Seinhardt (2005) contributed a timely article to the DNA Fingerprinting and Civil Liberties Project of the American Society for Law, Medicine, and Ethics, which provides an excellent overview of the issues leading to the ACLU's concerns.

In reflection of such serious concerns, some researchers have turned to the possibility of detecting the presence of THC in breath samples. The Colorado Legislature in 2014 allocated $250,000 to the state's Department of Economic Development to provide grant funding to a Colorado business (Lifeloc Technologies) which manufactures alcohol breathalyzers to work on a similar device for detecting THC. Likewise a Canadian corporation known as Cannabix is working on the development of such a device, as are analytic chemistry researchers in the Hill Lab at Washington State University who are working in a public/private partnership with Chemring Detection Systems of North Carolina to apply differential ion mobility spectrometry to the task of point-of-contact breath testing for THC.

Conclusion

In conclusion, it is quite apparent that the challenge posed to law enforcement by marijuana-impaired driving is a serious one, but it is also clear that potent countermeasures are in place or are being developed to meet that challenge. The numerous problems associated with amassing the necessary scientific evidence of dose response outcomes to sustain *per se* legal limits must be addressed in time, and the much more effective gathering of point-of-contact biological evidence must take place for the police to keep up with the problem of driving while high. While the social institution of the "designated driver" is now a well-established one, there is evidence that drivers who use cannabis are inclined to believe that it is safe to drive after consuming marijuana (O'Malley and Johnson, 2013). While cannabis may even be less impairing than alcohol, it is still the case that prudence would dictate that the designated driver concept be promoted among marijuana users recreating in groups.

Perhaps the future will bring a day when the designated driver norm is adopted by cannabis users and the patrol officers on duty will have ARIDE training certification and have at their disposal breathalyzers for *both* alcohol and drugs for the collection of point-of-contact evidence in cases of suspected impaired driving. That scenario could lead to both greater deterrence of drug-impaired driving and more effective arrest and prosecution of offenders. This would be a major accomplishment by the traffic safety community as it endeavors to meet its stated goal of Target Zero—namely, the avoidance of any traffic fatalities by 2030 through safer vehicles, more effective road engineering, more efficacious traffic law enforcement, and greater compliance by drivers with existing laws and regulations.

References

Anderson, D. M., Hansen, B., & Rees, D. I. (2013). Medical marijuana laws, traffic fatalities, and alcohol consumption. *Journal of Law and Economics, 56*(2), 333–369.

Asbridge, M., Hayden, J. A., & Cartwright, J. L. (2012). Acute cannabis consumption and motor vehicle collision risk: Systematic review of observational studies and meta-analysis. *British Medical Journal, 344*, e536.

Asbridge, M., Poulin, C., & Donato, A. (2005). Driving under the influence of cannabis and motor vehicle collision risk: Evidence from adolescents in Atlantic Canada. *Accident Analysis and Prevention, 37*, 1025–1034.

Bingham, C. R., Shope, J. T., & Zhu, J. (2008). Substance-involved driving: Predicting driving after using alcohol, marijuana, and other drugs. *Traffic Injury Prevention, 9*(6), 515–526.

Birkeland, S., Murphy-Graham, E., & Weiss, C. (2005). Good reasons for ignoring good evaluation: The case of the Drug Abuse Resistance Education (D.A.R.E.) Program. *Evaluation and Program Planning, 28*, 247–256.

Chu, M., Gerostamoulos, D., Beyer, J., Rodda, L., Boorman, M., & Drummer, O. H. (2012). The incidence of drugs of impairment in oral fluid from random roadside testing. *Forensic Science International, 215*, 28–31.

DRUID (Driving Under Influence of Drugs, Alcohol and Medicines). (2012). *Final report: Work performed, main results, and recommendations.* Berlin: European Union [Principal research group leaders H. Schulze, M. Schumacher, R. Urmeew, K. Auerback, A. Knoche, I.-M. Bernhoft, M. Hagenzieker, J. Alvarez, M. Pilgerstorfer, B. Zlender, & H. de Gier].

Elvik, R. (2013). Risk of road accident associated with the use of drugs: A systematic review and meta-analysis of evidence from epidemiological studies. *Accident Analysis and Prevention, 60*, 254–267.

Garvey, T., & Yeh, B. (2014, January 13). *State legalization of recreational marijuana: Selected legal issues. Report prepared for members and committees of Congress*. Washington, DC: Congressional Research Service.

Grotenhermen, F., Leson, G., Berghaus, G., Drummer, O. H., Kruger, H., Longo, M., Moskowitz, H., Perrine, B., Ramaekers, J. G., Smiley, A., & Tunbridge, R. (2007). Developing limits for driving under cannabis. *Addiction, 102*(12), 1910–1917.

Hall, W. (2014). What has research over the past two decades revealed about the adverse health effects of recreational cannabis use? *Addiction Monograph*, doi: 10.1111/add.12703.

Ingraham, C. (2014, February 9). Stoned drivers are a lot safer than drunk ones, new federal data show. *The Washington Post*.

Iversen, L. (2003). Cannabis and the brain. *Brain, 126*, 1250–1270.

Jones, A. W., Holmgren, A., & Kugelberg, F. C. (2008). Driving under the influence of cannabis: A 10-year study of age and gender differences in the concentrations of tetrahydrocannabinol in blood. *Addiction, 103*(3), 452–461.

Lachenmeier, D. W., & Rehm, J. (2015). Comparative risk assessment of alcohol, tobacco, cannabis and other illicit drugs using the margin of exposure approach. *Scientific Reports, 5*, 8126; doi:10.1038/srep08126.

Logan, B. K., Mohr, A., & Talpins, S. K. (2014). Detection and prevalence of drug use in arrested drivers using the Drager Drug Test 5000 and Affinition DrugWipe oral fluid drug screening devices. *Journal of Analytical Toxicology*, 1–7. doi:10.1093/jat/bku050.

Longo, M. C., Hunter, C. E., Lokan, R. J., & White, M. A. (2000). The prevalence of alcohol, cannaboids, benzodiazepines and stimulants amongst injured drivers and their role in driver culpability: Part II: The relationship between drug prevalence and drug concentration, and driver culpability. *Accident Analysis and Prevention, 32*(5), 623–632.

Lowry, J. (2015, February 6). Federal report: Fewer drivers drinking; More using drugs. *Denver Post*.

Maggitti, A., Logan, B. K., & McMullin, M. (2012). Tools, techniques and findings for the qualitative analysis of delta-9-tetrahydrocannabinoids in oral fluid. *Proceedings: American Academy of Forensic Sciences, XIX*, 474–475.

Mann, R. E., Adlaf, E., Zhao, J., Ialomiteanu, A., Smart, R. G., & Asbridge, M. (2007). Cannabis use and self-reported collisions in a representative sample of adult drivers. *Journal of Safety Research, 38*, 669–674.

Marks, D., & MacAvoy, M. (1989). Divided attention performance in cannabis users and non-users following alcohol and cannabis separately and in combination. *Psychopharmacology, 99*, 397–401.

Maschke, K. J. (2008). DNA and law enforcement. In M. Crowley (Ed.), *From birth to death and bench to clinic: The Hastings Center bioethics briefing book for journalists, policymakers, and campaigns* (pp. 45–50).Garrison, NY: The Hastings Center.

McGuire, F., Dawe, M., Shield, K. D., Rehm, J., & Fischer, B. (2011). Driving under the influence of cannabis or alcohol in a cohort of high-frequency cannabis users: Prevalence and reflections on current interventions. *Canadian Journal of Criminology and Criminal Justice, 53*(2), 247–259.

Miller, D. (2001, October 19). D.A.R.E. reinvents itself—with help from its social science critics. *Chronicle of Higher Education.*

Mosher, C., Pratt, T., Pickerill, M., Lovrich, N., & Gaffney, M. (2008). The importance of context in understanding biased policing: State patrol traffic citations in Washington State. *Police Practice and Research: An International Journal, 9*(1), 43–57.

National Center for Statistics and Analysis. (2015, January). *Early estimate of motor vehicle traffic fatalities for the first half (Jan–Jun) of 2014. (Crash Stats Brief Statistical Summary. Report No. DOT HS 812 093)*. Washington, DC: National Highway Traffic Safety Administration.

Nordrum, A. (2014, September). The new D.A.R.E. program: This one works. *Scientific American.*

O'Leary, B. (2014, February 4). Personal communication with National Highway Traffic Safety Administration office providing oversight of ARIDE program.

O'Malley, P. M., & Johnson, L. D. (2013). Driving after drug or alcohol use by U.S. high school seniors, 2001–2011. *American Journal of Public Health, 103*(11), 2027–2034.

ONDCP (Office of National Drug Control Policy). (2014). *National drug control strategy, 2014*. Washington, DC: Executive Office of the President.

Pan, W., & Bai, H. (2009). A multivariate approach to a meta-analytic review of the effectiveness of the D.A.R.E. program. *International Journal of Environmental Research and Public Health, 6*(1), 267–277.

Ramaekers, J. G., Berghaus, G., van Laar, M., & Drummer, O. H. (2004). Dose-related risk of motor vehicle crashes after cannabis use. *Drug and Alcohol Dependence, 73*(2), 109–119.

Ronen, A., Gershon, P., Drobiner, H., Rabinovich, A., Bar-Hamburger, R., Mechoulam, R., Cassuto, Y., & Shinar, D. (2008). Effects of THC on driving performance, physiological state and subjective feelings relative to alcohol. *Accident Analysis and Prevention, 40*, 926–934.

Rosen, C. (2003). Liberty, privacy, and DNA databases. *The New Atlantis: A Journal of Technology and Society, 1* (Spring), 37–52.

Rosenbaum, D. P., & Hanson, G. S. (1998). Assessing the effects school-based drug education: A six-year multilevel analysis of project D.A.R.E. *Journal of Research in Crime and Delinquency, 35*(4), 381–412.

Shellberg, T. (2003, November 20). DNA justice speaks. *Presentation for the American Prosecutors Research Institute.*

Simoncelli, T., & Seinhardt, B. (2005). California's Proposition 69: A dangerous precedent for criminal DNA databases. *DNA Fingerprinting and Civil Liberties: Second in a Series of Articles.* Boston: American Society for Law, Medicine and Ethics.

State of Missouri v. Tyler Gabriel McNeeley. No. 11-1425. (United States Supreme Court, 2013).

State of Washington v. Jasper Leeroy Beaty, No. 26328-9-11 (Wash. Ct. App. Feb. 20, 2002).

Terry-McElrath, Y. M., O'Malley, P. M., & Johnson, L. D. (2014). Alcohol and marijuana use patterns associated with unsafe driving among U.S. high school seniors: High use frequency, concurrent use, and simultaneous use. *Journal of Studies on Alcohol and Drugs, 75*(3), 378–389.

Toobin, J. (2007, August 6). An unsolved killing: What does the firing of a U.S. attorney have to do with a murder case? *The New Yorker.*

Wallach, P. (2014, August). Washington's marijuana legalization grows knowledge, not just pot: A report on the state's strategy to assess reform. *Brookings Center for Effective Public Management.*

Watson, S. (2011). Results first: Helping states apply objective data and independent analysis to policy decisions to get the best return on investment. Philadelphia and Washington, DC: Pew Center on the States, Pew Charitable Trusts.

West, S. L., & O'Neal, K. K. (2004). Project D.A.R.E. outcome effectiveness revisited. *American Journal of Public Health, 94*(6), 1027–1029.

9

Marijuana Enforcement and a Crime Analyst's Daydream

David A. Licate

This chapter will follow the thought process of a hypothetical crime analyst who has been tasked with determining if the "marijuana problem" should be a strategic priority for her police department. If marijuana enforcement is determined to be a strategic priority, the analyst is asked to recommend evidence-based responses to the problem. In her research, the analyst applies analytic frameworks and policing strategies learned through years of training, education, and her experience at the Midwestern Police Department. Midwestern PD self-identifies as a department that employs the intelligence-led policing strategy with heavy emphasis on data-driven and evidence-based practices. As the analyst researches the history and impact of cannabis prohibition, her mind wanders to the broader issues of policing effectiveness, legitimacy, and marijuana enforcement as a public policy.

The *2014 National Drug Threat Assessment Drug Summary* was discussed at the Midwest Police Department's monthly Citystat meeting. The *Summary*, created yearly by the US Drug Enforcement Administration, states:

> Marijuana is the most widely available and commonly abused illicit drug in the United States. According to the 2014 NDTS, 80 percent of responding agencies reported that marijuana availability was high in their jurisdictions. High availability levels are due to large-scale marijuana importation from Mexico, as well as increasing domestic indoor grows and an increase of marijuana cultivated in states that have legalized marijuana or passed "medical marijuana" initiatives. As a result, abuse among adolescents is increasing and the medical consequences of marijuana abuse are rising. Further, marijuana concentrates,

> produced with new and dangerous extraction methods that elevate their THC content, are an increasing concern to law enforcement and public health officials (p. 25).

In addition, the *Summary* reports:

- National level survey data show an increase in marijuana abuse among adolescents. The 2013 *Monitoring the Future* survey (MTF) reported more than one-third (36.4%) of 12th-graders used marijuana in the past year, an 11 percent increase over the past five years. MTF survey data also showed an increase in annual marijuana use for 10th- and 8th-graders. More than one-quarter (29.8%) of 10th-graders reported using marijuana in the past year, an increase of 12 percent from 2009, and 12.7 percent of 8th-graders reported using marijuana in the past year, an increase of 8 percent over the past five years (p. 28).
- Drug Abuse Warning Network (DAWN) data shows an increase in medical consequences resulting from marijuana abuse. According to DAWN, there was a 62 percent increase in marijuana-related emergency department (ED) visits from 2004 to 2011. In 2011, only cocaine-related ED visits outnumbered those for marijuana (p. 30).
- According to Treatment Episode Data Set (TEDS) data, marijuana-related primary treatment admissions averaged approximately 300,000 from 2002 to 2007. Between 2008 and 2011 admissions averaged approximately 350,000, a 17 percent increase (p. 30).

Although Midwest is not in a state with legalized marijuana in any form, it borders states that have eliminated marijuana prohibition. There is concern among Midwest command staff that marijuana from domestic growers will be smuggled in from the more permissive states. In addition, drug cartels may seek to expand operations in Midwest's state since they can provide cheaper, tax-free marijuana. The large national parks in Midwest's state have already been used to grow marijuana by both domestic and international producers. Some sites have been booby trapped, leading to injuries of campers. The Midwest PD is concerned that the increase in marijuana activity might lead to increases in other crimes associated with the drug market. At very least, Midwest expects an increase in drivers under the influence of marijuana. Midwest's command staff wants more information. The Midwest PD criminal intelligence analyst is tasked with gathering intelligence on the problem and making recommendations to be presented at the next Citystat meeting. Should marijuana enforcement be a strategic priority for the Midwestern Police Department and, if so, what evidence-based strategies should be used?

Crime Analysis and Policing Strategies

Although the "analysis of crime" has existed for a very long time, the assignment of professionals specifically tasked to perform crime analysis did not begin until the 1970s (Emig, Heck, & Kravitz, 1980). Santos (2012) provides a widely accepted definition of crime analysis:

> Crime analysis is the systematic study of crime and disorder problems as well as other police-related issues—including sociodemographic, spatial, and temporal factors—to assist the police in criminal apprehension, crime and disorder reduction, crime prevention, and evaluation (p. 2).

Crime analysis did not become common in large agencies until the 1990s when, among other factors, advanced information systems hardware and software became available to police departments (O'Shea & Nicholls, 2003; Pattavina, 2005). The 1990s would see the exhibition and diffusion of policing strategies that heavily relied on the analysis of crime data, such as New York City's Compstat program (Silverman, 2006; Police Executive Research Forum, 2013; Weisburd, Mastrofski, McNally, Greenspan, & Willis, 2003). Indeed, Midwestern PD modeled their Citystat program after the NYPD model. The Compstat model uses crime analysis and mapping as the foundation for strategic problem solving (Weisburd et al., 2003). Agencies hold monthly accountability meetings to insure that the identified problems are being addressed appropriately.

Midwest's analyst is intimately aware of the history of initiatives like Compstat. She understands that the recent history of policing strategies involves a search for an alternative to the Standard Model of Policing (SMP). As a crime analyst, she takes pride in the fact that all alternatives to the Standard Model require crime analysis to guide effective policing approaches to crime reduction (Santos, 2014). She understand that each alternative to the Standard Model has a lesson to share which may be helpful in analyzing the current problem.

The Standard Model of Policing relies primarily on reactive law enforcement tactics. The theoretical foundation for the SMP is deterrence theory. Potential criminals will be deterred by the presence of police officers on routine patrol and the investigative capacity to find perpetrators. The strategies used in the Standard Model of Policing include increasing the number of officers, rapid response to calls for service, conducting unfocused random motorized patrol, and general reactive arrest strategies (Sherman et al., 1997; Weisburd & Eck, 2004). Midwest's analyst learned about the limited effectiveness of the

SMP early in her education (Sherman et al., 1997; Skogan & Frydl, 2004; Telep & Weisburd, 2012; Weisburd & Eck, 2004). Although certain crimes may be deterred if the intervention is narrowly focused, the tactics of the SMP, such as routine preventive patrol, are usually too general to be effective.

SMP policing organizations operate in reactive "crisis mode" with little strategic direction. Consequently, individual units in SMP organizations may be unaware that they are working on the same cases or problems. Alternatives to the SMP, however, are mission-driven and require an enterprise-wide assessment of jurisdictional priorities. All organizational units map their strategies, tactics, and operations to the strategic priorities of the organization. Mission-driven organizations are much more efficient and effective than SMP organizations, a conclusion that the command staff at Midwestern PD had made years earlier.

The crime analyst at Midwest is familiar with policing approaches and their effectiveness. In seeking an approach to the marijuana problem in her jurisdiction, she knows that researchers have reviewed several of the alternatives to the SMP, but that the review is incomplete and ongoing (Weisburd & Eck, 2004; Telep & Weisburd, 2012). There have been individual meta-analysis produced through the Campbell Collaboration for hot spots policing (Braga, Papachristos, & Hureau, 2012), problem-oriented policing (Weisburd, Telep, Hinkle, & Eck, 2010), and "pulling levers" focused deterrence strategies (Braga & Weisburd, 2012). Currently, there are reviews taking place for community policing and disorder ("broken windows") policing. Despite her own agency's implementation, there is no systematic research to date on Compstat or intelligence-led policing.

The first credible alternative to the standard model of policing is community policing. The US Department of Justice's Office of Community Oriented Policing Services defines community policing as "a philosophy that promotes organizational strategies, which support the systematic use of partnerships and problem-solving techniques, to proactively address the immediate conditions that give rise to public safety issues such as crime, social disorder, and fear of crime" (COPS Office, 2013). The first key component of community policing is developing partnerships with the community to understand and respond to problems. In addition, community policing facilitates cooperation with the public and legitimacy of the police, so that partnerships are meaningful (COPS Office, 2013).

It has been difficult to evaluate community policing systematically as the concept is vague (Weisburd & Eck, 2004). Research results on specific programs or tactics of community policing including neighborhood watch, drug awareness programs, community meetings, storefront offices, and newsletters indicate no reduction in crime (Telep & Weisburd, 2012; Weisburd & Eck, 2004). The problem-solving component of community policing, however, has shown some promise. Midwestern's analyst understands that the real contribution of community policing is in the area of police legitimacy. The community policing approach builds police-community relationships that are essential for not only determining priorities, but also effective policing strategies. Midwest's analyst understands that much of the information she will need for her analysis will come from community partnerships and surveys.

Managing fear and disorder is an important component of community policing. Wilson and Kelling's (1982) "broken windows thesis" is the foundation of disorder (or broken windows) policing. The disorder approach to policing features strict enforcement of laws against disorderly behavior and minor offenses to prevent more serious crimes from happening (Sousa & Kelling, 2006). The research results of the effectiveness of broken windows policing have been mixed (Weisburd & Eck, 2004). A summary of studies in seven cities (Skogan, 1990, 1992) found no evidence that the strict enforcement of disorder ordinances reduced additional disorder or more serious crimes. New York City's "zero tolerance" variant of disorder policing was used intensively in the 1990s. Although many NYC officials concluded it was the reason crime rates dropped during that time, researchers have not rigorously evaluated these claims (Weisburd & Eck, 2004). Indeed, disorder policing in New York has been criticized for unnecessary attention to minor offenses, increases in police misconduct, and poor police–community relations. Midwestern's analyst understands that evaluations of disorder policing have demonstrated limited effectiveness. Furthermore, strict application of this strategy may damage community partnerships.

Problem-oriented policing (POP) is another alternative to the standard model of policing. Closely related to COP, but more focused, POP proactively identifies problems within the community and develops tailored responses that address underlying causes of the problems (Goldstein, 1990). The core component of POP is the problem-solving process, which is also an important component of community policing. POP's problem-solving process was operationalized by John Eck and William Spelman (1987) as the SARA model:

- **Scanning**—recognition of the problem
- **Analysis**—the causes and extent of the problem are explored, and the key actors identified

- **Response**—the nature and scope of this intervention will be determined by the nature and scope of the problem
- **Assessment**—evaluation of response

The SARA model includes scanning for problems in the community and prioritizing them for response, analyzing data to understand what conditions and opportunities created the problem, responding to the problem with specifically tailored police and non-police methods, and assessing whether the response worked correctly (Center for Problem-Oriented Policing, 2013). The Campbell review of POP found that this strategy had a modest, but significant, effect on crime reduction (Santos, 2014; Weisburd et al., 2010). Researchers conclude that even a superficial addressing of problems using the problem-solving process is enough to impact crime and disorder levels (Braga & Weisburd, 2006; Telep & Weisburd, 2012). Although more rigorous research needs to be conducted on POP efforts, the evidence so far shows that it is the most promising of the police strategies (Skogan & Frydl, 2004; Weisburd & Eck, 2004; Weisburd et al., 2010; Santos, 2014). Midwestern's analyst routinely examines problems using the SARA process. POP has taught her that targeting specific problems with narrowly designed solutions is most effective. POP responses are divided into three categories: place-based, offender-based, and problem-based.

One set of narrowly tailored place-based strategies has shown much promise. Hot spots policing is a place-based strategy that focuses policing resources in areas or "hot spots" that have disproportionately more crime than other areas within a jurisdiction (Braga et al., 2012; Telep & Weisburd, 2012; Weisburd & Eck, 2004; Santos, 2014). The research on the effectiveness of hot spots policing is rigorous and plentiful. The results show that police response to hot spots, whether they are individual dwellings, clusters of addresses, street segments, or blocks, is effective in reducing crime (Braga et al., 2012; Telep & Weisburd, 2012; Weisburd & Eck, 2004; Santos, 2014).

Critics of hot spots policing have commented that the strategy is only effective in the short-term, since crime returns after it is displaced. Others argue that displacement can be managed and is minimized by the diffusion of benefits derived from the policing intervention (Braga et al., 2012; Telep & Weisburd, 2012). Braga and Weisburd (2010) assert that hot spots policing can be effective in the long-term when coupled with more in-depth problem solving (i.e., not just identifying the hot spots but also understanding why they are "hot"). Crime analysis, particularly the use of crime mapping and spatial analysis, has an important role in identifying hot spots. Analysis is important in identifying hot spots because researchers have shown that police do not accurately identify hot spots or regularly agree on what is a hot spot in their respective areas of responsibility (Bichler & Gaines, 2005; McLaughlin, Johnson, Bowers, Birks, & Pease, 2006; Ratcliffe & McCullagh, 2001; Santos, 2014). Midwestern's analyst still gets surprised at how police officer perception of where and when crime occurs in their jurisdiction differs from the data on the incidence of crime. She takes pride in her ability to focus policing resources more effectively by providing timely and accurate intelligence on the distribution of crime.

While hot spots policing is a place-based response, Midwestern's analyst understands that offender-based responses such as "pulling levers" might be appropriate. Pulling levers (also known as focused deterrence) addresses serious offenders in high-crime areas of a city (Braga & Weisburd 2012). Focused deterrence was first implemented as a 1990s POP project in Boston. Much like Compstat, the strategy has diffused to many different communities across the country. In each community, offenders are identified through intelligence analysis. The offenders are then notified that they are being targeted. In many cases, offenders are provided with the opportunity to take advantage of rehabilitation, training, and social services to modify their criminal lifestyles. Individuals who choose to continue offending are targeted for arrest and enhanced penalties (Braga & Weisburd, 2012; Telep & Weisburd, 2012).

Midwestern's analyst recalls that the results of evaluations for the "pulling levers" response are positive in that they show a significant reduction in crime (Braga & Weisburd, 2012). As with POP, the problem-solving process is central in this approach, thus crime analysis is also central (Telep & Weisburd, 2012). Although the responses within this approach focus on individuals, the process of identifying the appropriate individuals involves identifying areas of disproportionately high crime (i.e., hot spots; Kennedy, Braga, & Piehl, 1998) and understanding the nature of crime and the relationship of the offenders to crime (Kennedy, Braga, and Piehl, 2001), both of which require crime analysis.

Regardless of policing strategy, analysis is key in determining priorities and designing place-based, offender-based, or situational responses. Understanding the significant role of analysis, the Midwestern PD has implemented a business model that places intelligence at its heart. Intelligence-led policing (ILP) is a strategy and business model that integrates the intelligence process with the operations and overall mission of a policing organization (Carter, 2009; Ratcliffe, 2008). As an integrative strategy, ILP fuses usually fragmented information collection and analysis processes within a policing organization and directs them toward specified crime and disorder reduction objectives. Like many other policing strategies, ILP originated in response to an inadequate deterrence-based standard model of policing. ILP incorporates useful elements of other policing strategies including the standard model of policing, problem-oriented policing, and community policing. Originally focused on targeting prolific offenders, hot spots, and threat groups, ILP has more recently added opportunity reduction, problem-solving, risk management, and other evidence-based techniques that have demonstrated long-term impact on crime and disorder (Licate, 2014). The ability of ILP to integrate many policing approaches into a coherent model is what attracted Midwestern PD and others to its adoption.

As an intelligence-led police department, the Midwestern PD has a formal and written information management plan (IMP). The IMP is a business plan that guides a focused series of processes for the intelligence function. This plan identifies priority problems and institutionalizes a process for monitoring the problems through the application of seven critical components (Ratcliffe, 2008; Carter, 2009; Licate, 2014):

- **Strategic Priority**—The agency must determine what problems receive priority. What problems are most important to the community?
- **Intelligence Requirements**—What additional information does the agency need to better understand each problem, its causes, and its effects?
- **Collection Plan**—Where (sources) and how (methods) will I get the additional information that I need to better understand the problem?
- **Analysis**—Collectively, what does the new information mean and what new insights does it provide about the problem?
- **Intelligence Products**—What actionable information do I need to tell other people in order to prevent or control the problem?
- **Operational Responses**—What explicit operational activities may be implemented to prevent or mitigate the priority problems? What resources are needed?
- **Process Review**—Was the information accurate and useful? Could the problem be altered as a result of the information? What will make the process better? (Carter, 2009)

Midwest's analyst understands the importance of well-defined Intelligence strategic priorities. Strategic priorities become the articulated criminal threats that must be monitored and managed by a policing agency in light of the impact these threats have on public safety and security. A strategic priority must be specified in the context of the local community and the policing agency's intent to manage that priority (Carter, 2009).

Defining intelligence priorities can become a complex process because law enforcement organizations have a wide range of potential responsibilities ranging from traffic control to counterterrorism. Resource limitations mean that these different responsibilities cannot be treated equally. Each responsibility must be given a priority that will guide the allocation of resources and the amount of organizational effort that will be devoted to addressing it. Midwestern's crime analyst has been asked to make a recommendation on how much of a priority marijuana enforcement should be in her jurisdiction.

Midwestern's analyst understands that 30 years of policing research has concluded that effective policing approaches are focused and systematic through the problem-solving process (Sherman et al., 1997; Telep & Weisburd, 2012; Braga & Weisburd, 2006; Weisburd & Eck, 2004; Weisburd et al., 2010; Santos, 2014). Although the idea of making greater use of evidence, information, and science in policing presented a significant challenge for the Midwestern PD, it was agreed that the benefits of evidence-based policing (police practices based on scientific evidence) were worth the investment. Midwestern PD has a culture supportive of the notion that information generated from systematic or scientific research should be regularly used by the police to make both strategic and tactical decisions. If this were not the case, the analyst's opinion on policing priorities and responses would not have been solicited.

The evidence-based approach assisted Midwestern in the advancement of police information and management systems that improved efficiency (and were a necessary component to intelligence-led policing). Further, evidence-based policing facilitated the transformation of Midwestern's policing culture from reactive to proactive. In short, evidence-based policing assisted in the transition from the Standard Model of Policing to a data-driven alternative. Finally, Midwestern PD staff believe that evidence-based approaches are more logical and effective, and strategies and tactics that are generated from information and based in scientific knowledge are more likely to reduce crime when employed (Lum, 2009). In sum, evidence-based strategies supported by systematic analysis and focused by place, offender, and/or problem are most successful (Lum, 2009; Santos, 2014).

Analyzing the Marijuana Issue

Midwestern PD's crime analyst has been tasked with determining if marijuana should be a strategic priority. To determine the best methods for defining the scope of the marijuana problem in her jurisdiction, she might turn to independent organizations such as the Problem-Oriented Policing Center (www.popcenter.org), university institutes and centers such as the Center for Evidence-Based Policing at George Mason University, or government research and statistics from sources like the National Criminal Justice Research Service (NCJRS), National Institute of Justice, and Bureau of Justice Assistance (BJA).

A search of the problem-oriented policing literature available at the Center for Problem-Oriented Policing reveals a paper collecting 1990s studies on policing drug hot spots (Jacobson, 1999) and one POP guide on responses to open-air drug markets (Harocopos & Hough, 2005). Both documents are consistent in their recommendations for dealing with drug markets. Both documents emphasize that understanding factors that contribute to the problem will help frame local analysis questions, determine good measures of effectiveness, recognize key intervention points, and select appropriate responses.

Midwestern's analyst understands that a detailed analysis of the problem in her area will help to design a more effective response and allow her to better predict the outcome of any action taken against the drug markets in her area. It is likely that the location of many markets are already known to operational personnel in her district. However, other key characteristics of the markets should be examined. For now, however, she is simply trying to determine if marijuana warrants the designation of strategic priority in the Midwestern PD.

Midwestern's analyst reads suggestions from the available POP Guide (Harocopos & Hough, 2005). The guide recommends a community policing tactic first. A community survey can identify residents' concerns, as well as trouble hot spots in the neighborhood. In addition, conducting a survey is good community policing approach that demonstrates police commitment and can help build relations between the police and local residents that might be useful in ultimately solving the problem.

The guide recommends that a dedicated telephone hotline for local residents is also useful for gathering intelligence. If the information provided is acted upon promptly, hotlines can help build confidence in the police. Midwestern's analyst reflects on the emerging utility of social media for generating intelligence. Citizens who would otherwise not call the police might be inclined to text information or leave it on the department's social media sites. In addition, many drug markets are conducting business online. Technically savvy investigators know how to tap this new source of intelligence.

Although technology is becoming increasingly important, systematic and well-recorded observations by an officer can be indispensable in defining the nature of the drug market and identifying some of the characteristics that allow drug-related sales to thrive in that area.

Other data sources that may be useful to identify discrete drug markets include:

- Narcotics sales arrests
- Citizen observation
- Calls for service
- Information on medical treatments for drug abuse (DAWN or TEDS data)

Midwestern's analyst goes on to read that drug markets vary in terms of size, drug type, and clientele. It is important to understand the conditions of each market and identify the reasons why the markets exist in the area. There might be a variety of situational and social factors contributing to the success of drug markets in a jurisdiction. The balance between supply reduction strategies and demand reduction strategies is likely to vary according to such factors (Harocopos & Hough, 2005). In any case, the Midwestern PD analyst has her work cut out for her.

Although her task is to define the problem and determine if it should be designated a strategic priority, Midwestern PD's analyst cannot avoid reading the available literature on successful responses. She understands that focusing on responses before adequately defining a problem can produce various inefficiencies and risk creating a solution in search of a problem (a problem for any agency in a political environment). She recalls the rise of street gang units in many jurisdictions that failed to demonstrate a gang problem. Well-meaning residents misidentifying groups of juveniles and calling city hall, the availability of grant money, opportunistic politicians, and bored line officers created a solution where a problem did not exist. As one evaluation noted, police departments typically were responding to political, public, and media pressure—not directly to the objective reality of the gang problem (Katz & Webb, 2003). The same evaluation found that gang units and gang unit officers were not practicing community or problem-oriented policing. In short, problems drive solutions in effective organizations and not vice versa.

Aware of the risks of examining solutions before defining the problem, the analyst's curiosity gets the best of her.

Jacobson (1999, p. 30–31) concludes that successful interventions have some things in common:

- **Intensity of intervention**—The use of proactive enforcement tactics in combination with alternative methods of crime prevention permits the weaknesses of certain approaches to be counter-acted by the strengths of others.
- **Leverage**—Situational policing of drug markets requires the creative use of levers by the police as they seek to persuade other agencies to work with them. In some cases, this will primarily be a matter of encouraging

potential partners to recognize that they have common interests and goals. In other cases, the police may have to draw on civil laws and regulations in obliging place managers to take actions against drug dealers and users.

- **Sustained action**—The likelihood that the beneficial impact of many initiatives will be eroded over time must always be borne in mind. Preventive strategies should incorporate components that will have at least some long-term effects upon drug market sites, and should be sufficiently flexible to respond to changing patterns of behavior among drug dealers and users.
- **Sensitivity to community relations**—Crime control initiatives that exacerbate existing tensions within neighborhoods may be counter-productive. When local residents and community organizations are involved in the development of strategies, efforts should be made to incorporate representatives of as many segments of the population as possible.
- **Evaluation**—Thorough process evaluations of initiatives should bring to light design and implementation problems as and when they arise, and may therefore assist with their resolution. Evaluations should also allow early mistakes to be avoided and achievements to be built upon in later phases of operations, and facilitate interchange concerning good practice between agencies and regions.
- **Situational crime prevention**—The term "situational crime prevention" refers to measures taken by the police and other agencies to reduce the opportunities for, and potential rewards of, crime committed in specific places. These measures focus on the nature of criminal events and the settings within which they occur, rather than on the motivations and profiles of offenders. Hence this is a highly pragmatic approach, which "seeks not to eliminate criminal or delinquent tendencies through improvement of society or its institutions, but merely to make criminal actions less attractive to offenders" (Clarke 1997, p. 2).

Midwestern PD's analyst is well versed in situational crime prevention methods. She understands that the implementation of situational crime prevention measures involves identification and modification of the physical and social variables that encourage criminal activity in high-crime locations (hot-spots). Variables may include a lack of formal or informal surveillance, poor management, easy access, and the presence of inadequately secured valuable items (Eck & Weisburd, 1995). In short, "crimes are created by the interactions of potential offenders with potential targets in settings that make doing the crime easy, safe and profitable" (Brantingham & Brantingham, 1995, p. 5). The police and other agencies may employ several tactics to discourage offenders from visiting high-crime locations. The chosen approaches will depend on the specific nature and setting of the crimes being committed.

The following issues should be addressed when considering the situational policing of drug markets (Jacobson, 1999, p. 4):

- identify and analyze drug hot-spots
- determine if police crackdowns, low-level enforcement, or situational initiatives are appropriate
- modify the environment of drug-dealing sites through various place management strategies
- monitor displacement: situational initiatives may produce changing patterns of, rather than reductions in, crime

Midwestern PD's analyst will need to answer some questions if she is to recommend action on the local marijuana problem. First, she will need information on the **nature of the drug market** in her jurisdiction (adapted from Harocopos & Hough, 2005, p. 16–18).

- Where is the drug market situated?
- Are there any clear geographical boundaries?
- Is it located near a transport hub or arterial route?
- Are there any physical or environmental characteristics that could encourage drug-related activity (e.g., vacant buildings, vacant lots, overgrown foliage, pay phones)?
- Are there suitable places for sellers to hide their drugs?
- What are the times of operation?
- Are there any particular days that are noticeably busier, for example, weekends or days when people receive their checks?
- What types of drugs are being sold?
- If several types of drugs are being sold, do sellers specialize in one particular drug or is there an overlap between markets?
- Is the market well-known as somewhere that drugs can be bought easily?
- How is the market advertised?
- Does the market have a reputation for violence?
- Is the market in fact violent? (Bear in mind that not all market-related violence will be reported to police).
- Where are drug transactions completed (e.g., on the street, in vehicles, elsewhere)?
- Are there places for people to use drugs once they have purchased them?

- How many open-air drug markets are operating in the jurisdiction?
- For how long has this particular drug market been operating?

Information about **market participants** (buyers and sellers) will be necessary for a complete analysis.

- How many sellers are operating in the area?
- Are sellers who are incarcerated or killed replaced easily and quickly by new sellers?
- Do sellers operate alone or use ancillary staff such as runners or lookouts?
- What is the structural organization of the market (e.g., is it fragmented—made up of freelance sellers with any alliance being on an ad hoc basis, or hierarchical—where organizations of sellers may dominate their local area and drive out competition)?
- What role do firearms play in the market?
- What proportion of customers is local to the area?
- If buyers travel to the market, how do they travel?
- Are buyers mainly serious or casual users?

In addition, Midwestern's analyst would gather information on the **current policing operations.**

- Have there been any preventive strategies used against drug markets in the area?
- What were the consequences of any previous enforcement?
- How was the market disrupted?
- How did the market adapt to enforcement?
- Did police activity lead to displacement?
- Aside from enforcement, what other actions have been taken by the police or other agencies to control the drug market?

In determining if marijuana enforcement should be a strategic priority, the analyst will have to gather information on the **impact of the drug market on the local community**.

- Does the local community consider the drug market to be a problem? (This could affect the level of support that can be expected from residents.)
- What activities and conditions are of concern specifically to citizens in the area (e.g., loitering, noise, traffic congestion, harassment, litter)?
- Have some areas become "no go" areas due to drug-related activity?
- Do local residents feel intimidated by drug sellers and their customers?

- Do local businesses feel that trade is being affected by drug-market activity? If so, how, specifically, has it been affected?
- Are some local businesses profiting from the drug trade (e.g., by selling products or services necessary to support the drug market)?
- What is the demand for drug treatment in the community?
- Do the police have any contact with local drug treatment providers?
- How has the drug market impacted health care providers (number of overdoses and illnesses)?

After a somewhat fruitful examination of the POP Center offerings on the subject and still distracted by responses, Midwestern PD's analyst visits the George Mason University's Center for Evidence-Based Policing. The center features the Evidence-Based Policing Matrix, which is an important tool for those seeking evidence-based responses to crime and disorder problems. The matrix includes evaluations of policing practices that meet a required level of rigor. In addition, the matrix allows the reader to view evaluated policing practices along various dimensions and levels. Most importantly, the matrix details which practices have been shown to be effective, seem promising, or actually make the problem worse (Lum, Koper, & Telep, 2011).

Midwest's analyst finds one systematic review of drug enforcement evaluations (Mazerolle et al., 2007). The results of the review indicate that proactive interventions involving partnerships between the police and third parties and/or community appear to be more effective than reactive/ directed approaches. The authors conclude that the general quality of research in drug law enforcement is poor, the range of interventions that have been evaluated is limited, and more high-quality research is needed across a greater variety of drug interventions. Midwestern's analyst would agree with the authors' assessment. Nearly a decade later, there were a few general evaluations of practices related to drug enforcement, but with one exception, none would be specific enough to be useful in Midwestern. The analyst saves an interesting article on the spatial analysis of "green teams" in responding to marijuana production. Should a response be warranted, this evidence-based and targeted method for responding to marijuana production with specialized interdiction teams might be useful (Malm & Tita, 2006).

Before delving into the Midwest PD's information systems and visiting personnel in various drug enforcement units to construct a local picture of the marijuana problem, the analyst conducts a web-based search on the subject of marijuana enforcement. She believes that having a better grasp on the overall issues will guide her records search and interviews of operational personnel. The analyst knows that specialized drug units are often reticent to share information with other units in Midwestern PD, let alone a civilian crime analyst. She must be as prepared and knowledgeable as possible when interviewing drug enforcement officers.

The analyst's web search reveals several articles resulting from the search "marijuana enforcement." She originally searched under "marijuana," however, this resulted in many articles and books on medical marijuana and marijuana legalization. Several newer books and magazine articles focused on the legalization efforts of several states and the implications of ending cannabis prohibition nationally (Martin & Rashidian, 2014; Hecht, 2014; Walker, 2014; Newsweek Special Edition, 2015). The analyst wondered why some states were legalizing medical and in some cases recreational marijuana when drug use threat assessments paint a dire picture. Recreational cannabis use was even legalized in Washington, DC. The analyst believed that the legalization movement should be considered when determining if Midwestern PD would make marijuana enforcement a strategic priority. After all, the DEA's National Assessment cited legalization in some states as a major cause of a growing problem. The analyst would have to order a few books on the subject. For now, she would continue her web search for peer-reviewed research articles.

The first article that catches the analyst's attention notes that between 1990 and 2002, the primary focus of the War on Drugs had shifted to low-level marijuana offenses (King & Mauer, 2006). During the study period, 82% of the increase in drug arrests nationally (450,000) was for marijuana offenses, and virtually all of that increase was in possession offenses. Marijuana arrests increased by 113% between 1990 and 2002, while overall arrests decreased by 3%. Of the nearly 700,000 marijuana arrests in 2002, 88% were for possession. Only 1 in 18 of these arrests resulted in a felony conviction. Most were dismissed or adjudicated as a misdemeanor. The analyst was shocked that so many resources, roughly $4 billion per year, were dedicated to minor marijuana offenses. The study went on to report that marijuana arrests constituted nearly half (45%) of the 1.5 million drug arrests annually. African Americans are disproportionately affected by marijuana arrests, representing 14% of marijuana users in the general population, but 30% of arrests.

The article concluded that the results of the study suggest that law enforcement resources are not being effectively allocated to offenses which are most costly to society. The investment of financial resources and personnel on marijuana offenses diverts funds away from other crime types and is, therefore, a questionable policy choice (King & Mauer, 2006).

A Policy Perspective

Midwestern's analyst was surprised to see the total number of marijuana arrests increase by 113% between 1990 and 2002 (King & Mauer, 2006). During the same period, all non-marijuana drug arrests increased by only 10%. Of the 450,000 increase in arrests for drugs, 82.4% was solely from marijuana arrests, and 78.7% from marijuana possession arrests. As of 2002, marijuana arrests comprised 45% of all drug arrests. Possession arrests constituted 88% of all marijuana arrests. While marijuana *trafficking* arrests declined as a proportion of all drug arrests during this period (from 6.1% in 1990 to 5.4% in 2002), the proportion for marijuana *possession* increased by two-thirds (24% in 1990 to 40% in 2002). The significant expansion of the drug war was fueled almost entirely by a focus on marijuana possession.

Midwestern's analyst was a bit confused. For the growth in the proportion of marijuana arrests for possession to make sense, marijuana use and marijuana market trends would have to run counter to all national crime trends during the period in question, including patterns in overall drug arrests. As this is rather unlikely, the growth in marijuana enforcement is better understood as the result of selective enforcement decisions. It appears that marijuana enforcement in the 1990s was not guided by data. Odd, thought the analyst, in a decade that invested significantly in community policing.

Midwestern's analyst thought that she must be missing something. Perhaps a dramatic decrease in the use of other drugs led law enforcement agencies to a shift of resources to marijuana. According to the data, there was a slight *increase* in the use of all illicit drugs by adult users between 1992 and 2001 (5.9% to 6.6%). Over that same period, emergency room admissions for heroin continued to increase. Thus, there are no explicit indications of dramatic shifts in drug use that might explain the law enforcement trend toward marijuana enforcement in the 1990s.

Her interest piqued, the analyst would continue her research, finally finding an article that explained the inconsistencies of 1990s marijuana enforcement. Geller and Fagan (2010) observed that arrests for marijuana possession in New York City increased more than tenfold since the mid-1990s, and remained high more than ten years later *despite the fact that possession of small quantities of marijuana has been decriminalized* in New York State since the late 1970s. The authors concluded that the rise in marijuana enforcement was partly attributable to the City's "Order Maintenance" policing strategy. New York City's disorder policing strategy was designed to aggressively target low-level offenses, usually through street interdictions known as "Stop, Question, and Frisk." New

York City's version of broken windows policing led to 2.2 million stops and arrests from 2004 to 2008. Further, Geller and Fagan (2010) also identified significant racial disparities in the implementation of marijuana enforcement, present in both stops and arrests. The disparities persist even when the researchers control for social structure, local crime conditions, and other types of stops.

The analyst goes on to read that the racial imbalance in marijuana enforcement is explained by targeted activity in places already subject to heightened scrutiny in the search for weapons. This link suggests that the policing of marijuana may be a pretext in the search for guns. If that is the case, there should be a significant relationship between marijuana enforcement activity and the likelihood of seizing firearms or other weapons. Geller and Fagan (2010), however, found no evidence of an increase in weapons seizures. The authors did note that a large proportion of marijuana enforcement activity by the NYPD lacked constitutional justification under either federal or New York law.

Geller and Fagan concluded that the racial skew, questionable constitutionality, and limited efficiency of marijuana enforcement in detecting serious crimes suggest a social burden disproportionately impacting non-white New Yorkers that is not offset by any substantial observed benefits to public safety.

Martin and Rashidian (2014) would also conclude that marijuana enforcement propagates racial inequality. The authors cite statistics indicating that blacks are nearly four times more likely than whites to be arrested for cannabis possession, although they use cannabis at comparable rates (ACLU, 2013). Martin and Rashidian would also be critical of New York City, stating that it has the highest number of arrests for marijuana possession in the country. Between 2002 and 2013, the NYPD made 5 million stop-and-frisks, or unannounced police pat-downs, on the street with the intention of finding guns. 86 percent of those stopped were black or Latino and 88 percent were innocent (ACLU, 2013). Less than two-tenths of a percent (.2) of all stops resulted in a gun seizure. The tactic has increased arrests for marijuana possession. In 2011, at the peak of stop-and-frisks in New York City, arrests for cannabis possession also peaked at 50,484.

The analyst would note that failed marijuana enforcement efforts were not just a big-city phenomenon. Recalling the systematic review she found earlier (Mazerolle et al., 2007), the analyst recalls an evaluation of marijuana enforcement in Kentucky. Potter et al. (1990) would declare proactive enforcement efforts in that state a failure. In fact, eradication efforts would make the marijuana problem worse by driving growers to produce greater quantities of higher quality marijuana. The authors would recommend leaving marijuana enforcement to federal agencies best equipped to deal with high-level traffickers. Local police, it was recommended, should manage any community complaints produced by the sale and use of marijuana through community and problem-oriented policing efforts.

Flynn (2004) would also find that marijuana enforcement efforts would actually make things worse. Stepped-up enforcement along the Mexican border can have the unintended consequence of creating the kind of environment that is conducive to terrorists and criminals by creating a demand for those who are in the business of arranging illegal crossings. Further, the expenditure of hundreds of millions of dollars in homeland security funding would result in no arrests of terrorists. Instead, success on the border would be evaluated by the amount of drugs seized and illegal immigrants captured. Flynn argues that the War on Terrorism rapidly devolved into a drug war on the southern border. Instead of marijuana enforcement as a pre-text for gun enforcement in the inner city, terrorism enforcement is a pre-text for drug enforcement on the border. Instead of inner city African Americans suffering the weight of disproportionate marijuana enforcement, it is Mexican nationals who are being labeled as criminal immigrants. It is no different in the big city, a rural environment, or on the border: focusing on low-level producers and possessors of marijuana is extremely expensive with little impact on serious crime. Indeed, enforcement efforts may actually encourage criminal behavior.

Midwestern's crime analyst was now concerned about the possible negative consequences of marijuana enforcement for her jurisdiction. It is difficult to implement any form of community policing when the community feels that they are unfairly being targeted by police. Further, intelligence-led policing efforts rely on good relations with the community. The community is an essential partner in communication about crime problems and solutions. If marijuana enforcement is deemed a priority, it will have to focus on high-level traffickers and market disruption to be effective. It will have to avoid constitutionally questionable tactics that erode police legitimacy in the community. The analyst wonders if this can be accomplished. Is proactive marijuana enforcement worth it? Will it impact serious crime or simply divert resources from more worthy priorities?

As Midwestern's analyst wonders about alternatives to marijuana enforcement, a day dream takes her back to college. Specifically, to her public policy analysis class. Public policy analysis is a rational, systematic approach to making policy choices in the public sector (Walker, 2000; Clemmons & McBeth, 2001). It is a process that generates information on the consequences that would follow the adoption of various policies. The purpose of public policy analysis is to assist policymakers in choosing a course of action from among complex alternatives under uncertain conditions. Policy analysis is not meant to replace the judgment of the policymakers (any more than an X-ray or a blood test is meant to replace the judgment of medical doctors). Rather, the goal is to provide a better basis for the exercise of that judgment by helping to clarify the problem, presenting the alternatives, and comparing their consequences in terms of the relevant costs and benefits. As Santos articulates (2014), analysis is the diagnosis and not the cure.

The complex and uncertain world of public policymaking requires applying what in marketing theory terms might be called "customer-based marketing," rather than "technology-based marketing" (Walker 2000). In technology-based marketing, the product is designed first and a market/customer sought out second. In this case, marijuana enforcement is the adopted policy alternative or product. Customer-based marketing seeks to understand the customer first and then create the product second. This meshes well with a community policing strategy in which problems are identified by the community and police in partnership.

The key factor in choosing which style of marketing, or policy approach in this case, is the cost of failure. When the cost of a failed product (policy) is relatively low, technical marketing is preferred. When the cost of failure is high, customer marketing is preferred. So, in providing decision support for public policymakers, a choice must be made: are you involved in technology-based marketing or customer-based marketing? For most real-world policy problems, a customer-based approach is more appropriate. This means starting with the problem, not with the product. The policy analysis process is customer based. Indeed the intelligence-led policing process begins with defining priority problems, not with marketing a solution.

The Midwestern analyst continues to dream about her policy analysis class. Perhaps the policy analysis process will best inform her recommendation. The policy analysis process generally involves performing the same set of logical steps (Walker, 2000; Clemmons & McBeth, 2001).

Step 1. **Identify the problem**. This step will constrain what follows. The analyst must identify the questions or issues involved and the context within which the policies will have to function. At this stage, the analyst must clarify constraints on possible courses of action, identify the people who will be affected by the policy decision, and decide on the initial approach.

Step 2. **Identify the objectives of the new policy**. In general, a policy is a set of actions taken to solve a problem. If the policy meets certain objectives, the problem is considered solved. In this step, the policy objectives that must be reached to solve the problem are determined.

Step 3. **Decide on criteria** (measures of performance and cost) with which to evaluate alternative policies. Determining the degree to which a policy meets an objective involves measurement. This step involves identifying consequences of a policy that can be estimated (quantitatively or qualitatively) and that are directly related to the objectives. Policy criteria include the following:

- **Effectiveness**—Likelihood of achieving policy objectives.
- **Efficiency**—The achievement of policy benefits in relation to costs (least cost for most benefit).
- **Equity**—Fairness in the distribution of the policy's costs and benefits across groups in society.
- **Liberty**—Extent to which the policy restricts individual rights and freedoms.
- **Political Feasibility**—The extent to which public officials support the policy.
- **Social Acceptability**—The extent to which the public will accept the policy.
- **Administrative Feasibility**—The likelihood that an agency or department can implement the policy well.
- **Technical Feasibility**—The availability of technology needed to implement the policy.

Step 4. **Select the alternative policies to be evaluated.** All worthwhile policy alternatives are listed, so consequences can be easily compared. If a policy is currently implemented, it should be included as the "base case" to determine how much of an improvement can be expected from the other alternatives.

Step 5. **Analyze each alternative.** Determine the consequences that are likely to follow if the alternative is implemented. The consequences are measured in terms of the criteria chosen in Step 3. This step usually involves using a model or matrix to facilitate comparison of alternatives and is performed for several possible future scenarios.

Step 6. **Compare the alternatives in terms of projected costs and benefits.** This step involves examining the estimated costs and benefits for each of the scenarios and choosing a preferred alternative. If none of the alternatives examined is good enough to be implemented (or if new aspects of the problem have been found, or the analysis has led to new alternatives), return to Step 4.

Step 7. **Implement the chosen alternative.** This step involves obtaining acceptance of the new policy (both within and outside the government), training people to implement the policy, and performing other tasks to put the policy into effect.

Step 8. **Monitor and evaluate the results.** This step is necessary to make sure that the policy is actually accomplishing its intended objectives. If it is not, the policy must be modified, terminated, or a new analysis performed.

Back to Reality

The Midwestern PD analyst continues to ponder if marijuana enforcement should be a strategic priority for the Midwestern PD using the policy analysis framework. First, what are the dimensions of the marijuana problem in Midwestern? Is there a marijuana problem? If so, what are the objectives of marijuana enforcement? Are there other alternatives to the marijuana problem than enforcement?

From her research, the consequences of marijuana enforcement do not hold up well against policy criteria. There is little research on the effectiveness of marijuana enforcement in reducing crime or discouraging drug use. Therefore, efficiency appears to be low with significant investment of time, personnel, and funding for little impact. Most discouraging, marijuana enforcement historically has scored low on the equity and liberty criteria, with the burdens of the policy falling disproportionately on one particular group. Although the policy is politically feasible and some politicians will openly support marijuana enforcement, social acceptability appears to be waning. One can wonder how long politicians will support a program against the prevailing winds of public opinion.

Finally, is marijuana enforcement administratively feasible for a police department with the above concerns in place? Can a police department implement a policy that erodes their relationship with the community? Without effective community partnerships, can the police effectively engage in any form of intelligence-led policing? Will making marijuana enforcement a priority effectively limit the Midwestern PD's ability to respond to other priorities? Should the focus be on citizen complaints about community disruptions caused by specific drug-related activities? Should enforcement activities be left to federal agencies better equipped to target high-level drug entrepreneurs while avoiding low-level growers and dealers? If Midwestern PD chooses marijuana enforcement, will it be capable of disrupting the economy of the local drug market by disrupting its finances and enforcing money laundering laws? Will Midwestern PD be ready to engage the political corruption and police misconduct that often accompanies proactive drug enforcement activities? In short, when all consequences are considered, is marijuana enforcement the best alternative to the marijuana problem in Midwestern PD?

The door to the crime analysis office opens, bringing Midwest's analyst back to the moment. The captain asks if she will need a projector for maps and statistics at the upcoming CityStat meeting or if she will be using handouts. The captain wants to know the title of her presentation for the meeting's agenda. The analyst pauses for a moment: "Marijuana Enforcement and a Crime Analyst's Daydream."

References

America Civil Liberties Union. (2013, June). The war on marijuana in black and white: Billions of dollars wasted on racially biased arrests. Retrieved from https://www.aclu.org/billions-dollars-wasted-racially-biased-arrests.

Bichler, G., & Gaines, L. (2005). An examination of police officers' insights into problem identification and problem solving. *Crime & Delinquency, 51*, 53–74.

Braga, A. A., Papachristos, A. V., & Hureau, D. M. (2012). The effects of hot spots policing on crime: An updated systematic review and meta-analysis. *Justice Quarterly, 31*(4), 633–663.

Braga, A. A., & Weisburd, D. L. (2012). The effects of focused deterrence strategies on crime: A systematic review and meta-analysis of the empirical evidence. *Journal of Research in Crime & Delinquency, 49*, 323–358.

Braga, A. A., & Weisburd, D. (2010). *Policing problem places: Crime hot spots and effective prevention.* New York: Oxford University Press.

Braga, A. A., & Weisburd, D. L. (2006). Problem-oriented policing: The disconnect between principles and practice. In D. L. Weisburd and A. Braga (Eds.), *Police innovation: Contrasting perspectives* (133–154). Cambridge, UK: Cambridge University Press.

Brantingham, P., & Brantingham, P. (1995). Criminality of place: Crime generators and crime attractors. *European Journal on Criminal Policy and Research, 3*(3), 5–26.

Carter, D. (2009). *Law enforcement intelligence: A guide for state, local, and tribal law enforcement agencies* (2nd Ed). Washington, DC: Office of Community Oriented Policing Services.

Center for Problem-Oriented Policing. (2015). The SARA model. Retrieved from http://http://www.popcenter.org/about/?p=sara. 3/10/15.

Clarke, R. V. (1997). *Situational crime prevention: Successful case studies* (2nd ed.). New York: Harrow and Heston.

Clemons, R. S., & McBeth, M. K. (2001). *Public policy praxis: Theory and pragmatism: A case approach*. Upper Saddle River, NJ: Prentice Hall.

Eck, J. E., & Weisburd, D. (1995). Crime places in crime theory In J. E. Eck & D. Weisburd (Eds.), *Crime and place: Crime prevention studies*, Volume 4. Monsey, New York: Criminal Justice Press.

Eck, J., & Spelman, W. (1987). *Problem-solving: Problem-oriented policing in Newport News*. Washington, DC: Police Executive Research Forum.

Emig, M., Heck, R., & Kravitz, M. (1980). *Crime analysis: A selected bibliography*. Washington, DC: US National Criminal Justice Reference Service.

Flynn, S. 2004. *America the vulnerable: How our government is failing to protect us from terrorism*. New York: HarperCollins.

Geller, A., & Fagan, J. (2010). Pot as pretext: Marijuana, race, and the new disorder in New York City street policing. *Journal of Empirical Legal Studies, 7*(4), 591–633.

Goldstein, H. (1990). *Problem-oriented policing*. New York: McGraw-Hill.

Harocopos, A., & Hough, M. (2005). *Drug dealing in open-air markets*. DIANE Publishing.

Hecht, P. (2014). *Weed land: Inside America's marijuana epicenter and how pot went legit*. Berkeley, CA: University of California Press.

Jacobson, J., & Webb, B. (1999). *Policing drug hot-spots*. Home Office Police Research Group.

Katz, C. M., & Webb, V. J. (2003). *Police response to gangs: A multi-site study*. Washington, DC: National Institute of Justice.

Kennedy, D. M., Braga, A. A., & Piehl, A. M. (2001). *Reducing gun violence: The Boston Gun Project's Operation Ceasefire*. Washington, DC: National Institute of Justice.

Kennedy, D. M., Braga, A. A., & Piehl, A. M. (1998). The (un)known universe: Mapping gangs and gang violence in Boston. In D. Weisburd & T. McEwen (Eds.), *Crime mapping and crime prevention* (Crime Prevention Studies, 8: 219–262. Monsey, NY: Criminal Justice Press.

King, R. S., & Mauer, M. (2006). The war on marijuana: The transformation of the War on Drugs in the 1990s. *Harm Reduction Journal, 3*(6).

Licate, D. (2014). Intelligence-led policing. In G. Moore (Ed.), *Encyclopedia of US intelligence*, New York: Auerbach Publications.

Lum, C., Koper, C., & Telep, C. (2011). The evidence-based policing matrix. *Journal of Experimental Criminology, 7*(1), 3–26.

Lum, C. (2009). Translating police research into practice. *Ideas in American Policing, 11* (August). Washington, DC: Police Foundation.

Malm, A. E., & Tita, G. E. (2006). A spatial analysis of green teams: A tactical response to marijuana production in British Columbia. *Policy Sciences, 39*(4), 361–377.

Martin, A. & Rashidian, N. (2014). *A new leaf: The end of cannabis prohibition.* New York: The New Press.

Mazerolle, L., Soole, D., & Rombouts, S. (2007). Drug law enforcement: A review of the evaluation literature. *Police Quarterly, 10*(2), 115–153.

McLaughlin, L., Johnson, S. D., Bowers, K. J., Birks, D. J., & Pease, K. (2006). Police perceptions of the long- and short-term spatial distribution of residential burglary. *International Journal of Police Science & Management, 9*(2), 99–111.

Newsweek Special Edition: Weed Nation. (2015, February/March).

Office of Community Oriented Policing Services. (2015). Community policing defined. Retrieved from http://www.cops.usdoj.gov/.

O'Shea, T. C., & Nicholls, K. (2003). Police crime analysis: A survey of US police departments with 100 or more sworn personnel. *Police Practice & Research, 4*, 233–250.

Pattavina, A. (2005). *Information technology and the criminal justice system.* Thousand Oaks, CA: Sage.

Police Executive Research Forum. (2013). *Compstat: Its origins, evolution, and future in law enforcement agencies.* Washington, DC.

Potter, G., Gaines, L., & Holbrook, B. (1990). Blowing smoke: An evaluation of marijuana eradication in Kentucky. *American Journal of Police, 9*(1), 97–116.

Ratcliffe, J. H. (2008). *Intelligence-led policing.* New York: Willan.

Ratcliffe, J. H., & McCullagh, M. (2001). Chasing ghosts? Police perception of high crime areas. *The British Journal of Criminology, 41*, 330–341.

Santos, R. B. (2014). The effectiveness of crime analysis for crime reduction: Diagnosis or cure?" *Journal of Contemporary Criminal Justice, 30*, 147.

Santos, R. B. (2012). *Crime analysis with crime mapping.* Thousand Oaks, CA: Sage.

Sherman, L. W., Gottfredson, D., MacKenzie, D. L., Eck, J., Reuter, P., & Bushway, S. (1997). *Preventing crime: What works, what doesn't, what's promising. A report to the attorney general of the United States.* Washington, DC: US Department of Justice, Office of Justice Programs.

Silverman, E. (2006). Compstat's innovation. In D. L. Weisburd & A. Braga (Eds.), *Police innovation: Contrasting perspectives* (267–283). Cambridge, UK: Cambridge University Press.

Skogan, W. (1992). *Impact of policing on social disorder: Summary of findings*. Washington, DC: US Department of Justice, Office of Justice Programs.

Skogan, W. (1990). *Disorder and decline: Crime and the spiral of decay in American neighborhoods*. New York: Free Press.

Skogan, W., & Frydl, K. (2004). *Fairness and effectiveness in policing: The evidence*. Washington, DC: The National Academies Press.

Sousa, W., & Kelling, G. (2006). Of 'broken windows,' criminology, and criminal justice. In D. L. Weisburd & A. Braga (Eds.), *Police innovation: Contrasting perspectives* (77–97). Cambridge, UK: Cambridge University Press.

US Department of Justice, Drug Enforcement Administration. (2014). *National Drug Threat Assessment Summary*.

Telep, C., & Weisburd, D. (2012). What is known about the effectiveness of police practices in reducing crime and disorder? *Police Quarterly, 15*, 331–357.

Walker, J. (2014). *After legalization: Understanding the future of marijuana policy*. Washington D.C: FDL Writers Foundation.

Walker, W. E. (2000). Policy analysis: A systematic approach to supporting policy making in the public sector. *Journal of Multi-Criteria Decision Making, 9*, 11–27.

Weisburd, D., & Eck, J. (2004). What can police do to reduce crime, disorder, and fear? *The Annals of the American Academy of Political and Social Science, 593*, 42–65.

Weisburd, D., Mastrofski, S. D., McNally, A. M., Greenspan, R., & Willis, J. J. (2003). Reforming to preserve: Compstat and strategic problem solving in American policing. *Criminology & Public Policy, 2*, 421–456.

Weisburd, D., Telep, C., Hinkle, J., & Eck, J. (2010). Is problem-oriented policing effective in reducing crime and disorder? Findings from a Campbell systematic review. *Criminology & Public Policy, 9*, 139–172.

Wilson, J., & Kelling, G. (1982). Broken windows: The police and neighborhood safety. *Atlantic Monthly, 24*(9), 29–38.

10

What Are the Legal Implications of Marijuana Legalization?

Andrea Walker, Brianne Posey, and Craig Hemmens

Marijuana Legalization: Trends and Implications

Marijuana is the most commonly used illegal drug in the world (National Institute on Drug Abuse Health, 2014). The demand for it has created an enormous black market; widespread legalization could eliminate this black market and reduce the "crime" and "criminals" associated with marijuana. The most recent statistics reveal there were 750,000 arrests for marijuana possession (American Civil Liberties Union, 2015). The penalties for a marijuana possession conviction vary by state, from small to large fines, to a misdemeanor or even a felony conviction. Legalization would have a significant impact on other areas of the law as well.

In this chapter we examine questions regarding marijuana legalization in areas such as higher education, employment, family law, transportation, and community corrections. We examine the implications for the state governments that may be in violation of federal drug laws. Legalization on a state-by-state basis is a prime example of our federal society at work, where the states are free to experiment with different approaches to a particular issue.

From Criminalization to Legalization

Historically, the cannabis plant (from which the drug is harvested) has been used for purposes such as fiber for clothing, paper, and rope (Malleis, 2012). Additionally, Conboy (2000) notes that marijuana has been used for medical purposes for at least 5,000 years, and domestically was "recognized by US physicians for its medicinal value as early as 1840, and included in the *United States*

Pharmacopoeia as a treatment for lack of appetite until 1942" (p. 601). Furthermore, the recreational consumption of marijuana has not always been a crime in the United States. According to McBride, Terry-McElrath, Harwood, Inciardi, and Leukefeld (2009), by the 1930s the United States had transformed from "a relatively open market approach to drugs to one that was strongly moralistically prohibitionist" (p. 72). This was partly due to the Harrison Act of 1914. While the law "only regulated and taxed production, importation, distribution, and use of drugs such as opium and coca leaf derivatives, it was interpreted as de facto prohibition" (p. 72). With the passing of the Marijuana Tax Act in 1937, the possession and use of marijuana became a federal crime in the United States.

By the end of the 1960s, the rise in marijuana use by young adults was apparent, partly due to the media coverage of the Civil Rights Movement (McBride, et al., 2009). The increased marijuana use did not go unnoticed by the federal government. In the Controlled Substance Act of 1970, Congress increased resources allocated to combating illegal drug activity, leading to an increase in the number of arrests for possession of illegal substances, including marijuana (Duncan, 2009; Mosher, 2011). In contrast to the federal government's move to increase sanctions for marijuana possession, states like Ohio and California modified their state penal codes in the 1970s to lower the penalties for simple possession of marijuana (Single, 1989).

By the mid-1990s, various states, cities, and counties throughout the United States had begun decriminalizing the personal use of marijuana by adults; examples include cities such as Denver and New York City, as well as the state of Maine (Grinspoon, 1994; Nadelmann, 2004; Kilmer, Caulkins, Pacula, MacCoun, & Reuter, 2010). Other jurisdictions have made the detection of, and arrest for, personal use and/or possession of marijuana by adults a low priority for law enforcement. Such an offense is now supposed to be dealt with by a civil citation and fine rather than criminal punishment (Damrogonplasit & Hsiao, 2009; Duncan, 2009). For example, in 2004, voters in Oakland, California, passed Measure Z, essentially decriminalizing simple possession of marijuana and making the crime a low propriety for the Oakland Police Department (King & Mauer, 2006; Oakland City Council Clerk, 2005). California attempted to pass Proposition 19 in 2010, legalizing personal marijuana use; however, the voters did not pass the proposition.

In 2012, Washington and Colorado enacted laws legalizing the simple possession of marijuana. Since then, other states (e.g., Alaska) have followed Washington and Colorado's lead. Clearly, there is a movement toward lessening sanctions for simple marijuana possession. There are several reasons for this change in political and public perception surrounding marijuana use.

Impetus for Change

A strong argument for the legalization of marijuana is related to the rising national arrest and incarceration rates for those convicted of simple possession. For example, arrest rates for illegal drug possession increased from 600,000 in 1980 to over 1.5 million by 2002 (Shepard & Blackley, 2005, p. 324). Arrests for marijuana encompass roughly half of the 1.5 million annual drug arrests, far exceeding the numbers for harder drugs, such as heroin or cocaine (King & Mauer, 2006, p. 1186). As the fight against drugs increased, so did the arrests rates for marijuana possession (Castellano & Uchida, 1990; King & Mauer, 2006; McBride, Terry-Elrath, Harwood, Inciardi, & Leukefeld, 2009; Mosher, 2011). Arrest rates for marijuana possession are four times higher than arrests rates for marijuana trafficking and 52% higher than those made for all other illicit drugs combined (Mosher, 2011, p. 371).

In 1992, Tony Serra, a California criminal defense attorney, argued that marijuana users were being "savaged" by marijuana laws and were exposed to severe and "inequitable" criminal sanctions (as cited in Boire, 1993, p. 5). Eventually, over 70% of the public would agree with Mr. Serra's conclusions (Nadelmann, 2004, p. 1). There are many reasons public sentiment has changed with regard to the dangers of marijuana as a drug, and the possible consequences of the continued enforcement of strict marijuana laws.

The increased focus of law enforcement on minor drug offenses reduces resources that could be used in fighting violent crime (Rosenthal et al., 2003). With state and local governments worrying over every penny in today's economic climate, the cost of strict enforcement of simple marijuana possession has come into question (Damrogonplasit & Hsiao, 2009; Duncan, 2009; Kilmer et al., 2010; Rosenthal, et al., 2003). Furthermore, skyrocketing state incarceration rates for low-level drug offenders have forced many jurisdictions to rethink their drug enforcement policies (Duncan, 2009; Kilmer et al., 2010; King & Mauer, 2006; Rosenthal et al., 2003). There is also a fast-growing national trend to minimize criminal sanctions for drug use and to treat drug offenders for their addiction, instead of punishing and incarcerating them (Damrogonplasit & Hsiao, 2009; Husak, 2006; King & Mauer, 2006; McBride et al., 2009).

Along with increased public support, the medical community has also played a role in the changing viewpoint on marijuana. The American Medical Association (2009; hereinafter "AMA") has acknowledged that marijuana does, in fact, have a legitimate medicinal purpose and can be used to alleviate the discomfort of cancer patients as well as those who suffer from anxiety. Though the use of marijuana may have negative side effects (such as some minor forms of memory loss, lowered cognitive abilities, and increased learning impairments; Covey, Wenzel, & Cheer, 2014), the AMA believes that the therapeutic benefit to the drug may outweigh the risk of its consumption by patients. Twenty-three states have legalized marijuana for medicinal purposes, though it is still regulated by each state (Malleis, 2012). Thus far, however, the federal government has refused to acknowledge the AMA's findings and is still actively pursuing adults possessing marijuana for personal use regardless of whether it is for medicinal purposes.

However, taking the movement for medicalization and decriminalization of marijuana a step further, the states of Washington, Alaska, Oregon, and Colorado, as well as the District of Columbia, have all recently passed measures and initiatives to legalize the personal use and possession of marijuana. Both liberal and conservative states have passed, or are working towards passing, medical marijuana laws and even eliminating laws that prohibit possession of small amounts of marijuana (Hickenlooper, 2014). The national trend leaning toward decriminalization and legalization of marijuana seems clear. Accordingly, the issue is ripe for discussion and investigation.

Since the explosion of marijuana use by young adults in the 1960s, researchers have been examining the possible dangers associated with personal use of marijuana, both in terms of the effect of the drug on the user as well as any possible consequences for the rest of society (Grinspoon, 1994). With the simple possession of marijuana becoming more accepted throughout the country, researchers and practitioners are now faced with the challenge of anticipating what issues will arise in light of the seemingly growing trend of the legalization of marijuana by the states. We now turn to an examination of some of these issues.

Employment

The legalization of marijuana has definitely complicated things for employers in both Colorado and Washington. Many employers, especially those with strict anti-drug policies, have questioned how these new laws will affect their employer obligations, workplace policies, workplace standards, and employer limitations. Further, employers in both states are questioning how they can maintain a drug-free workplace when marijuana use is lawful. In short, the answers to these questions are that the employers hold all the cards. Employers may make decisions that are best for their company, their other employees, and their consumer base.

The War on Drugs, Criminalization of Marijuana, and Workplace Usage

On June 18, 1971, President Nixon declared a "War on Drugs." This declaration was a response to the alarming increase of drug and alcohol related crimes and fatalities in America during that time (Benavie, 2012). This war also prompted President Nixon to sign the Reorganization Plan Number 2 in 1973, which required all taxable employers to report all employees who consumed illegal drugs while on the job to the authorities.

Since the passing of Amendment 64 in Colorado and Initiative 502 in Washington, the legalization of marijuana has decriminalized work-place cannabis use. However, there are still restrictions on workplace usage. The substance may not be used indoors in the state of Colorado. Indoor cannabis use is a violation of Colorado's Clean Indoor Air Act (2006) (Pacula et al., 2014). In Washington, public smoking indoors is prohibited following Washington's statewide public smoking ban in 2005 (Pacula et al., 2014).

Prior to legalization in these states, employers were to report workplace substance use to authorities and drug charges would most likely follow. Now in both Colorado and Washington, smoking marijuana in the workplace is still prohibited; however, no drug charges may be filed. Smoking in the workplace is a violation of workplace rules or an infraction that is punishable by fine only (Rodd, 2014). This has further complicated the War on Drugs. Since the beginning employers have played a crucial role in fighting the War on Drugs. The employers were to report the drug use of employees. This not only allowed for a drug-free workplace, but it allowed for an extra pair of eyes for the government to prosecute individuals guilty of using controlled substances (Lyman, 2010). However, in many aspects the decriminalization of marijuana has weakened the function of employers in fighting the War on Drugs.

Termination of Job Based on Positive Marijuana Test

In 1988 the Drug-Free Workplace Act created strict requirements that employers of government organizations and those who work with vulnerable populations (children, inmates, the elderly, etc.) to conduct alcohol and drug testing. Failure to comply with these regulations can result in significant penalties for both employers and employees. Furthermore, this law gives employers the power to terminate employees for having a controlled substance in their system. This has not only allowed employers to have control over what their employees do during work hours but after work hours as well (i.e., an individual consumes an illegal drug on Sunday and tests positive on Monday). The legalization of marijuana in Colorado and Washington has shifted this dynamic somewhat.

Currently, in both states employers may still terminate an individual's employment as the result of a positive drug test. However, this right is being challenged. Some have argued that employers still have the right to enforce their company's drug and alcohol policies and that all employees must adhere to those policies. On the other side, some have argued that as marijuana is legal, as long as it was not consumed at work, employers should not be able to terminate employees who use it. This argument is causing many controversies at both the state and federal level. An example of this is the case of Brandon Coats. Brandon Coats was a Denver, Colorado, resident and quadriplegic who was fired by Dish Network after failing a drug test in 2010. Coats took his case to the Colorado Supreme Court and argued that his marijuana smoking was allowed under a Colorado state law intended to protect employees from being fired for legal activities off the clock. The company argued that because marijuana remains illegal at the federal level, medical marijuana is not covered by the state law. The Colorado Supreme Court has yet to issue a ruling in this case, but the decision will have significant implications for drug testing and employer termination policies (Mascia, 2010).

Similar questions have arisen as to whether employees who refuse to be drug tested can be terminated. Consent must be provided in order for a drug test to be conducted. However, the United States Supreme Court has ruled that employers have the power to enforce penalties for failure to complete a drug test when prompted by employers or law enforcement. The legalization of marijuana has caused many to challenge this ruling. One example is Michael Boyer. Michael Boyer, a Spokane, Washington, resident, became the first Spokane resident to buy recreational marijuana. His purchase was televised on various media outlets. The same day TrueBlue Labor Ready, his employer, ordered Boyer to take a drug test. He was then terminated. TrueBlue later reinstated Moyer and explained that he did not violate workplace policies as he did not report to work impaired (Goldstein, 2014). Although Moyer was reinstated, many other have argued that because some companies hold prejudices against marijuana, if an employee knows that they are going to test positive for the substance, that they should be able to opt out of drug testing.

As of now termination for a failed drug test remains murky in both states. What is and what is not protected by law in terms of marijuana use and employer's termination policies has been vaguely defined by the legislatures. This vagueness has caused confusion over whether marijuana is workplace appropriate.

Denial of Job Based on Positive Marijuana Test

Drug testing is a crucial component of today's hiring process. The presence of a controlled substance in one's system is cause for denial of a job following the passage of the Drug-Free Workplace Act. So does this mean that employers can deny employment due to the presence of a legal drug in one's system, such as marijuana? The answer is yes and no.

In terms of medical marijuana, the answer is no. Rulings in both Colorado and Washington create exceptions for medical marijuana use. In *Beinor v. Industrial*, the Colorado Court of Appeals affirmed that the Colorado state constitution protects a worker from being discriminated against for using marijuana for medical purposes (Byrd, 2012). Employers cannot discriminate against employees who test positive for marijuana when it is prescribed by a physician. Furthermore, it is important to note that while employers may not discriminate against potential employees who use medical marijuana, *Beinor v. Industrial* also states that this does not include unemployment benefits. Employers still have a right to deny unemployment benefits due to a violation of zero-tolerance drug policies (Byrd, 2012).

In Washington the conflict between the legalization of marijuana and workplace regulations has not as yet been so clearly defined. Washington State law does not force employers to refuse workers who use marijuana for medical reasons and with a prescription. Rather, it requires employers to explain to candidates their drug policy and why they are being denied employment.

In terms of recreational use of marijuana, neither Colorado nor Washington marijuana laws prohibit employers from denying potential candidates from employment for testing positive for marijuana. Currently employers are allowed to keep enforcing zero-tolerance drug policies. However, this may be subject to change. In 2014 Washington, DC, joined Washington and Colorado in legalizing medical and recreational marijuana use. In December of 2014, the DC City Council unanimously passed temporary legislation that prohibits an employer from drug-testing potential employees for marijuana before a conditional job offer has been made. Currently, in Washington and Colorado drug testing of applicants and employees for marijuana is still generally permitted. However, as many individuals have deemed denial of employment due to marijuana testing discriminatory, this type of job screening process may be subject to change.

Marijuana and Workplace Safety

As both Washington and Colorado have passed legislation legalizing marijuana for adult recreational use, arguments that marijuana is similar to or even safer than alcohol and cigarettes have been made. This has caused confusion as to how workplace safety is affected by marijuana legalization. Many questions have arisen. Can one effectively perform job tasks while under the influence of marijuana? Should employers be able to determine if an individual is "too high" to be at work? Should employers be required to provide workers compensation for employees injured on the job while under the influence of marijuana?

To understand workplace safety, it is important to first understand how marijuana affects the body. The main active ingredient in marijuana is Delta-9 Tetrahydrocannabinol, commonly known as THC. THC is a proactive chemical in cannabis that alters transmitters in the brain and spinal cord (Martin-Santos et al., 2010). The potency and effect of marijuana are directly related to the THC content.

The levels of THC consumed in mainstream marijuana have experienced a drastic evolution throughout the years. The marijuana used in the 1960s and 1970s had a very low THC content of 2–3% (Booth, 2005). Since the mid-1990s, THC content has been consistently in the 12–15% range (Booth, 2005). Most marijuana today has undergone hybridization to enhance its effects. As a result it is not uncommon for cannabis to be routinely at 25–35% THC content (Cascini, Aiello, & Di Tanna, 2012).

What does this mean? The higher the percentage of THC, the more acute the "high" is. Additionally, THC affects the "volume control" in the brain that regulates pleasure, mood pain, appetite, motivation, and memory, among other cognitive functions. The most common effects of marijuana use are:

- Delayed decision-making
- Erratic cognitive function
- Diminished concentration
- Distortions in time
- Visual distance tracking
- Impaired memory
- Paranoia
- Drowsiness

The higher the THC content, the more intense and prolonged these effects are (Anderson et al., 2010).

In Colorado, THC content has no limitation under the new law. If inhabitants in Colorado desire to consume 100% THC, it is their right to do so.

However, in terms of workplace safety, the law requires that workers are to treat marijuana the same as prescription drugs such as Vicodin or Percocet, which can impair mental and physical abilities and affect worker safety. In Washington, this has been left to the discretion of the employer. If an employer suspects that an employee is impaired on the job, they may take action; however, the issue becomes blurred when a worker shows no impairment but nonetheless tests positive for marijuana.

In addition, many have begun to examine how the legalization of marijuana effects workers' compensation. Employer liability has been around in the United States since 1855, and workers' compensation is a form of insurance providing wage replacement and medical benefits to employees injured in the course of employment. Most state workers' compensation laws allow an employer to use the so-called "intoxication defense." The intoxication defense is the employer's claim that a work-related injury was the result of alcohol, drugs, or medication use by the employee. In both Washington and Colorado employers may dispute workers' compensation if there is reliable proof that the injury was a direct result of marijuana-related impairment (Hickox, 2011).

However, if there is another contributing factor present, for example, a wet floor, defective machinery, or an equipment malfunction, this could invalidate an intoxication defense. In these cases, coverage could apply even if such use is against company policy. An intoxication defense may be complicated by the fact that marijuana can stay in a person's system for days. Following an accident, an employee could test positive for marijuana even if he or she had used the drug during off hours and was not impaired at work. This means that it can be extremely difficult for employers and workers compensation courts to determine whether an employee was actually impaired at the time of an injury.

In sum, all substances, legal or illegal, have the potential to impact safety in the workplace. Impaired employees are not safe employees. One of the challenges with marijuana is that a "presence-in-system" drug screen may not necessarily indicate impairment. Proponents will claim an individual cannot be impaired past four hours of the use of marijuana; however, medical science has proven that consistent THC levels maintained in the body at 15 ng/mL can negatively impact a driver's ability to multi-task and respond appropriately to stimulus (Hartman & Huestes, 2012).

As marijuana legalization increases, it is crucial that employers understand the negative impact of impairment on an employee's job performance. Employers should ask questions such as, how high is too high? Should high-functioning drug users be exempt? These may sound like bizarre questions to consider, but the Cannabis Industry Council has promised to bring lawsuits over such issues and fight for an individual's right to work high, as long as that person's job performance is not negatively impacted.

Finally, employers must be prepared to deal with reasonable cause or cause for suspicion situations in which a potentially impaired employee is required to undergo drug and alcohol testing. Just as one would not find it acceptable for an employee to be performing job duties while intoxicated, the employer will need to exercise vigilance to understand marijuana impairment and keep the same standards, regardless of the challenges. In Colorado and Washington, it is clear that taking every precaution to protect workplaces from accidents, lost time, lost productivity, high employee turnover, and other liabilities is increasingly necessary in the changing culture of perceptions about recreational drug use.

Higher Education

With the legalization of recreational marijuana in certain states, institutions of higher education are faced with a dilemma. Simply stated, how will legalization be regulated (if at all) on their campuses and at their school functions? Educational institutions must rely on federal funding in order to sustain campus and administrative operations as well as academic and athletic programs (Washington State University, 2014). The Federal Drug-Free Schools and Communities Act requires that all higher education institutions abide by federal drug laws, including the prohibition of marijuana use or possession on college campuses. Therefore, college campuses in states where marijuana legalization has occurred have to decide if they will follow the new state law or continue to abide by federal law. What we are seeing, thus far, is that state schools are maintaining the federal prohibition of marijuana on their campuses (e.g., Washington State University) and during their school functions and activities (e.g., athletic events); though enforcement of the federal marijuana prohibition on certain campuses may be becoming more lax with the enactment of new state laws (Sullivan-Moore & Turkewitz, 2014).

Aside from the issues of federal funding, colleges in the states that have legalized simple possession of marijuana have stated that the possession and consumption of marijuana on campus is at odds with their institution's academic standards and may be a risk to public safety (Colorado College, 2014; Washington State University, 2014). Marijuana is an intoxicant, and could be viewed as having the same deleterious effects of alcohol, prompting colleges and universities to limit its access on campus and during school functions. Furthermore, Covey et al. (2014) have argued that prolonged marijuana use can contribute to memory loss, cognitive impairment, drug socialization, and reinforced cues to continue such behavior. In light of studies such as these, schools may prohibit the use of marijuana on the grounds of the safety and well-being of their faculty, staff, and students. For example, Colorado College (2014) has stated that it will not change its stance with regard to the prohibition of marijuana on campus because the college "seeks to foster a healthy learning environment" and the administration believes that the consumption of marijuana is contrary to that goal.

Universities not only have concerns about academic standards, public safety, and drug use on their campuses, but they also have conduct standards that are required for their athletic programs and of student athletes. Furthermore, the National Collegiate Athletic Association's (hereinafter "NCAA") rules and regulations prohibit the use of drugs by student-athletes. For obvious reasons, this prohibition includes performance-enhancing drugs; however, it also includes recreation drugs such as cocaine, methamphetamine, and, relevant to our purposes here, marijuana (National Collegiate Athletic Association, 2014). Universities who are members of the NCAA (such as Washington State University and the University of Colorado, both in the Pac-12 Conference) must be concerned about risking their standings in the NCAA by student abuse of marijuana.

Insurance and Marijuana

As states have begun to legalize marijuana, insurers are being forced to consider the impact on their business. The reality is that accidents happen every day. Whether it is injury or illness, insurance protects one from the harsh financial burdens of accidents or injury. How does the availability, access, and cost of insurance change when a controversial subject such as marijuana is thrown into the mix? The answer is deeply imbedded in money, medicine, and politics.

Medical Marijuana

Medical marijuana differs from other forms of marijuana in three ways. First, medical marijuana has been prescribed by a physician while other forms that are sold in dispensaries or on the streets have not been. Second, medical marijuana does not have psychosocial effects. Usually street marijuana contains higher levels of the chemical as tetrahydrocannabinol (THC). This usually produces psychosocial effects or gets an individual "high," while medical marijuana contains low levels of THC and higher levels of the chemical cannabidiol (CBD). CBD does not produce the "high" effect (Wang et al., 2008). Third, medical marijuana has no additives, while street marijuana may be cut with other hallucinogens such as ecstasy or opium. In addition to recreational use, both Colorado and Washington permit the use of marijuana as a medical treatment. Accordingly, the use of medical marijuana has become a controversial topic among health care personnel and politicians.

The history of medical marijuana use dates back many centuries. Cannabis was first used in Taiwan for fiber starting about 10,000 years ago. Zuradi (2006) explains that in China the use of cannabis as medicine was probably a one of the earliest developments of medicine. During this time cannabis was also used a used as an anesthetic for its numbing abilities. In the 1500s Egyptians used cannabis to treat sore eyes. Surviving texts from ancient India explain that cannabis was used to treat insomnia, headaches, a whole host of gastroin-testinal disorders, and to relieve the pain of childbirth (Aldrich, 1997). Historically, Greeks have used cannabis to treat nose bleeds and inflammation.

In the mid-nineteenth century, medical interest in the use of cannabis began to grow in the West. By the twentieth century there were over 2,000 cannabis medicines. Then, during the Great Depression, America's views on medical marijuana began to shift. In 1937, the United States passed the first federal law against cannabis. The law was passed unanimously by Congress despite objections from the American Medical Association (AMA).

In the 1970s and 1980s there was some push for acceptance of medical marijuana. Activists and medical personnel began to rally for the right to utilize the drug for treatment purposes. In 1976 the federal government created the Investigational New Drug (IND) compassionate access research program. This program allowed patients to receive up to nine pounds of cannabis from the government each year. In 1988, the DEA's Chief Administrative Law Judge, Francis Young, admitted that medical usage of the drug was safe if controlled. Young stated in a press conference that "[m]arijuana, in its natural form, is one of the safest therapeutically active substances known ... It would be unreasonable, arbitrary and capricious for the DEA to continue to stand between those sufferers and the benefits of this substance" (Bostwick, 2012). However, the DEA still refused to regulate legal usage of the drug for medical purposes.

Then the Medical Cannabis Movement began in 1989. After the outbreak of HIV/AIDS in the United States, the FDA was flooded with new applications for the drug from doctors and patients. Medical cannabis was used as a trial drug to alleviate side effects of HIV/AIDS. The drug proved to be helpful for many patients. However, in 1991, the Public Health Service announced that the program would be suspended because it undermined federal prohibition. Furthermore, the DEA concluded that despite the successful medical marijuana trials for HIV/AIDS patients and centuries of documented safe use, cannabis would remain classified in America as a Schedule I substance. The DEA further explained that the drug "had a high potential for abuse and no accepted medical value" (Inciardi, 2012).

Health care advocates continued to resolve this issue through legal and administrative means throughout the 1990s. In 1997, the Office of National Drug Control Policy commissioned the Institute of Medicine (IOM) to conduct a comprehensive and longitudinal study of the medical efficacy of cannabis therapeutics. In 2005 cannabis was determined by the IOM to be a safe and effective medicine. It was later determined by numerous states that patients should have access to the drug and that the government should expand avenues for research and drug development (Watson, Benson, & Joy, 2000). This also was the birth of controversy surrounding health care aspects of the drug.

Health Care Coverage and Medical Marijuana

While medical marijuana is a legal medicine for treating such ailments as AIDS, various cancers, and glaucoma, it is not covered by health insurance plans. Currently marijuana is classified as a Schedule 1 substance under the Federal Controlled Substances Act. Furthermore, it will most likely be a long time before health insurers include medical marijuana on their prescription formularies, for a wide array of reasons. First and foremost, health insurers do not have the authority to challenge the law. While state laws may be implemented for certain substances, health care providers must abide by federal laws (Jost, 2010). Second, medical marijuana has not been approved by the DEA or FDA. Many health care providers do not want to cover drugs that are both banned by the DEA and have not been approved by the FDA. This stems from fear of being legally and financially liable for adverse effects of the drug (Cohen, 2009).

This has caused a financial burden on many individuals who are prescribed medical marijuana. As health care providers do not cover medical marijuana, most patients are paying entirely out of pocket for medical marijuana. This can cause the average patient several hundred dollars per month or more, depending on the type and severity of their illness. On average, medical marijuana can cost roughly $350 for a six-week supply. In 2010, there were about 369,000 registered medical marijuana users in Washington and Colorado. An estimated 600,000 are presently using the drug for their ailments, and a projected 900,000 more individuals are potential candidates based on the wide variety of health problems it can supposedly treat (Bowles, 2012). The financial burden of the price of medical marijuana and the lack of support from the federal government will become a pressing issue.

Insurance Coverage in the Marijuana Business

As the legalization of marijuana has increased, the need for insurance for marijuana providers has increased. Insurance coverage for establishments that have a license to sell marijuana is generally granted to greenhouses and dispensaries. This has opened up a relatively new demand for insurance in both Colorado and Washington. While health care providers do not cover medical cannabis, almost every establishment that sells medical marijuana legally is required by the state to have insurance for their crops. This has created a paradox and further controversy as the government demands that business buy insurance for cannabis; however, most health care providers refuse to list cannabis as covered under insurance.

Laws in certain states allow patients to grow their own marijuana at a specified quantity, while others require that patients purchase their supply in controlled amounts through a dispensary. In order to do either, patients are typically required to obtain a physician's recommendation and register with the state. Both methods are bound by state law to limit the amount an individual can have at once, allowing a supply for a certain number of days in some areas, and ounces in others.

Family Law/Divorce

Cases involving parental custody and marital dissolutions are particularly sensitive. Historically, these proceedings could expose a husband or wife to the loss of the custody of their children or grounds for a divorce, based on their use of marijuana. Unfortunately, there appears to be no uniformity among states in terms of determining the specific amount of marijuana use (medicinal or recreational) that can constitute grounds for the removal of children, loss of child custody in divorce proceedings (Malleis, 2012), or even solely as grounds for divorce (for example, *see, Carambat v.Carambat*, 2011). As with many family law issues, it seems to be handled in a case-by-case basis, on the grounds of what is in the best interest of the child, or in the case of grounds for divorce, the spouses. It is foreseeable, however, that these issues will arise more often now that recreational marijuana has been legalized in some states.

Child Custody

Child custody decisions and case law have consistently favored the notion of the "best interest of the child," though there is no single definition of that standard on which courts can rely (Malleis, 2012). The Colorado Court of Appeals has stated that "what constitutes endangerment to a particular child's physical or emotional health is a highly individualized determination" (*see, In re the Marriage of Catherine Parr, f/k/a Catherine Lyman and David Lyman*, 2010). The California Court of Appeals has also made it clear that denial of parental rights based on accusations of substance abuse must be decided on by "independent corroboration" and that a court may not require drug testing of one parent to corroborate the accusations of another (*see, Wainwright v. The Superior Court of Humboldt County, et al.*, 2000). Obviously, a parent who is a substance abuser and has minor children is a cause for serious concern for family law courts. When couple files for divorce, the use of such substances may be used by one spouse to discredit the other, as well as sway the court in terms of child custody orders. Not surprisingly, issues of marijuana use and child custody have been already been addressed in various state court family law proceedings. These issues range from supervision of any visitation time to complete the denial of visitation or custody, based on a parent's use of marijuana (medicinal or recreational).

California Family Code section 3011(d) requires that judges consider a parent's habitual or recreation use of illegal drugs when determining where to place the child in custody proceedings, and even the denial of child visitation. The imperative word here is *illegal*. According to the new laws of several states, the use of recreational marijuana is no longer illegal. Because the legalization of recreational marijuana is in its infancy, we do not know yet how courts will rule in child custody cases wherein one parent is a *legal* recreational user of marijuana. However, we can look to rulings made in similar cases, such as where one parent's custody was challenged based on the use of medicinal marijuana.

The Colorado Court of Appeals overturned a trial court's decision to supervise and limit a father's visitation time with his child based on his medicinal marijuana use (*see, In re the Marriage of Catherine Parr, f/k/a Catherine Lyman and David Lyman*, 2010). Specifically, the court found that because the father did not use marijuana in the presence of this child, his conduct did not warrant limiting his visitation opportunities. However, this is not the case in every child custody matter that involves the use of marijuana. Malleis (2012), for example, discusses a case in which a father in Washington was ordered to comply with limited, supervised visitation with his two children based on his state-sanctioned medicinal marijuana use. In one state, the use of medicinal marijuana use is not considered grounds for limiting visitation or custody, and in another state, it is considered possible endangerment to the child and potential grounds for denial of visitation or custody. These contradictory rulings serve to illustrate the challenges that the legalization of recreational marijuana forces family law courts in these states to face. One can hypothesize, however, that overall the courts will rule in custody cases involving the use of marijuana similar to past rulings in cases involving the use of alcohol: on a case-by-case basis, and always in the best interest of the child.

Grounds for Divorce

States have granted the dissolution of a marriage on various legal grounds including that a spouse is an alcoholic or drug addict (*Ashburn v. Ashburn*, 970 So. 2d 204, Miss. Ct. App. 2007). Substance abuse (including the use of marijuana) can have a negative effect on a marriage, and may even contribute to the dissolution of that marriage. Yamaguchi & Kandel (1985; 1997) found that the use of marijuana may be correlated with intimate partner selection and decisions about child bearing; moreover, that people who regularly use marijuana (prior to and during marriage) are more likely to dissolve their marriages. These findings have important implications for family law courts who must preside over dissolution proceedings.

With the legalization of recreational marijuana, there is little doubt that family law courts will be faced with an increase of divorce filings that involve accusations regarding recreational marijuana use. Interestingly, in *Carambat v. Carambat* (2011), the Mississippi Supreme Court ruled that a spouse's habitual use of marijuana was grounds for divorce, even though the complaining spouse knew of the other's drug use and that use had preceded the marriage. The court's reasoning was that even though the wife knew that the husband was a habitual user prior to marriage, his continued use of the drug had a deleterious effect on their marriage and therefore constituted grounds for dissolution.

The issue of whether one spouse knew of another spouse's recreational use of marijuana prior to and during the marriage may be moot, if courts decide to treat divorce causes of action for marijuana use in the same way that divorce causes for alcohol abuse are treated. Again, the court would be relying on the assumption that the substance abuse contributed to the dissolution of the marriage. Alcohol abuse has repeatedly been used as grounds for divorce (provided that corroborating evidence is available), and there is no reason to believe that marijuana abuse (even if it is recreational and legal under state law) will be dealt with any differently.

Marijuana Transportation

One issue that arises regularly when discussing the legalization of marijuana in Colorado and Washington is transportation. While it is legal to purchase and possess marijuana in both Colorado and Washington, it still remains illegal to do so in neighboring states. What happens if someone purchases marijuana in a state where it is legal and then travels to a state where it is illegal? Likewise, what happens if someone purchases marijuana in a state where it is illegal and then travels to a state where it is legal? What are the legal limitations of the transportation of marijuana between states? These questions further complicate the decriminalization of the drug.

Transportation within Colorado

Colorado has specific regulations pertaining to the transportation of marijuana. A person 21 years of age or older may legally possess and transport up to one ounce of marijuana for personal use within the state (Oesterle & Collins, 2011). If you are driving within Colorado, you may carry up to the legal limit of marijuana in your car. However, neither the driver nor passengers may smoke marijuana in the vehicle. It is illegal to ride a bike while under the influence of marijuana and you may not smoke on trains or buses (Blake & Finlaw, 2014).

Colorado has different laws for flying with possession of marijuana. If you are flying from Colorado to another state you may not travel with marijuana, even if you are traveling to Washington or another state where it is legal. This is because airport security is conducted by the Transportation Security Administration, a federal agency. Marijuana is still a controlled substance under federal law and possession of marijuana is a crime under federal law. Furthermore, the federal government does not have to honor state laws that conflict with federal law (Simbro, 2014).

Transportation within Washington

Like Colorado, Washington has specific regulations regarding personal use of marijuana.In Washington, persons over the age of 21 may legally possess up to 1 ounce of marijuana for personal consumption, or up to 16 ounces of solid marijuana infused products (like edibles). Anything over 16 ounces of solid marijuana infused products, or 72 ounces of liquid marijuana infused products is a felony. (Utter & Spitzer, 2013).

Washington law forbid drivers from operating a motor vehicle if they impaired by a drug, be it legal or illegal. Furthermore it is illegal to smoke marijuana while driving (Utter & Spitzer, 2013).

Similarly to Colorado, you may not fly with marijuana in Washington. While the state laws regarding marijuana have changed, federal laws have not. The federal government bans marijuana, even medical marijuana, on aircraft, whether in a carry-on, a checked bag, or any package being shipped by air.

Transportation Outside of Washington and Colorado

Colorado and Washington were the first states to make the production, processing, purchase, and possession of marijuana for medical and recreational use by adults legal. Oregon and Alaska would follow this trend in 2014. Additionally, 23 states currently have legalized only medical marijuana. However, there are still a number to states that outlaw either marijuana for recreational use or outlaw both medical marijuana and marijuana for recreational use.

You may not transport marijuana into states where it is illegal. You may legally possess marijuana for personal use in Colorado that you had purchased in Washington. However, you may not transport that marijuana through the neighboring states that you would have to drive through to get it there (Garvey & Yeh, 2013).

Offenders under Community Supervision

Persons who are subject to community correctional supervision (e.g., probation or parole) are often required to abstain from alcohol throughout their supervision and may be subject to random or routine urinalysis testing to ensure their compliance (Hamilton & Campbell, 2013). Akin to the restrictions also placed on the general public, the use of illicit drugs is always prohibited for those who have been placed under supervision. Drug tests for probationers and parolees may be ordered and conducted as a condition of their release (Kleiman, 2011). With the simple possession of marijuana now legal in a few states, the question of marijuana use and persons under community supervision will surely come before the courts. It can be assumed that the use of marijuana by people on community supervision will ultimately be handled similarly to how alcohol use is currently supervised by community corrections officers. Thus, similar to alcohol use and community supervision, offenders who are on supervised release and who have shown a propensity in the past for abusing the drug (and when this abuse can be linked to their criminal behavior) will be barred from consuming the drug during their period of supervision (Kleiman, 2011).

A considerable amount of fiscal resources are spent by jurisdictions on community supervision, and released offenders who commit technical violations (such as testing "dirty" on a drug test) are a large portion of the current prison population (Kleiman, 2011; Hamilton & Campbell, 2013). It is possible that lessening the supervision requirements with respect to simple marijuana possession could result in a possible decrease in the need for drug testing, hence freeing up possible resources to be allocated to other areas of community supervision. It also may help decrease the number of offenders returned to custody because of technical violations based on marijuana charges.

Local Government Opt-Out Options

When California initially considered legalizing marijuana back in 2010, there were several petitions proposed; one of those (The Tax, Regulate and Control Cannabis Act) included language that required every county in the state to allow dispensaries to open within their jurisdictions (Patton, 2010). The Tax, Regulate, and Control Cannabis Act did not make it on the ballot. Instead, it was replaced with Proposition 19 (The Regulate, Control and Tax Cannabis Act), which did not include language requiring the allowance of dispensaries within all California jurisdictions (Patton, 2010). Though California did not ultimately pass either version of the law, an interesting question is raised. Should counties be required to allow marijuana dispensaries to open up within their jurisdiction?

Shortly after the legalization of marijuana in Washington, some counties banned marijuana dispensaries within their jurisdiction. Eventually, the issue did make its way through the courts. In the matter of *MMH, LLC v. Fife* (2014), the Pierce County Superior Court ruled that the county had the right to refuse to allow dispensaries within its jurisdiction. Washington State's attorney general's office agreed with the county, and filed a brief stating that there is nothing in the new law that required all counties to allow dispensaries. Furthermore, the attorney general noted that to do so would risk possible intrusion from the federal government, while leaving out the requirement clause lessens the chance of interference (Washington State Attorney General's Office, 2014). Several cases (e.g., *Americanna Weed, LLC v. City of Kennewick*, 2014; *Emerald Enterprises & John M Larson v. Clark County*, 2014) have been filed in Washington since, and every court thus far has ruled in favor of local governments' prohibition. The first case, *MMH, LLC v. Fife*, has been appealed to the Washington State Supreme Court. The court is expected to decide whether or not it will hear the case this year (Washington State Attorney General's Office, 2014).

Retroactivity

It was estimated that on any given day in 2004, there were over 100,000 people behind bars for marijuana offenses (Nadelmann, 2004). Even more alarming, the Drug Policy Alliance (2015) states that roughly 88% of drug charges across the United States were charges of possession only. Recognizing this, one of the previously proposed marijuana petitions in California (The Tax, Regulate and Control Cannabis Act, 2010) required that their marijuana legalization laws be applied retroactively (Patton, 2010). This meant that those who were already convicted and sentenced to custody for the crime of simple marijuana possession would be released from custody. That petition never made it onto the ballot, and the subsequent Proposition 19 (which also ultimately failed to gain enough votes) did not include a retroactivity provision.

Washington and Colorado also have no such retroactivity provisions in their marijuana legalization statutes. Persons in custody in those states for simple possession will remain there, possibly to serve the remainder of their sentences. It is difficult to know exactly what effect enacting these kinds of new laws retroactively might have on incarceration rates (but one could reasonably assume that incarceration rates would go down) or on budgets for these jurisdictions (e.g., how much money would it save to release all of the inmates in custody for simple possession of marijuana?). It remains to be seen, therefore, how many states that eventually legalize marijuana possession will include a requirement that the new laws be applied retroactively, thereby effectively releasing an untold number of persons within state and local custody.

Conclusion

Marijuana legalization is in its early days. But if news reports are to be believed, other states are soon to follow the lead of Colorado and Washington. As with any significant policy change, there will be a host of expected and unexpected consequences. In this chapter we have provided an overview of some of the areas that have already experienced some major changes as a result of marijuana legalization. These are just the tip of the iceberg, however. More changes, some still unknown and certainly unintended, are likely to appear in the coming years.

What we do know, even in these early days, is that marijuana legalization will have a widespread impact on civil and criminal law. On the criminal law side, society's draconian response to illegal drug use led to mass incarceration, and criminal convictions for drug possession changed the course of many lives. On the civil law side, illegal drug use has long had a number of potentially serious repercussions, from loss of a job to loss of child custody. With the legalization of marijuana, these criminal and civil penalties fall away. At the same time, marijuana legalization creates potential new problems, such as the impact on life and health insurance policies and benefits. As more states legalize marijuana, these and other issues will be raised and the courts and state legislatures will have to respond. We live in interesting times.

References

Aldrich, M. (1997). History of therapeutic cannabis. *Cannabis in medical practice.* Jefferson, NC: McFarland, 35–55.

American Civil Liberties Union. (2015). *Marijuana Arrests By the Numbers.* Retrieved from https://www.aclu.org/gallery/marijuana-arrests-numbers.

American Medical Association, Council on Science and Public Health. (2009). *Report 3: The use of cannabis for medicinal purposes.* Retrieved from http://www.ama-assn.org/resources/doc/csaph/csaph-report3-i09.pdf.

Americanna Weed, LLC v. City of Kennewick, Benton Co. Sup. Crt No. 14-2-02226l-1 (2014).

Anderson, D. M., & Rees, D. I. (2014). The legalization of recreational marijuana: How likely is the worst case scenario? *Journal of Policy Analysis and Management, 33*(1), 221–232.

Anderson, B. M., Rizzo, M., Block, R. I., Pearlson, G. D., & O'Leary, D. S. (2010). Sex, drugs, and cognition: Effects of marijuana. *Journal of psychoactive drugs, 42*(4), 413–424.

Ashburn v. Ashburn, 970 So. 2d 204 (Miss. Ct of App, 2007).

Benavie, A. (2012). *Drugs: America's holy war.* Routledge.

Blake, D., & Finlaw, J. (2014). Marijuana legalization in Colorado: Learned lessons. *Harv. L. & Pol'y Rev., 8*, 359–471.

Boire, R. (1993). *Marijuana law.* Berkeley, CA: Ronin Publication.

Bostwick, J. M. (2012, February). Blurred boundaries: The therapeutics and politics of medical marijuana. *Mayo Clinic Proceedings, 87*(2), 172–186.

Bowles, D. W. (2012). Persons registered for medical marijuana in the United States. *Journal of Palliative Medicine, 15*(1), 9–11.

Byrd, G. (2012). State medical marijuana statutes: A gateway to employee discrimination and wrongful termination.

California Family Code section 3011(d). Retrieved from http://www.leginfo.ca.gov/cgi-bin/displaycode?section=fam&group=03001-04000&file=3010-3011.

Carambat v. Carambat, 72 So.3d 505 (Sup. Ct of Miss, 2011).

Cascini, F., Aiello, C., & Di Tanna, G. (2012). Increasing delta-9-tetrahydrocannabinol (-9-THC) content in herbal cannabis over time: Systematic review and meta-analysis. *Current Drug Abuse Reviews, 5*(1), 32–40.

Castellano, T. & Uchida, C. (1990). Local drug enforcement, prosecutors, and case attrition. *American Journal of Policing, 9*, 133–162.

City of Oakland Clerk Website. *Report regarding Measure Z,* Retrieved from http://clerkwebsvr1.oaklandnet.com/attachments/11052.pdf.

Cohen, P. J. (2009). Medical marijuana: The conflict between scientific evidence and political ideology. Part one of two. *Journal of Pain and Palliative Care Pharmacotherapy, 23*(1), 4–25.

Colorado College. (2014). Policy on Marijuana. Retrieved from https://www.coloradocollege.edu/offices/presidentsoffice/colorado-college-policy-on-marijuana.dot.

Conboy, J. R. (2000). Smoke screen: America's drug policy and medical marijuana. *Food & Drug Law Journal, 55,* 601–617.

Covey, D., Wenzel, J., & Cheer, J. (2014). Cannabinoid modulation of drug reward and the implications of marijuana legalization. *Brain Research.* Retrieved from http://dx.doi.org/10.1016/j.brainres.2014.11.034.

Daily, M. B. (2012). *Colorado MMC legal compliance: For Colorado dispensary owners: The critical legal information.* Anne Holland Ventures Inc.

Dalton, C. (1997, Winter) Domestic violence, domestic torts and divorce: Constraints and possibilities. *New England Law Review, 31*(2), 319–395.

Davis, A. C., & O'Keefe, E. (2014, December 9) Congressional spending deal blocks pot legalization in DC. *Washington Post.* Retrieved from http://www.washingtonpost.com/local/dc-politics/congressional-budget-deal-may-upend-marijuana-legalization-in-dc/2014/12/09/6dff94f6-7f2e-11e4-8882-03cf08410beb_story.html.

Department of Housing and Urban Development. (2014). Public housing program. Retrieved from http://portal.hud.gov/hudportal/HUD?src=/topics/rental_assistance/phprog.

Drug Policy Alliance (2015). *Drug war statistics.* Retrieved from http://www.drugpolicy.org/drug-war-statistics.

Duncan, C. (2009). The need for change: An economic analysis of marijuana policy. *Connecticut Law Review, 41*(5), 1701–1740.

Emerald Enterprises v. Clark County. Cowlitz Superior Court Case No.14-2-00951-9. (2014).

Garvey, T., & Yeh, B. T. (2013, April). State legalization of recreational marijuana: Selected legal issues. In *Congressional Research Service Report for Congress.*

Goldstein, S. (2014). Mike Boyer, Spokane, Wash. man fired for buying legal pot, is rehired. *The Daily News.*

Gonzales v. Raich et al., 545 U.S. 1 (2005).

Grinspoon, L. (1994). *Marijuana reconsidered.* San Francisco, CA: Quick American Archives.

Hamilton, Z. K., & Campbell, C. M. (2013). A dark figure of corrections: Failure by way of participation. *Criminal Justice and Behavior, 40*(2), 180–202.

Hartman, R. L., & Huestes, M. A. (2013). Cannabis effects on driving skills. *Clinical Chemistry, 59*(3), 478–492.

Healy, J. (2014). Nebraska and Oklahoma sue Colorado over marijuana law. *The New York Times.*

Hickenlooper, J. W. (2014). Experimenting with pot: The state of Colorado's legalization of marijuana. *Milbank Quarterly, 92*(2), 243–249.

Hickox, S. A. (2011). Drug testing of medical marijuana users in the workplace: An inaccurate test of impairment. *Hofstra Lab. & Emp. L J, 29,* 273.

Husak, D. (2006). *Do marijuana offenders deserve punishment?* In M. Earleywine, (Ed.), *Pot politics: Marijuana and the cost of prohibition,* (pp. 189–207), New York, NY: Oxford Publishing.

In re the Marriage of Catherine Parr, f/k/a Catherine Lyman and David Lyman, No. 09CA0854 (Colorado Ct of App Div. I, 2010).

Inciardi, J. A. (2008). *The War on Drugs IV: The continuing saga of the mysteries and miseries of intoxication, addiction, crime and public policy (4th Edition).* New York: Prentice Hall.

Jost, T. S. (2010). Can the states nullify health care reform? *New England Journal of Medicine, 362*(10), 869–871.

Kilmer, B., Caulkins, J., Liccardo Pacula, R., MacCoun, R., & Reuter, P. (2010). Altered state? Assessing how marijuana legalization in California could influence marijuana consumption and public markets. Santa Monica, CA: RAND Drug Policy Research Centre.

King, R., & Mauer, M. (2006). The war on marijuana: The transformation of the War on Drugs in the 1990s. *Harm Reduction Journal, 3*(6), 1186–1202.

Kleiman, M. A. (2011). Justice reinvestment in community supervision. *Criminology & Public Policy, 10*(3), 651–659.

Lyman, M. D. (2010). *Drugs in society: Causes, concepts and control.*

Malleis, D. (2011). High price of parenting high: Medical marijuana and its effects on child custody matters. *University of La Verne Law Review, 33,* 357–392.

Martin-Santos, R., Fagundo, A. B., Crippa, J. A., Atakan, Z., Bhattacharyya, S., Allen, P., & Mascia, J. (2010). Medical use of marijuana costs some a job. *The New York Times.*

McBride, D., Terry-McElrath, Y., Harwood, H., Inciardi, J., & Leukefeld, C. (2009). Reflections on drug policy. *The Journal of Drug Issues,* 71–88.

MMH, LLC., v. Fife, Peirce County Superior Court Case No. 14-2-10487-7, (2014).

Mosher, C. (2011). Convergence or divergence? Recent developments in drug policies in Canada and the United States. *American Review of Canadian Studies, 41*(4), 370–386.

Nadelmann, E. A. (2004). Drug prohibition in the United States: Costs, consequences, and alternatives. *Science, 245*, 939–947.

National Collegiate Athletic Association (2014). 2014–15 NCAA Banned Drugs. Retrieved from http://www.ncaa.org/health-and-safety/policy/2014-15-ncaa-banned-drugs.

National Institute on Drug Abuse (2014). *Drug Facts: Nationwide Trends*. Retrieved from http://www.drugabuse.gov/publications/drugfacts/nationwide-trends.

New York Times. Retrieved from http://www.nytimes.com/2014/11/02/education/edlife/legally-high-marijuana-on-campus-colorado.html/.

Oesterle, D. A., & Collins, R. B. (2011). *The Colorado State Constitution*. Oxford University Press.

Pacula, R. L., Kilmer, B., Wagenaar, A. C., Chaloupka, F. J., & Caulkins, J. P. (2014). Developing public health regulations for marijuana: Lessons from alcohol and tobacco. *American Journal of Public Health, 104*(6), 1021–1028.

Patton, M. (2010). Legalization of marijuana: A dead-end or the high road to fiscal solvency? *Berkeley Journal of Criminal Law, 15*, 163–204.

Rodd, E. (2014). Light, smoke, and fire: How state law can provide medical marijuana users protection from workplace discrimination. *Boston College Law Review, forthcoming.*

Rosenthal, E., Kubby, S., & Newhart, S. (2003). *Why marijuana should be legal.* Philadelphia, PA: Running Press Publishers.

Scottie, L. (2014). *Washington city sued over its ban on marijuana businesses.* Aljazeera America.

Shepard, E., & Blackley, P. (2005). Drug enforcement and crime: Recent evidence from New York State. *Social Science Quarterly, 86*(2), 323–342.

Simbro, A. M. (2014). Sky's the limit: A modern approach to airport security, *Ariz. L. Rev., 56*, 559.

Single, E. (1989). The impact of marijuana decriminalization: An update. *Journal of Public Health Policy, 10*(4), 456–466.

Sullivan Moore, A., & Turkewitz, J. (2014, October 29). Legally high at a Colorado campus.

Thomson v. Thomson, 661 SE2d 130 (SC Ct. App. 2008).

United States Pardon Attorney. (1996). *Civil disabilities of convicted offenders.* Washington, DC: United States Department of Justice.

Utter, R. F., & Spitzer, H. D. (2013). *The Washington State Constitution*. Oxford University Press.

Wainwright v. Superior Court of Humboldt County, 84 Cal. App. 4th 262; 100 Cal. Rptr. 2d 749 (2000).

Wang, T., Collet, J. P., Shapiro, S., & Ware, M. A. (2008). Adverse effects of medical cannabinoids: A systematic review. *Canadian Medical Association Journal, 178*(13), 1669–1678.

Washington State Attorney General's Office. (2014). Retrieved from http://www.atg.wa.gov/pressreleases.aspx?current=2014#.VMLKYZUtF1s.

Washington State University. (2014). Retrieved from https://news.wsu.edu/2012/12/05/wsu-outlines-parameters-for-initiative-502-marijuana-law/#.VMLK35UtF1s.

Yamaguchi, K., & Kandel, D. B. (1985). On the resolution of role incompatibility: A life event history analysis of family roles and marijuana use. *American Journal of Sociology*, 1284–1325.

Yamaguchi, K., & Kandel, D. B. (1997). The influence of spouses' behavior and marital dissolution on marijuana use: Causation or selection. *Journal of Marriage and the Family*, 22–36.

11

Marijuana Businesses in Colorado: Three Hurdles for Success

Nancy E. Marion

Introduction

Voters in Colorado have supported legalized marijuana use for many years. In 2000, citizens passed Amendment 20 that altered the state constitution to allow for the medical use of marijuana. This change permitted qualifying patients or caregivers to legally possess up to six marijuana plants or two ounces of useable marijuana for medical purposes. In 2012, Colorado voters again chose to change the state constitution when they passed a second ballot initiative, Amendment 64. This time, the change allowed for the recreational cultivation and use of marijuana among adults aged 21 or older within the state. The sections of the constitution that permit marijuana use are found in Article XVIII. Section 14 of that article is titled "Medical Use of Marijuana for Persons Suffering from Debilitation Medical Conditions" and Section 16 is titled "Personal Use and Regulation of Marijuana (Recreational)."

The newest initiative, Amendment 64, allows for marijuana to be legally sold and used for recreational purposes starting on January 1, 2014. The law stipulates that users must be 21 years of age or older and cannot use the drug in a public place. Users are permitted to grow their own marijuana, up to six plants per adult, but the plants must be kept in an enclosed, locked space that is not open or public. No more than three of those plants can be in the flowering stage at one time. A person who cultivates their own marijuana is prohibited from selling it. In order to grow the drug for retail sale or open a store, a person must apply for, and be granted, a license from the state. Growers and sellers must track all marijuana purchased and sold and file monthly sales records with the state. Visitors to the state may purchase and use marijuana while in the state but cannot transport it to another state. Amendment 64 also allows people to grow industrial hemp, which does not contain the same psychoactive components that are used for medical and recreational use. Hemp is typically used in industrial applications to manufacture products such as clothing, food, paper, and fuel.

After Amendment 64 was passed, it was necessary for the governor and the state legislature to change the state laws to reflect the vote. It was also necessary to establish new policies outlining how sales of recreational marijuana would be implemented. To begin the process, the state's governor, John Hickenlooper, signed Executive Order B 2012-004 on December 10, 2012, to establish a Task Force on the Implementation of Amendment 64. The members of the task force were asked to identify the legal, policy, and procedural issues that needed to be addressed in order to implement the ballot initiative fully and effectively.

On March 13, 2013, the task force issued a report entitled *The Task Force Report on the Implementation of Amendment 64: Regulation of Marijuana in Colorado* that included 58 recommendations regarding the process by which recreational marijuana should be legally grown, sold, and taxed in the state. The recommendations had many goals: to limit the distribution and consumption of marijuana to anyone over 21 years of age, to promote the health and safety of youth, to promote entrepreneurship, to propose a new financing structure, to determine appropriate taxation of marijuana sales, to set requirements for licensing and operations, to educate citizens about the effects of marijuana, to specify rules for home cultivation, and to provide guidance for employers and employees. Among the recommendations in the report were the creation of a system for state and local licensing of those who sought to cultivate or sell marijuana; the establishment of a Marijuana Enforcement Division; creation of application fees for licenses, licensing fees, and operating fees; establishment of a viable tax structure for marijuana sales; development of rules to oversee legal cultivation and manufacture of the drug; creation of new rules for transportation of marijuana and a mechanism to destroy marijuana that cannot be sold; establishment of new regulations regarding the legal purchase of marijuana by residents and visitors; creation of requirements for packaging and labeling of marijuana; establishment of provisions for marijuana education for professionals, youth, and the public about the effects of marijuana; development of recommendations for support of law enforcement efforts; establishment of new rules regarding driving while under the influence of alcohol or drugs such as marijuana; developing proposed revisions needed for the state criminal code; and developing new provisions regarding industrial hemp.

Based on the recommendations of the task force, the Colorado legislature passed new laws that amended the Colorado Revised Statutes. Governor Hickenlooper signed many of these proposals in May 2013. The laws regarding medical marijuana are found in CRS 12-43. 3-101 et seq. and those defining recreational (or retail) marijuana is found in CRS 12-43. 4-101 et seq.

As outlined in the task force recommendations, the state legislature created a new agency, the Marijuana Enforcement Division, and gave it the authority to oversee implementation of the new laws. Found within the Colorado Department of Revenue, the new agency was given the responsibility to implement legislation, develop rules, and enforce compliance with the new laws regarding recreational marijuana. The agency has the authority to grant licenses to those who seek to work in the field of either medical or recreational marijuana. They also are responsible for approving dispensary licenses. The agency personnel conduct background checks that are required for those who grow or sell marijuana. The mission statement of the agency is simple: "Our mission is to responsibly administer and enforce medical and retail marijuana laws and regulation in a fair and equitable manner by implementing efficient and effective fiscal management policies, operable enforcement strategies and collaborative partnerships with stakeholders that establish public trust and value in the agency" (Colorado Department of Revenue, 2015).

In September 2013, the state Department of Revenue formally adopted rules for creating and overseeing the establishments that would sell recreational marijuana to customers. Local governments also passed licensing requirements that would be in addition to the state requirements.

In January 2014, the governor of Colorado made it clear that he would ensure that recreational marijuana would be permitted, but only in a way that protects the citizens of the state. In his State of the State address, Hickenlooper said, "Just as we must implement the voters' wishes on marijuana, we are obligated to make sure that children and parents understand brain development and the risks of underage use. We are committed to a safe, regulated and responsible environment. This will be one of the great social experiments of this century, and while not all of us chose it, being first means we all share a responsibility to do it properly" (Gov. Hickenlooper, January 9, 2014).

As a result of the new amendments and laws regarding legalized sale and use of marijuana for both medical use and recreation in Colorado, there have been economic ramifications to both the individuals who live in the state and to the state itself. New businesses abound. But these new businesses are facing three major hurdles that block their success: federal laws, taxes, and banking. This article describes some of the businesses that are proliferating in the new legalized marijuana market in Colorado, and how these three hurdles are preventing marijuana-related business from thriving.

New Businesses

After changes were made in Colorado's state constitution and statutes to legalize the recreational use of marijuana, a new market for products and services that cater to this industry quickly emerged. New business opportunities for interested entrepreneurs are almost endless. There has been an explosion of new businesspeople who are seeking to take advantage of the new laws, making the marijuana business one of the fastest-growing and most lucrative industries in the state. In fact, the cannabis market is currently valued at approximately $1.53 billion. Moreover, estimates place of value for the five-year national market potential at $10.2 billion ("Cannabis Industry," 2014; O'Connor, 2014). The dramatic expansion of marijuana retailers and pot-based companies has been referred to as the "green rush."

Estimates by the Marijuana Industry Group, an organization formed in 2014 between the University of Colorado Boulder Business Research Division and BBC Research and Consulting, indicate that there are currently around 10,000 people who are directly employed by the emerging marijuana business. Currently in Colorado, the marijuana industry comprises approximately .4% of the total number of people employed in the state. These estimates may even be too low, as they do not include those people who are indirectly involved in the marijuana industry, such as accountants or attorneys, nor does it include restaurants that have developed and serve marijuana-enhanced food items to customers (Lopez, 2014). These jobs, the agency points out, are all revenue-producing jobs.

One of the primary emerging businesses revolves around growing the plant itself. The cultivation process has created a multitude of business opportunities from seeds, soil, growing lights, containers, and warehouse space (which costs up to four times as much now as it did before Proposition 64 was passed). There is now a need for a massive amount of the drug in the state. In 2014, the Marijuana Policy Group estimated that the total demand for marijuana by residents of Colorado to be approximately 121.4 metric tons. The estimated demand for marijuana by visitors to the state was estimated to be approximately 8.9 metric tons. In total, this means that there is an estimated demand for marijuana in Colorado of 130.3 metric tons each year.

Once the plant is grown, processors need to prepare the product for sale. This involves bud trimmers, who trim the cannabis after it is harvested. The product must be labeled for sale and packaged, and then marketed to users. The product needs to be delivered to stores and retail outlets using a transportation system that meets requirements set forth by the law (Huff, 2013). At those outlets, employees called bud tenders help customers choose the strain of marijuana that is best for them. Stores that sell paraphernalia such as pipes and other methods to ingest the product are needed. Pot critics rate the stores, dispensaries, and the pot itself. If someone has questions regarding any of these steps, a new group called Cannabis University, Inc., has emerged to provide seminars to those with questions.

Other marijuana businesses are popular as well. There are now coffee shops, bakeries, and restaurants that sell cannabis-infused treats ranging from chocolates, gummies, cookies, and pies, to marinara sauce, oils, pizza, and pot-based soda. THC-laced edibles are one of the fastest growing markets. Edibles are popular because they can be more discrete for those users who do not want to be seen smoking marijuana—there are fewer social taboos associated with edibles. It is also thought that edibles have fewer health risks when compared to smoking marijuana. In addition, users report that the effects of edible marijuana are quite different from those experienced after smoking marijuana. The high experienced from eating the drug takes longer to appear and is reportedly more mild. Thus, many edibles retailers are reaching out to first-time users who are just beginning to use marijuana.

In some cases, however, the edibles produced in bakeries can be extremely potent, especially for those people who are not used to smoking marijuana. A major concern with edibles is the danger that the baked goods will be consumed by children. To prevent this from happening, the state established new rules for edibles. Now these products must be sold in smaller portions, must be more clearly marked and must be delivered in child proof packaging. They have established a serving size as being ten milligrams. Those edibles with higher doses can still be sold in larger packages but must be scored or marked in a way that is easy to separate the portions.

One example of a company that produces edibles is Simply Pure, which produces medicated edibles that are currently available in many marijuana dispensaries throughout the state. Dixie Elixirs and Edibles is another company that manufactures candies, sodas (mandarin, red currant, and sarsaparilla flavored), vape pens, massage oils, bath salts, and lotions laced with THC. One of their best selling items is Dixie Rolls, a THC-enhanced chocolate candy wrapped in silver wrappers (Kamin and Warner, 2014).

Another new product being produced by entrepreneurs is marijuana wax, a concentrated, pure THC in "shatter" that is packaged into one gram increments. The packages are sold from $30 to $50 on the retail market. To make the shatter, the producer separates the crystal-coated strands called trichomes that are found on high-quality marijuana flowers and trimmings from the plant. The trichome is the part of the marijuana plant that contains all of the oil, THC, and cannabinoids that cause a user to feel "high" after ingesting the drug. As the producers separate the trichomes from the marijuana plant, an amber-colored paste remains. The paste is spread on a pan and baked in an oven for about 24 hours. The result is a potent marijuana concentrate, referred to as "shatter." Shatter contains about 80 or 90% THC. About 50 to 55 pounds of source material will yield about five pounds of shatter (Evans, 2014). The product has become very popular among users and quickly sells out when available in retail stores.

A different entrepreneur in the marijuana business field created a website that gives users the opportunity to rate marijuana dispensaries across the state. The site, called Weedmaps.com, makes a profit by charging dispensaries for access to information about retail stores. The dispensaries are given the opportunity to respond to reviews that are posted on the site. Dispensaries can also pay for having professional photos and videos taken and posted on-line for viewers to watch. It has been estimated that this business will see sales of $30–$40 million a year (Wells, 2013).

The insurance industry is one of the indirect employers that has been affected by marijuana legalization. Many insurance companies are watching the trends in marijuana use and business operations, and attempting to determine what coverages, if any, they could offer to businesses that grow and/or sell marijuana products (directly or indirectly) for either medical or recreational purposes. These companies, like other businesses, need insurance for a host of issues, such as workers' compensation, business interruption, theft, products liability, cargo insurance, business owners' policy coverage, equipment breakdown, and cyber liability (O'Connor, 2014).

Another indirect marijuana business in Colorado is tourism. Marijuana tourism is now big business in Colorado as many users have flocked to the state to purchase and use marijuana legally and safely. While tourists and non-residents are not legally permitted to purchase the drug in medical marijuana dispensaries, they are permitted to shop in recreational stores (although they cannot transport the drug to another state) (Wyatt, 2014a). A visitor is permitted to purchase 1 ounce at a time from a retail store, but since there is no formal record of purchases, a non-resident can make multiple purchases each day. However, a person cannot legally possess more than one ounce of marijuana at any given time, regardless of whether they are a resident, unless they are a registered medical marijuana patient.

One study of the emergence of the marijuana tourism industry showed that 40% of the customers in recreational marijuana shops in Denver were visitors to the state. In the popular ski towns of Aspen and Breckenridge, the number increased to 90%. Based upon sales tax reports filed with the Colorado Department of Revenue for January 2014, the total marijuana sales in these mountain communities saw an increase of over 100% (Light, Orens, Lewandowski, & Pickton). This has led some residents of these towns to be concerned about the effect of marijuana sales on the town's reputation. They do not want to become known as "pot havens" and risk alienating those visitors who are opposed to the drug's legalization.

One example of a marijuana tourism business is My 420 Tours, whose name plays on the "420" reference to marijuana. The company does not sell marijuana to its customers, but does arrange for guests to sample a variety of different marijuana products. Those who book the tour visit locations throughout Colorado that are central to the marijuana industry that will give the guest a view of the different marijuana activities. Tourists will visit a growing operation, and a company that manufactures edibles. They may also take part in a cooking class to learn more about using marijuana as an ingredient in a wide variety of food products. During the tour, as guests may ingest marijuana, they are provided with private transportation and hotel accommodations in a marijuana-friendly hotel.

To support these existing businesses or even ones that do not yet exist, different gatherings were held as a way to increase knowledge about legal marijuana in the state. In April 2014, Colorado's fifth annual Cannabis Cup was held. This is a travelling trade show sponsored by *High Times* magazine that allows for booths to display their products to others. At this event, there were about 250 booths from different dispensaries, with plenty of samples for people to try the product. There were also representatives from marijuana growers. Workshops on subjects such as cultivation were popular, as were seminars relating to the business of legal marijuana. There were also seminars about the use of concentrates. Performers such as Snoop Lion (also known as Snoop Dogg), the rappers Wiz Khalifa and Mac Miller, and the band Slightly Stoopid, appeared. Those interested had the opportunity to take a bus tour of recreational marijuana centers (i.e., pot shops) (Harris, 2014).

A related event, which occurred on May 22, 2014, was the Colorado Cannabis Summit. This was a meeting directed toward business entrepreneurs to discuss issues relevant to the emerging field. They discussed issues regarding training of employees, human resources, safety, security, marketing, taxes, and issues relevant to the management of the emerging businesses (Hendee, 2014).

It is clear that Amendment 20 and Proposition 64 had major impacts on the businesses surrounding marijuana in Colorado. The number of new business opportunities is endless, including businesses directly involved with the marijuana market and those more indirectly involved. The description provided here includes only a portion of the businesses that have emerged. However, as a burgeoning business opportunity, these new businesses are facing three primary issues: federal laws, taxes, and banking.

Federal Laws

Many critics of Colorado's laws permitting medical and recreational marijuana use are quick to point out that marijuana remains illegal under the federal law and all of the newly emerging businesses are violating federal statutes. This means that they could be raided by the Drug Enforcement Administration and shut down at any time, regardless of the fact that they have obeyed state laws. The owners and employees could be punished by fines and imprisonment and their property (e.g., homes, cars, bank accounts) seized by the federal government.

At the same time, the federal government under President Barack Obama has indicated that they will support the decision of the voters and not challenge the state law. This was made clear in a memo dated August 29, 2013, written by James Cole, the US Deputy Attorney General. In the memo, titled "Guidance Regarding Marijuana Enforcement," Cole indicated that federal drug enforcement agencies are unlikely to enforce federal law prohibiting marijuana cultivation, use, and possession (as described in the Controlled Substances Act) in those states where marijuana has been legalized. This is dependent upon state regulation and control being functional. Despite this edict, a change in administration could very well mean a change in this policy. While businesses are being allowed to thrive under the Obama administration, this could change under a new president after the next national election, or any after that.

Taxes

One essential question that had to be resolved before the laws allowing for recreational marijuana could be implemented in Colorado revolved around the tax structure for sales of the drug. Colorado has a Taxpayers' Bill of Rights that requires voter approval for all tax increases. It also requires that money be returned to taxpayers if actual taxes collected earn more than the estimated figure posed to voters during a campaign (Associated Press, 2014c). In November 2013, voters approved a proposed tax structure for recreational marijuana that included both an excise tax and special sales taxes on retail marijuana. This proposal appeared on the ballot under Proposition AA, which passed by a wide margin.

According to Proposition AA, there would be a 10% state sales tax on recreational marijuana on top of the existing 2.9% state sales tax. This would be in addition to any local taxes imposed. There would also be an excise tax of 15%

Table 1. Projected Retail Marijuana Revenue by Task Force Members

	FY 2013–14	FY 2014–15
2.9% Sales Tax	$5,624,900	$17,770,793
10% Additional Sales Tax (not including 15% local share)	$16,486,777	$52,086,807
15% Excise Tax	$11,422,770	$45,958,948
Fees	$1,688,663	$1,962,413
Other	$54,141	$68,696
Total	**$35,277,251**	**$117,847,657**

Table 2. Projected Medical Marijuana Revenue

	FY 2013–14	FY 2014–15
2.9% Sales Tax	$10,344,290	$10,001,306
Fees	$4,977,926	$5,682,787
Other	$77,876	$112,396
Total	**$15,400,092**	**$15,796,489**

on marijuana sales that would be used to fund public school construction projects. The excise tax is imposed on the first sale or transfer from a retail marijuana cultivation facility to a retail marijuana store, retail marijuana product manufacturing facility, or to another retail marijuana cultivation facility. The proposed tax would be calculated on the basis of the category of the retail marijuana product (i.e., flower, trim, or immature plant) being sold or transferred. There would be no excise tax on medical marijuana (Colorado Department of Revenue, 2015).

Before the law was implemented in January 2014, the governor's task force made projections concerning the potential revenue from the recreational and medical marijuana sales. Table 1 represents the projected funds resulting from recreational marijuana after accounting for direct and indirect costs to the Department of Revenue as well as appropriations made from the Marijuana Cash Fund legislation, as provided by the task force. Table 2 presents the similar projections for medical marijuana.

Other estimates of tax revenue from the sale of marijuana were made by other officials in the state. They estimated that revenue generated from the sale of marijuana would be somewhere around $67 million. This estimate was made public in the "Blue Book" voting guide distributed to voters prior to the election, as required by the constitution of the state. In June 2014, a prediction on the retail marijuana tax collections estimated that value would be lower than what was estimated (Colorado Office of State Planning and Budgeting, 2014).

Once the sale of recreational marijuana began in Colorado, any business that sold marijuana and marijuana infused products was required to file sales tax information electronically each month. According to data gathered by the Colorado Office of State Planning and Budgeting, the state's revenue was increased by the sales tax on recreational marijuana. Revenue data shows that Colorado made roughly $2 million in marijuana taxes in January 2014. The Department of Revenue indicates that $14.02 million worth of recreational marijuana was sold in the first month it was legal (Associated Press, 2014c).

Tables 3, 4, and 5 show the sales tax revenues from medical and recreational marijuana in the first months after Proposition 64 became operational.

According to Governor Hickenlooper, the tax revenue from the legal marijuana market far exceeded the state's predictions. The governor indicated that sales and excise taxes would produce $98 million, far more than the estimated

Table 3. 2014 Sales Taxes to Marijuana Cash Fund (2.9% Rate)

Month	Reported Sales Tax Medical	Reported Sales Tax Recreational	Total Reported Sales Tax
January	913,519	416,690	1,330,209
February	1,022,176	438,253	1,460,429
March	999,900	569,505	1,569,405
April	919,982	639,728	1,559,710
May	927,330	642,124	1,569,454
June	830,861	700,107	1,530,968
July	838,711	821,078	1,659,789
August	935,807	956,973	1,829,780
September	908,630	886,915	1,795,545
October	928,329	888,250	1,816,579

Source: Colorado Department of Revenue; Prepared by Office of Research and Analysis, "State of Colorado, Marijuana Taxes, Licenses, and Fees Transfers and Distribution."

Table 4. 2014 Retail Marijuana Sales Tax (10% Rate)

Month	Local Government Distribution	Marijuana Cash Fund Transfer	Total Retail Marijuana Sales Tax
January	210,269	1,191,534	1,401,568
February	212,674	1,210,786	1,434,916
March	285,215	1,613,861	1,898,685
April	330,057	1,864,829	2,217,607
May	315,356	1,787,025	2,070,577
June	368,231	2,086,648	2,473,627
July	443,498	2,513,164	2,970,183
August	496,211	2,811,874	3,307,078
September	443,937	2,515,663	2,940,346
October	488,236	2,766,687	3,244,159

Source: Colorado Department of Revenue; Prepared by Office of Research and Analysis, "State of Colorado, Marijuana Taxes, Licenses, and Fees Transfers and Distribution."

Table 5. 2014 Retail Marijuana Excise Tax (15% Rate)

Month	Public School Capital Construction Assistance Fund Transfer	Collections Not Yet Allocated	Total Retail Marijuana Excise Tax
January	195,318	32	195,318
February	339,531	84	339,615
March	609,887	20	609,907
April	732,406	1,945	734,351
May	1,135,718	(70)	1,135,718
June	963,551	6,086	969,637
July	1,399,496	(1,566)	1,397,930
August	1,458,036	6,760	1,464,796
September	1,456,528	(8,423)	1,446,105
October	1,718,909	6,364	1,718,273

Source: Colorado Department of Revenue; Prepared by Office of Research and Analysis, "State of Colorado, Marijuana Taxes, Licenses, and Fees Transfers and Distribution."

$79 million presented to voters during the campaign to legalize the drug (Wyatt, 2014b).

However, another report indicated that marijuana was not bringing in the expected revenue. This report found that voters were told that the state would collect $33.5 million in the first few months of the new law. But there were some factors that led to this value being less than originally predicted. First, many users continue to purchase their marijuana from the illegal (black) market because it is cheaper. Second, it is estimated that more people are using medical marijuana, which is taxed less that recreational marijuana (and is also cheaper for the user) (Lobosco, 2014). Finally, it is thought that some users are growing their own marijuana, and thus not paying taxes to the state.

In fact, the tax structure in Colorado has added to the costs of the drug. When the sales of marijuana became legal in January 2014, a pot shop charged nearly twice the amount for recreational marijuana than they would charge for medical marijuana. Because of the high taxes, those customers purchasing recreational marijuana were charged $45 for an eighth of an ounce whereas those purchasing medical marijuana were charged $25 for an identical amount (Vekshin, 2014).

Spending

While there is some debate over the exact tax revenue figures, there is no doubt that there is revenue to the state from legal marijuana. The question then, is how the money will be spent. As defined in the law, the first $40 million of the excise tax must go to school construction. The rest will be spent by state lawmakers.

According to the laws passed by the legislature, any revenue collected from the new tax is placed into the state's General Fund. The money will then be transferred to a "Marijuana Tax Cash Fund" that will be used to support the regulation and enforcement of the recreational marijuana industry. A portion of the cash fund will be distributed to local governments in areas where retail marijuana sales occur. Called the "marijuana rebate," 15% of the money generated from the retail marijuana sales tax will be distributed to the local governments based upon the percentage of retail marijuana sales that occur in their local communities (Colorado Office of State Planning and Budgeting, 2014).

In February 2014, Governor Hickenlooper announced his plans for spending the revenue collected from marijuana sales. He sought to spend $99 million of the money in different priority areas, including $45.5 million for youth marijuana use prevention and deterrence programs, $40.4 million for substance abuse treatment programs, $12.4 million for public health initiatives, $29 million on enforcement, $1.8 million on regulatory oversight, and $200,000 on statewide coordination efforts (Associated Press, 2014a). The governor also proposed a $5.8 million, three-year, statewide media campaign that would focus on the health risks associated with marijuana use. Under his plan, the state's Department of Transportation would receive $1.9 million for a media campaign called "Drive High, Get a DUI" (Associated Press, 2014c). Before it becomes effective, the governor's spending proposal must be approved by the state legislature (Associated Press, 2014b).

In addition to the governor's requests, other state-wide departments requested money from the Marijuana Cash Fund. These included:

- The Department of Public Health and Environment requested $3.7 million for a three-year, statewide marijuana education campaign to educate Coloradans on the impact of marijuana.
- The Department of Public Safety requested $373,667 to gather and analyze information on the illegal production, sale, and distribution of marijuana in Colorado. The department also proposed a plan to develop a comprehensive intelligence framework that would help identify future threats to public safety related to illegal drug activity.
- The Department of Education requested $11 million for mental health and substance abuse prevention programs in public schools. They also requested funds to provide grants to public schools as a way to increase the availability of school health professionals to educate students regarding the dangers of marijuana use. They also requested $6 million for additional school resource officers.
- The Governor's Office requested $190,097 to establish a Drug Policy Office that would be responsible for coordinating the state's regulatory, road, and public safety, as well as the public health response to legal marijuana use.
- Department of Health Care Policy and Financing requested $42.3 million for an enhanced substance use disorder program that would add intensive outpatient services and inpatient/residential treatment for those individuals who use marijuana for health issues; they also sought an additional $13 million to provide school based prevention and early intervention for marijuana substance use and disorder services in schools.
- The Department of Human Services requested $32.2 million for substance abuse service initiatives, including $10 million to fund marijuana, prescription drug, and alcohol abuse prevention for youth and grants to local communities to implement evidence-based prevention programs for underage marijuana, alcohol, and prescription drug misuse; $7 million for 105 additional beds in the Intensive Residential Treatment for

Substance Use Disorders to treat marijuana misuse; $6 million for the Collaborative Management Program for prevention, intervention, and treatment of marijuana use; $5 million for the Tony Grampsas Program, for grants that target the prevention of marijuana use; and $4.1 million for the Colorado Access to Recovery Program that provides community support so that those people leaving substance abuse programs can continue their treatment in their communities.

- The Department of Law requested $456,760 to develop in-house expertise on state and local marijuana retail regulations as a way to provide training for regulators and peace officers.
- The Department of Public Health and Environment requested $8.7 million for five health initiatives. These included a statewide marijuana education campaign with a website to educate Coloradans on the impact of marijuana; a registry to collect data on drivers suspected of driving under the influence of drugs or alcohol; a Healthy Kids Colorado Survey that examines the relationships between marijuana use and school performance; a monitoring program to observe marijuana-related health issues through the state; and a one-year pilot project to determine the correlation between marijuana use during pregnancy and birth defects.
- The Department of Revenue: requested $1,840,000 for programming required for retail marijuana sales and excise taxes.
- The Department of Transportation: requested $1,875,000 to fund the "Drive High, Get a DUI" campaign for marijuana-impaired driving awareness (State of Colorado, Office of the Governor, 2014).

Banking

The third issue restricting marijuana businesses revolves around the inability of such industries to open and maintain accounts in banking institutions. To some, the issues revolving around banking are considered the biggest challenge facing the new and growing cannabis industry. The problem is simply that business owners are unable to open accounts because their industry revolves around an illegal endeavor.

The problem is centered around a law passed in 1970, the Bank Secrecy Act, which was originally created as a way to deter money laundering by illegal organizations, including drug dealers. The law requires that banks report large deposits of cash that are believed to be linked to illegal activity, including drugs. Any bank that accepts large deposits that are potentially the result of illegal activity may be charged with money laundering and face harsh penalties or even revocation of their banking license. Since these new businesses in Colorado are making a profit based on activities that are illegal under federal law, most banks will not allow marijuana business owners to open accounts, nor will they approve start-up loans (Wells, 2013).

This problem is evidenced by the fact that the two largest banks in Colorado, Wells Fargo Bank and FirstBank, announced that they would not offer new loans to landowners with preexisting leases with marijuana businesses. They claimed that any property used as collateral for a loan is subject to federal drug-seizure laws, which makes the loans a risk.

Because of this, the marijuana industry is largely an all-cash business. Transactions are all done with cash. Successful business owners have no place to put their profits and must rely on safes located in their homes or offices. Clearly, this poses an increased safety risk to business owners because there are large amounts of cash readily available, making this a potential problem for law enforcement. The restrictions on banking make it virtually impossible for these business owners to thrive as a normal endeavor.

The Obama administration recognized that this discrepancy in the baking regulations could lead to an increased risk of crime (particularly robbery and theft) as well as inefficient accounting of sales. He asked that new rules be developed for bankers to allow them to legally accept cash deposits from established, legal marijuana businesses in Colorado. On February 14, 2014, a "Guidance" was published by the Financial Crimes Enforcement Network ("FinCEN"), part of the US Department of the Treasury. Their goal was to help financial institutions provide services to businesses in the marijuana industry while still following federal law.

According to the new rules, any bank doing business with a marijuana dispensary, retail store, or other business must prove, among other things, that the marijuana never makes it into the hands of children, that the marijuana is not trafficked into another state, that the business-owner has no ties to a drug cartel, and that the drug is not used on federal property. It is very difficult for banks to comply with these rules and guarantee these things will not occur. Even though the federal government has issued statements of clarification that allow financial transactions related to marijuana, the laws outlawing large deposits remain on the books, and banks remain hesitant to deal with marijuana businesses.

The FinCEN report reiterated the need for banks to file a Suspicious Activity Report, or SAR, with the federal government, if there is reason to believe there are illegal acts being committed. This might happen if the bank knows, suspects, or has reason to suspect that a particular transaction involves funds derived from illegal activity. They may also suspect that the activity is intended to evade federal regulations.

Bankers were asked to fill out different types of SAR reports. One of those is a "Marijuana Limited" SAR in which the banker believes the business does not violate a stipulation in the Cole Memo (a document from the Department of Justice that outlines when the federal government will enforce federal anti-marijuana laws). In this report, the bankers will indicate that they are filing the report only because the business is engaged in a marijuana-related business, but that no additional suspicious activity has been identified. A "Marijuana Priority" SAR report will be filed by a bank if they believe that the business violates a stipulation of the Cole Memo. This report will indicate the possible violations, including the dates, people involved, and any other relevant information. A third type of SAR is a "Marijuana Termination" report, which should be filed if the bank seeks to end a relationship with the business in order to comply with the law.

The FinCEN report indicated that a bank is not required to accept transactions from marijuana businesses. Instead, a bank's decision to open or close an account should be made by each individual institution. A financial institution should consider whether a marijuana-related business being considered for a loan or account violates one of the priorities mentioned in the Cole Memo. According to the Guidance, there are possible indicators that a company is violating the Cole Memo. These are listed in Table 6.

On July 18, 2014, the US House of Representatives acted on legislation geared toward making it easier for banks to do business with marijuana businesses. They voted in favor of an amendment, referred to as the "Heck" amendment, that prevents the Securities and Exchange Commission and the US Treasury from penalizing banks that lend money to businesses and otherwise participate in other banking activities with marijuana-based businesses in Colorado and other states where it is legalized.

The legislature in Colorado has also approved a bill aimed at providing newly legalized marijuana businesses access to basic banking services ("Colorado Could Have," 2014). In December 2014, the Fourth Corner Credit Union was granted a charter by state banking regulators to serve marijuana businesses, but the bank would still need approval from the National Credit Union Administration, a federal agency.

Conclusion

The passage of Proposition 64 in Colorado has opened up endless opportunities for new businesses in the state. However, these businesses are limited by three primary concerns: federal laws outlawing marijuana, high taxes, and

Table 6. Indicators of Cole Memo Violations

- A customer appears to be using a licensed marijuana business as a front to launder money derived from other criminal activity. This may be indicated if a business has a higher profit than would be expected, if the business receives substantially more revenue than its local competitors, if the business is depositing more cash than is expected given the amount of revenue it is reporting for tax purposes; if the business is not able to demonstrate that its profit is derived from the sale of marijuana; if there is rapid movement of funds, or deposits by third parties with no connection to the accountholder.
- The business is unable to produce documentation to demonstrate that it is licensed and operating in compliance with state law.
- Review of publicly available databases about the business, its owner(s), manager(s), or other related parties, reveals information such as a criminal record, involvement in the illegal purchase or sale of drugs, violence, or other potential connections to illicit activity.
- The business engages in international or interstate activity, including by receiving cash deposits from places outside of the state, or makes or receives frequent or large interstate transfers.
- The owner(s) or manager(s) of a marijuana-related business live in another state.
- A marijuana-related business is located on federal property or the marijuana sold by the business was grown on federal property.

Source: US Department of Treasury, Financial Crimes Enforcement Network; "BSA Expectations Regarding Marijuana Related Businesses." February 14, 2014. www.fincen.gov.

banking limits. The uncertainties presented by these issues can hinder many from becoming part of the new industry and can also put a damper in the industry's growth.

The fact that marijuana remains illegal under federal law certainly hinders successful business. Any emerging marijuana business is currently violating federal law. Even though the current presidential administration is not enforcing federal statutes banning the drug, this could change at any time. The DEA could begin raiding and confiscating all marijuana, equipment, property, and money associated with the industry. Those who have established businesses risk losing everything, including their investments, if this were to happen. Potential investors may be uneasy about beginning a business or providing needed capital for businesses knowing that it could be seized by the government at any time and used as evidence to prove illegal behavior.

This concern became more real after a lawsuit was filed with the US Supreme Court in December 2014, by the states of Nebraska and Oklahoma. Officials in these states have asked the federal court to invalidate the law permitting legalized marijuana in Colorado. These officials argue that Colorado's law harms other states by facilitating the transportation of the drug into the states where marijuana remains illegal. They reiterate that marijuana is illegal under federal law, and that Colorado's law undermines the federal Constitution. If the Supreme Court decides to hear the case, it could decide that Colorado's laws are inconsistent with federal laws and are therefore unconstitutional. This would open the door to federal enforcement of anti-marijuana laws.

Another burden on marijuana business is the high taxes imposed on the sale of the drug. The excessive taxes on every sale of marijuana or marijuana product may drive some users to purchase the marijuana illegally on the black market, where it is untaxed and therefore much cheaper. Moreover, the product is also available through medical marijuana dispensaries at the untaxed and cheaper rates. Clearly, when users purchase the drug illegally, it cuts into the profits of the legal operations. At this point, legitimate marijuana businesses must compete with a cheaper product that is readily available to customers.

In order to reduce the black market sales (and maintain tax revenues for the state), the law enforcement in the state will need to continue to crack down on illegal purchases. Even though sale of the drug is now legal, it does not mean that police can stop investigating and arresting those who are selling and buying marijuana illegally. The law enforcement operations must continue to concentrate on the underground sales of the drug. The alternative is to reduce the high taxes now imposed on the drug so that the cost of the legal product is less prohibitive to those seeking to use it.

The third burden, the lack of banking options, is also prohibitive to businesses. Because marijuana is illegal under federal law, banks cannot open checking accounts or deposit profits, creating an all-cash business. This is clearly a significant roadblock for operating any business as it becomes difficult to purchase equipment or product without credit. It also opens businesses up to theft by employees or criminals. Some officials have recognized the increased possibility of skimming, whereby sales are inaccurately reported to the government and a portion of the money is stolen. Banks must be permitted to accept large cash deposits and transactions by marijuana-based companies. Until then, law enforcement must pay careful attention to possible crimes caused by excessive amount of cash found in stores and homes.

While the legalization of marijuana has opened up endless opportunities for new business endeavors in Colorado, significant obstructions remain. In the years to come, these issues must be resolved if the industry is to thrive. Other states that are considering legalizing the drug should look to take these concerns into account as they make new laws and regulations for marijuana sales in their own states.

References

Associated Press. (2014b, February 19). Colorado governor reveals plan to spend marijuana tax revenue. Fox News. Retrieved from http://www.foxnews.com/politics/2014/02/19colorado-governor-reveals-plan-to-spend.

Associated Press. (2014c, February 19). Colorado governor marijuana tax spending plan. *Toledo Blade*. Retrieved from http://www.toledoblade.com/Nation/2014/02/19/Colorado-governor-marijuana-tax-spending.

Associated Press. (2014a, March 10). Colorado marijuana taxes net state $2 million. Fox News. Retrieved from http://www.foxnews.com/us/2014/03/10/colorado-marijuana-taxes-net-state-2-million.

Cannabis industry creates rise in new markets. (2014, January 24). PR.com. Retrieved from http://www.pr.com/press-release/538773.

Colorado could have a first-of-its-kind bank for marijuana businesses. (2014, May 13). *Inquisitr*. Retrieved from http://www.inquisitr.com/1249377/colorado-could-have-a-first-of-its-kind.

Colorado Department of Revenue. (2015). Stakeholders—Marijuana enforcement. Retrieved from https://www.colorado.gov/pacific/enforcement/stakeholders-marijuana-enforcement.

Colorado Department of Revenue, Taxation Division. (2015). Marijuana taxes. Retrieved from https://www.colorado.gov/pacific/tax/marijuana-taxes-file.

Colorado Office of State Planning and Budgeting. (2014, September). The Colorado economic outlook: Economic and fiscal review. Retrieved from http://www.colorado.gov/cs/Satellite/OSPB/GOVR/1218709343298.

Evans, B. (2014, August 9). Concentrated marijuana fastest growing sector in Colorado retail pot industry. *Summit Daily*. Retrieved from http://www.summitdaily.com/news/12541102-113/mouser-marijuana-grow-concentrates.

Harris, R. L. (2014, April 4). In Colorado, Cannabis Cup time. *New York Times*. Retrieved from http://intransit.blogs.nytimes.com/2014/04/04/in-colorado-cannabis-cup-time/.

Hendee, C. (2014, April 29). Colorado Cannabis Summit seeks to set standards for marijuana industry. Retrieved from http://www.bizjournals.com/denver/news/2014/04/29/colorado-cannabis-summit-seeks.

Hickenlooper, J. (2014, January 9). The state of our state is strong. Retrieved from http://www.colorado.gov/cs/Satellite/GovHickenlooper/CBON/1251649620018.

Huff, E. A. (2013, June 24). New wave of business opportunities involving medicinal, nutritional marijuana sweep Colorado. Retrieved from http://www.naturalnews.com/040920_marijuana_business_opportunities_Colorado.htm.

Kamin, S., & Warner, J. (2014, June 11). Don't eat the whole thing. *Slate.* Retrieved from http://www.slate.com/articles/news_and_politics/altered_state/2014/06/marijuana_edibles.

Light, M. K., Orens, A., Lewandowski, B., & Pickton, T. Colorado Department of Revenue and the Marijuana Policy Group. (2014). Market size and demand for marijuana in Colorado. Retrieved from http://www.colorado.gov/cs/.

Lobosco, K. (2014, September 2). Colorado is missing $21.5 million in pot taxes. CNN Money. Retrieved from http://money.cnn.com/2014/09/02/news/economy/marijuana-taxes-colorado/index.html.

Lopez, G. (2014, May 20). Legal marijuana created thousands of jobs in Colorado. *Vox.* Retrieved from http://www.vox.com/2014/5/20/5734394/legal-marijuana-created-thousands-of-jobs.

O'Connor, A. (2014, October 2). Marijuana insurance industry: How high can it go? *Insurance Journal.* Retrieved from http://www.insurancejournal.com/news/national/2014/10/01/342142.htm.

State of Colorado, Office of the Governor. (2014, November 3). Governor John Hickenlooper's budget speech. Retrieved from http://www.colorado.gov/cs/Satellite?blobcol=urldata&blobheader=application%2Fpdf&blobkey=id&blobtable=MungoBlobs&blobwhere=1251943287907&ssbinary=true.

US Department of Treasury, Financial Crimes Enforcement Network "BSA Expectations Regarding Marijuana Related Businesses February 14, 2014. Retrieved from www.fincen.gov.

Vekshin, A. (2014, January 7). Marijuana prices double in Colorado. *Albuquerque Journal.* Retrieved from http://www.abqjournal.com/332172/news/marijuana-prices-double-in-colorado.html.

Wells, J. (2013, December 16). Marijuana related business sees growth as pot legalization spreads. NBC News. Retreived from http://www.nbcnews.com/business/consumer/—marijuanarelated-business-sees-growth-pot-legalization-spreads-f2D11750342.

Wyatt, K. (2014a, October 9). New at the pot shop: Milder marijuana for novices. Yahoo News. Retrieved from http://news.yahoo.com/pot-shop-milder-marijuana-novices-043641944.html.

Wyatt, K. (2014b, February 19). Governor: Colorado pot market exceeds tax hopes. *Denver Post.* Retrieved from http://www.denverpost.com/marijuana/ci_25180402/colorado-governor-reveals-pot-tax.

12

Legally High on Campus?

Kelley A. Cronin

Introduction

The passage of Amendment 64 by the state legislature of Colorado in 2012 legalized recreational use of marijuana by adults, and set the rest of the country on a movement to follow in their footsteps. While the trend towards legalization on the state level is expanding, possessing and using marijuana remains a crime under federal law. The potential impact on colleges and universities has opened up a new dialogue about marijuana laws and how they will affect campus life, research, and operations (Schutier, 2014). This chapter will examine the ramifications of new marijuana laws for colleges and discuss some of the programs that have been created to prepare students for a country where pot is legal.

Marijuana: The Campus Culture

The popularity of marijuana on college campuses can be traced to the counterculture of the 1960s, where antiestablishment was the dominant theme and smoking pot became a symbol of rebellion against authority. During this time, more lenient attitudes towards the drug emerged. Marijuana use became widespread in the upper middle class and was popularized by baby boomer "hippies," many of whom also worked to reduce legal penalties (Warf, 2014). The film *Reefer Madness* and "420 parties" contributed to a campus culture where smoking pot was not only socially acceptable, but often viewed as a rite of passage. At the same time, studies about marijuana use on college campuses began to emerge. Messer (1969) sought to determine how data on marijuana use compared with different types of students as defined by peer group ratings. Messer collected data on 344 college students (62% of whom had smoked marijuana) in a survey which allowed students to categorize one another by types. Those types were then summarized into three categories: "hippies," "political activists," and "academic-types" (or "succeeders"). The results found that 61.7% of "hippies" used marijuana more than five times in a month, compared to "political activists" at 24.3% and "succeeders" at only 4.2%. Messer concluded that the data was more useful in describing a student culture, rather than student types. He also determined that the use of drugs such as marijuana is highly associated with the establishment of an "important subcultural student movement."

Changes in public opinion and efforts to decriminalize and legalize cannabis have contributed to the current presence of marijuana in college life. While the college party scene has always been associated with underage drinking, the use of marijuana has increasingly become part of that landscape. One reason for this increased use is that marijuana is both readily available and socially acceptable. Previously attached stigmas that only "hippies" or "stoners" use it have faded away. Today, many young people view the use of marijuana as no different than the use of alcohol.

Nationally there is an upward trend in cannabis use among college students, many of whom were pre-exposed to the drug in high school or middle school. Research indicates that daily marijuana use is now at the highest rate among college students in more than three decades (Wadley, 2014). Scholars at the University of Michigan conduct the nationwide Monitoring the Future (MTF) study, a nationally funded research program that looks at historical and developmental changes in substance abuse and related attitudes of full-time college students one to four years beyond high school ("Monitoring the Future," 2013). Since 1980, the Monitoring the Future study has tracked substance use by college students, but the level has varied over time. In 2008, researchers compared annual marijuana usage among college students in a longitudinal study comparing past 30-day and past-year users (Higher Education Center for Alcohol, 2008). The results concluded that the percentage of past 30-day marijuana users increased from 13% in 1993 to 17% in 2001, while, the past-year marijuana users rose from 23% in 1993 to 30% in 2001 (Higher Education Center for Alcohol, 2008). In 2013, this number jumped to 36% (Wadley, 2014).

Federal Law and the Drug Free Schools and Communities Act Amendment of 1989

The federal government still considers the use of cannabis illegal and colleges and universities do not want to jeopardize their federal funding for research or student financial aid. Under the Drug Free Schools and Communities Act Amendment of 1989 Policy (Public Law 101-226), colleges may not knowingly and willingly allow substance use on campus (US Department of Education, 2006). The act also mandates that any college or university receiving federal funding must adopt a program to prevent use of illegal drugs by students and employees. At a minimum, the act requires each institution of higher education distribute to all of its students and employees the following:

- A statement of standards of conduct that clearly prohibits the unlawful possession, use, or distribution of drugs and alcohol by students and employees on the institution's property or as part of any of its activities;
- A description of applicable legal sanctions under local, state, or federal law for the unlawful possession or distribution of illicit drugs and alcohol;
- A description of the health risks associated with the use of illicit drugs and the abuse of alcohol;
- A description of available drug or alcohol counseling, treatment, or rehabilitation or re-entry programs;
- A statement that the institution will impose sanctions on students and employees who violate its standards of conduct relating to illicit drugs and alcohol, and a description of those sanctions.
- Institutions must conduct a biennial review of its program to determine effectiveness, execute needed changes, and ensure that disciplinary penalties are always met (US Department of Education, 2006).

Additionally, college dormitory contracts typically have clauses that prohibit possession or use of illegal drugs. Infractions of these rules result in expulsion from the dorms and the canceling of the housing contracts. In many cases, parents are not refunded their money.

In compliance with the Drug Free Schools and Communities Act Amendment of 1989 Policy (Public Law 101-226), most colleges and universities include in their websites information concerning federal, state, and local laws and the various sanctions for breaking them. Federal trafficking penalties are specifically laid out as federal law and may trump state legalization for many colleges (DiBlasio, 2012). Table 1 illustrates some of the information provided on the Boston University website about federal drug laws and their penalties. It is a modified example of the types of information being published in accordance with the Drug Free Schools and Communities Act Amendment of 1989.

Table 1. Federal Drug Laws and Penalties

The possession, use, or distribution of illegal drugs is prohibited by federal law. Strict penalties exist for drug convictions, including mandatory prison terms for many offenses. The following information, although not complete, is an overview of federal penalties for first convictions. All penalties are doubled for any subsequent drug conviction.

A. Denial of Federal Benefits
21 U.S.C. 862
A federal drug conviction may result in the loss of federal benefits, including school loans, grants, scholarships, contracts, and licenses. Federal drug trafficking convictions may result in denial of federal benefits for up to five years for a first conviction. Federal drug convictions for possession may result in denial of federal benefits for up to one year for a first conviction and up to five years for subsequent convictions.

B. Forfeiture of Personal Property and Real Estate
21 U.S.C. 853
Any person convicted of a federal drug offense punishable by more than one year in prison shall forfeit to the United States any personal or real property related to the violation, including houses, cars, and other personal belongings. A warrant of seizure is issued and property seized at the time an individual is arrested on charges may result in forfeiture.

C. Federal Drug Trafficking Penalties
21 U.S.C. 841
Penalties for federal drug trafficking convictions vary according to the quantity of controlled substance involved in the transaction. The list below is a sample of the range and severity of federal penalties imposed for first convictions. Penalties for subsequent convictions are twice as severe.

If death or serious bodily injury results from the use of a controlled substance which has been illegally distributed, the person convicted on federal charges of distributing the substance faces a mandatory life sentence and fines ranging up to $8 million.

Persons convicted on federal charges of drug trafficking within 1,000 feet of a university (21 U.S.C. 845a) face penalties of prison terms and fines which are twice as high as the regular penalties for the offense, with a mandatory prison sentence of at least one year.

D. Federal Drug Possession Penalties
Persons convicted on federal charges of possessing any controlled substance face penalties of up to one year in prison and a mandatory fine of no less than $1,000 up to a maximum of $100,000. Second convictions are punishable by not less than 15 days but not more than two years in prison and a minimum find of $2,500. Subsequent convictions are punishable by not less than 90 days but not more than three years in prison and a minimum fine of $5,000.

Substance	Amount	Penalty-First Conviction
Marijuana	50–100 kg	**Prison:** up to 20 years
Hashish	10–100 kg	**Fine:** up to $1 million
Hashish Oil	1 gm.	

Source: Boston University campus safety website. Retrieved at: http://www.bu.edu/safety/alcohol-drugs/laws/.

Campus Life under New Laws

The legal environment of marijuana is rapidly changing and the impact for college campuses around the country has yet to be fully determined. Four states—Washington, Colorado, Oregon, and Alaska—and the District of Columbia have passed social use laws (Martin, 2014). Other states are experiencing legalization movements and college officials are looking for guidance on how to redefine or maintain existing policies. Lessons can be drawn from colleges and universities in Washington State and Colorado and their handling of both recreational and medical marijuana use under new laws.

Washington State

The passage of Initiative 502 (I-502) in November 2012 made Washington State one of the first to legalize marijuana use for recreational use. Under the new state law, adults 21 and older are authorized to possess and use marijuana-related paraphernalia and any combination of the following: one ounce of useable marijuana; 16 ounces of marijuana-infused product in solid form; or 72 ounces of marijuana-infused product in liquid form. Using marijuana or marijuana-infused products in public is illegal. Possession in amounts greater than 40 grams is a felony offense and driving under the influence of marijuana is prosecutable (University of Puget Sound, 2012). However, the University of Puget Sound student life website makes the following disclaimer:

> As a federally-funded institution, the University of Puget Sound will follow federal law when it comes to the sale, possession, and use of marijuana or marijuana-infused products. The production, sale, possession, and use of marijuana or marijuana-infused products are prohibited on campus (University of Puget Sound, 2012).

At Central Washington University (CWU), marijuana is not allowed in any facility on the campus. This policy has remained unchanged since legalization (Allmand, 2014). The school's policy also takes into account that marijuana use is still against federal law, and that allowing pot on campus could put federal funding in jeopardy (Allmand, 2014). To complicate matters, even if someone is over 21 and found in possession, he or she may still face disciplinary actions under student codes of conduct.

Colleges and universities in Washington previously dealt with this issue in 1998 when the state approved the use of medical marijuana. It too was banned, forcing those who wanted to use it for medical reasons to live off-campus. In response, Washington State University waived its requirement that all freshmen had to live in the dorms (Geranios, 2012). Despite the ban on campus, students with medical marijuana cards were reportedly being allowed to consume marijuana brownies in the dorms for medical reasons (Geranios, 2012). Recent changes to the federal government's ban on medical marijuana will alleviate some of these complications (Halper, 2014). However, until legalization occurs nationwide, colleges and universities will still have to comply with federal law.

Colorado

Through the passage of Amendment 64, Colorado joined Washington State in the legalization of marijuana for people age 21 and older. Colorado, however, also legalized the growing of cannabis for personal use. Under the new law, entrepreneurs may produce and sell marijuana at retail and small-scale home productions (up to six plants or 12 plants per household) (Halper, 2014). This, however, does not translate into plants growing on dormitory windowsills. Colleges and universities across Colorado continue to ban the use and production of pot on their campuses because, like Washington, the new laws are trumped by the national Drug-Free Schools and Communities Act Amendment of 1989 (Palmer, 2014). At the University of Denver campus, no additional regulations were created after the amendment passed. Since marijuana was already a banned substance, new policies and procedures were not needed. Colorado State University went beyond posting the new information to their website and used student-focused media accounts to communicate the new marijuana regulations. Information was also posted in the residence halls and on-campus media outlets were used to convey how the changes would impact student lives (Palmer, 2014).

For many of these colleges, campus security efforts have not changed simply because the law has. Because substance abuse was banned previously, campus police have maintained a watchful eye on such activity. Furthermore, the NCAA still bans drugs and has strict drug testing policies. The NCAA banned drug and testing policies are not tied to whether a substance is legal for general population use, but rather whether the substance is considered a threat to student-athlete health and safety (Palmer, 2014).

While most colleges in Washington and Colorado maintain nothing has changed in terms of the ban on marijuana use, some off-campus police departments have indicated they will no longer arrest or ticket students who are 21 and older and using marijuana (Gerianos, 2012). The University of Colorado at Boulder police no longer ticket people who are legal under state law to possess marijuana, however, students could still face Office of Student Conduct discipline ("Know the Rules," 2014). Students under the age of 21 caught with either marijuana or alcohol receive a Minor in Possession ticket from either the university or city police. Those students facing a violation of the Student Code of Conduct receive a hearing with a less-stringent burden of proof. A university conduct officer reviews the facts and decides whether the student should be held responsible for the actions of which he or she is accused ("Know the Rules," 2014). In addition to student disciplinary proceedings, people under 21 can face penalties from the criminal courts. The most common offense—possession of marijuana—may result in a fine up to ninety-nine dollars ("Know the Rules," 2014). For struggling college students, these fines can become a financial hardship.

Challenges for College and University Officials

Legalization of cannabis might evoke images of smoke-filled dorm rooms and students regularly attending classes high, but the reality is it will not change many of the policies currently established on college campuses. A conflict exists between state laws, public opinion, and current federal statute. The federal government still considers cannabis a controlled substance and federal laws have not been changed. This presents a problem for colleges and universities on how to navigate legalization within a confusing legislative environment. Clarity is needed as more states put the issue on their ballots and expect passage. The challenge for college and university officials is to recognize the current culture of marijuana use while maintaining compliance with federal law.

Searching for Ways to Respond

Universities across the country are searching for ways to respond to the legalization of cannabis on their campuses. Marijuana is the most abused substance and tailor-made programs are few. Most programming has been modeled after alcohol treatment programs, but some argue that these do not adequately capture the marijuana experience (Sullivan Moore & Turkewitz, 2014). For example, in a typical program for experienced marijuana smokers, students will answer questions which are adapted from an index of alcohol-related problems such as: Has the student ever passed out after using? Got into a fight? What they are not being asked is: Are you eating too much? Coughing too much? Are you experiencing problems with sleep, motivation, memory, and attention? (Sullivan Moore & Turkewitz, 2014). The marijuana experience is much different from that of the binge drinker or alcoholic and requires a program that can help students recognize their problems.

In an effort to address the narrowed focus of these programs, colleges and universities are creating specific programming for marijuana users. For instance, the University of North Carolina at Wilmington provides a program—BASICS-Marijuana—to help students explore their marijuana use in a nonjudgmental environment (University of North Carolina Wilmington, n.d.). The goal of the program is to reduce risky behaviors and harmful consequences of abuse. The sessions are conducted one-on-one with a trained facilitator and the student. The program is usually completed in three one-hour sessions (University of North Carolina Wilmington, n.d.). At Boston College, MODE (Marijuana and Other Drug Education) is an alcohol and drug education program which is offered in 90-minute sessions. The emphasis is on prevention and self-reflection while encouraging healthier choices around marijuana use (Boston College, n.d.). The program charges a fifty dollar administrative fee for those attending as the result of a disciplinary hearing or court imposed sanction.

Over 600 universities and colleges across the country use the San Diego State University sponsored program—eCHECKUP TO GO (eCHECKUPTOGO, n.d.). These programs are designed to motivate individuals to reduce their level of marijuana use by using personalized information about their own behavior and risk factors. The entire program is online based, offering prevention and intervention services. The program begins with a self-administered survey which takes 20–30 minutes to complete. These are self-guided and do not require a face-to-face meeting with a counselor or administrator. If students are determined to need further reflection, they may be asked to complete a companion program, "Personal Reflection," which takes an additional 15–20 minutes (eCHECKUPTOGO, n.d.). The primary goal of the program is to reduce levels of marijuana use and abuse on college campuses with a special focus on first-year students and chronic users. The program also seeks to strengthen a culture of safety and health by providing links to campus and community resources (eCHECKUPTOGO, n.d.).

Marijuana Programs as Retention Strategy

Some colleges have been adding programs specifically designed for marijuana users as a retention strategy. According to a University of Maryland 2013 report, marijuana users, even those who use infrequently, are more likely to drop out of college (Arria et al., 2013). The researchers used data from the College

Life Study, an ongoing research on health-related behaviors among college students. Over a period of four years, they tracked 1,133 participants. All of the students attended the same university located in the mid-Atlantic region of the United States (Brophy Marcus, 2013). Beginning in the student's freshman year, students participated in a series of questionnaires and interviews, even if they did not continue to attend the university. Enrollment and graduation data were acquired from university records that the students agreed to share. The authors of the report found that 71% of the students had remained "continuously enrolled" over the 4-year period. Those who left had various reasons, from transferring to another college to simply leaving altogether. The researchers decided to use the term "discontinued enrollment" instead of the traditional term, "dropout," to describe this group. The study concluded that marijuana use was a predictor for discontinued enrollment (Brophy Marcus, 2013).

While the results of the University of Maryland report suggest marijuana use is linked to discontinued enrollment, there has been little research to date on the effectiveness of such programs on retention and graduation rates (Sullivan Moore & Turkewitz, 2014). As more institutions look for ways to address the problems of drug abuse and retention, studies should be conducted to reflect the possible correlation of the two.

Preparing Students for Legalization

Institutions of higher education in states where marijuana is legalized are already moving from a punitive stance to a more educational approach (Sullivan Moore & Turkewitz, 2014). The tone clearly has changed in these states, but other states are following with programs that educate students and employees on responsible use of marijuana. In Colorado, rather that telling people not to use the drug, officials at colleges and the state health department are working to get the public educated about the facts so they know how to use the drug responsibly (Culp-Ressler, 2015). The Colorado state campaign "Good to Know" is paid for out of recreational marijuana tax dollars. The message seeks to relay basic information about Colorado's marijuana laws, such as the prohibition of public use and the ban on giving it to children (Ingold, 2015). Colorado State University is addressing the public for the first time through a program entitled, "Recreate Responsibly" (Bishop, 2014). The campaign takes a comedic approach, addressing common misconceptions about marijuana use. Posters with simple messages are placed around campus, one of which reads, "Peanut butter and jelly fish? Nasty combination. So is marijuana and alcohol" (Bishop, 2014). Other posters deal with other misconceptions such as driving under the influence, prohibition on campus, and knowing your limits.

Some colleges have taken the preparation efforts to another level, developing research around the issue of legalization. Humboldt State University in California created The Humboldt Institute for Interdisciplinary Marijuana Research (Martin, 2014). Here, a collection of faculty and students conduct research about cannabis policy (Martin, 2014). The mission of the institute is to "improve the economic, social, physical, and environmental health of individuals and communities through the interdisciplinary scientific study of marijuana" (Eschker, Meisel, & Grabinski, 2014). Research focuses on issues of legalization and the impact it will have on economic and sociological factors.

Other institutions are adding courses on the topic of marijuana to their offerings. At Oregon State University, a sociology course, "Marijuana Policy in the 21st Century," explores the policy issues facing the state following the legalization of recreational use in November 2014 ("New Marijuana Policy," 2015). Students enrolled in the course work with policymakers and stakeholders to address some of the major questions legalization has presented. At Santa Clara University School of Law, a new class focuses on the numerous legal issues that could arise should California legalize cannabis ("California University," 2015). Moritz College of Law at The Ohio State University offers a course entitled, "Marijuana Law: Policy and Reform" ("Marijuana Class," 2015). The University of Denver has recently announced it is adding a class on representing marijuana clients—the first ever in the country (Migoya, 2015).

The popularity of these courses coincides with the shift in public opinion about cannabis and the legalization efforts that have begun to make their way across the United States. As more states legalize recreational use, college curriculums are sure to reflect these issues in their course offerings.

Conclusion

Campus officials around the country are working to increase awareness about the effects of cannabis and the impact legalization will have on their students. In places where marijuana use has been legalized, campus police have reported a decrease in the number of related citations (Sullivan Moore & Turkewitz, 2014). However, laws or no laws, students are going to continue to do what they do. The social culture of college age students is permeated with alcohol and marijuana use. To expect this to end is unrealistic and while legalization may complicate governing on college campuses, most officials state that they will maintain a drug-free environment.

The challenge for institutions of higher education will be to navigate a legal landscape that is quickly transforming. While compliance under the Drug Free Schools and Communities Act Amendment of 1989 prohibits marijuana use on campus, educational approaches should be utilized to address the changing culture. Preparing students and employees for an environment where pot is legal will undoubtedly be a huge task, but it also presents an opportunity for creating a new culture on campus: one of responsibility and accountability.

References

Allmand, C. (2014, August 16). Marijuana on campus: Looking at Washington's marijuana culture. *The Daily Record News.* Retrieved from http://www.dailyrecordnews.com/members/marijuana-on-campus-looking-at-washington-s-marijuana-culture/article_6d67b3ec-24d5-11e4-8f13-0019bb2963f4.html.

Arria, A., Caldeira, K. M., Bugbee, B. A., Vincent, K. B., & O'Grady, K. E. (2013) The academic opportunity costs of substance abuse during college. The University of Maryland. Retrieved from http://www.cls.umd.edu/docs/AcadOppCosts.pdf.

Associated Press. (2015, February 12). California university to offer marijuana policy class. *Washington Times.* Retrieved from http://www.washingtontimes.com/news/2015/feb/12/california-university-to-offer-marijuana-policy-cl/print/.

Bishop, D. (2014, September 16). Colorado state campaign strives to educate students about marijuana despite conduct prohibition. *The Collegian Central—Colorado State University.* Retrieved from: http://www.collegian.com/2014/09/colorado-state-campaign-strives-educate-students-marijuana-despite-conduct-prohibition/89115/.

Boston College, n.d. MODE (Marijuana and Other Drug Education). Retrieved from http://www.bc.edu/offices/ade/eiep/mode.html.

Boston University. State and Federal Laws and Sanctions Concerning Drugs and Alcohol. Retrieved from http://www.bu.edu/safety/alcohol-drugs/laws/.

Brophy Marcus, M. (2013, March 22). Even a little pot use ups college dropout risk. *U.S. News and World Report.* Retrieved from http://health.usnews.com/health-news/news/articles/2013/03/22/even-a-little-pot-use-ups-college-dropout-risk.

Culp-Ressler, T. (2015, January 7). 'Good to Know' campaign educates Colorado residents on responsible weed use. *ThinkProgress.* Retrieved from www.thinkgprogress.org.

DiBlasio, N. (2012, November 12). Schools are blunt about new pot law: Not on our campus. *USA Today*. Retrieved from http://www.usatoday.com/story/news/nation/2012/11/10/marijuana-university-colorado-washington/1692827/.

eCHECKUPTOGO. n.d. Retrieved from http://www.echeckuptogo.com/usa/programs/coll_mj.php.

Eschker, E., Meisel, J., & Grabinski, J. (2014). College students working in the marijuana industry. Humboldt Institute of Interdisciplinary Marijuana Research, Humboldt State University. Retrieved from http://www2.humboldt.edu/hiimr/.

Geranios, N. (2012, November 28). Pot legalization no free ride to smoke on campus. *The Seattle Times*. Retrieved from http://www.seattletimes.com/seattle-news/pot-legalization-no-free-ride-to-smoke-on-campus/.

Halper, E. (2014, December 16). Congress quietly ends federal government's ban on medical marijuana. *LA Times*. Retrieved from http://www.latimes.com/nation/la-na-medical-pot-20141216-story.html.

Higher Education Center for Alcohol and Other Drug Abuse and Violence Prevention. (2008). Marijuana use among students at institutions of higher education. Retrieved from www.highereducation.org.

Ingold, J. (2015, January 6). New Colorado marijuana public education campaign takes lighter tone. *The Denver Post*. Retrieved from http://www.denverpost.com/news/ci_27262040/new-colorado-marijuana-public-education-campaign-takes-lighter-tone.

Johnston, L.D., O'Malley, P.M., Miech, R.A., Bachman, J.G., and Schulenberg, J.E. (2013). *Monitoring the Future National Survey Results on Drug Use, 1975–2013, Volume 2: College Students and Adults age 19–55. 2013.* Retrieved from http://www.monitoringthefuture.org/pubs/monographs/mtf-overview 2013.pdf.

Know the rules on drinking and drugs at CU-Boulder. (2014, August 22). ColoradoDaily.com. Retrieved from http://www.coloradodaily.com/welcome back_campuslife/ci_26322410/know -rules-drinking-and-drugs-at-cu-boulder.

Marijuana class takes hazy place in college curriculum. (2015, February 15). *CBSDenver*. Retrieved from http://denver.cbslocal.com/2015/02/15/marijuana-law-classes-take-hazy-place-in-college-curriculum/.

Martin, A. (2014). Want to toke on campus? Not so fast. *The Atlantic*. Retrieved from www.theatlantic.com.

Messer, M. (1969). The predictive value of marijuana use: A note to researchers of student culture. *Sociology and Education, Winter, 42*(1).

Migoya, D. (2015, January 18). University of Denver adds pot business to law school curriculum. *The Denver Post*. Retrieved from http://www.denverpost.com/marijuana/ci_27338213/university-denver-adds-pot-business-law-school-curriculum.

New marijuana policy course offered at Oregon State University. (2015, January 15). *Oregon State University News and Communications.* Retrieved from http://oregonstate.edu/ua/ncs/archives/2015/jan/new-marijuana-policy-course-offered-oregon-state-university.

Palmer E. (2014, February 28). Not so fast: You still can't smoke pot at Colorado colleges. *U.S. News and World Report.* Retrieved from http://www.usnewsuniversitydirectory.com/articles/marijuana-remains-banned-at-colorado-colleges_13754.aspx#.VPD2X_nF-So.

Schutier, L. (2014). Update: Marijuana on campus—Yes, it is *STILL* illegal (But HEMP *may* be okay). National Association of College and University Attorneys, *NACUANotes, 12*(3).

Sullivan Moore, A., & Turkewitz J. (2014, October 29). Legally high at a Colorado campus. *NY Times.* Retrieved from http://www.nytimes.com/2014/11/02/education/edlife/legally-high-marijuana-on-campus-colorado.html?_r=0.

US Department of Education Report. (2006, July). Complying with the Drug Free Schools and Campuses. Regulations: A Guide for University and College Administrators. Washington, DC. Retrieved from http://www.higheredcompliance.org/resources/resources/dfscr-hec-2006-manual.pdf.

University of North Carolina Wilmington, Office of Dean of Students, Division of Student Affairs, n.d. Standard university responses to drug offenses. Retrieved from http://uncw.edu/studentconduct/documents/AlcoholDrugs.MinimumSanctions.11.5.13.pdf.

University of Puget Sound. (2012). Washington State laws on marijuana. Retrieved from http://www.pugetsound.edu/student-life/counseling-health-and-wellness/substance-abuse-prevention/washington-state-laws-on-marijuana/.

Wadley, J. (2014, September 8). College students' use of marijuana on the rise, some drugs declining. University of Michigan News Release. Retrieved from http://ns.umich.edu/new/releases/22362-college-students-use-of-marijuana-on-the-rise-some-drugs-declining.

Warf, B. (2014). High points: An historical geography of cannabis. *Geographical Review, 104*(4), 414–438.

About the Authors

Ericka Christensen is a PhD candidate in The School of Politics, Philosophy, and Public Affairs at Washington State University.

Kelley A. Cronin is an associate professor at Notre Dame College of Ohio. Her research interests include homeland security policies and politics and administrative theory as it relates to policing. Previously, she worked in municipal government and local law enforcement.

Cheyenne Foster is a PhD student in the Department of Criminal Justice and Criminology at Washington State University. Her interests include corrections, gender and justice, drug policy, and qualitative methods. She is also a Wonder Woman fanatic who enjoys examining the parallels between the comics and feminist theory.

Edward L. W. Green is a doctoral candidate in the Department of Sociology, Anthropology, and Social Work at Kansas State University.

Craig Hemmens is the chair and a professor in the Department of Criminal Justice and Criminology at Washington State University. He holds a JD from North Carolina Central University School of Law and a PhD in criminal justice from Sam Houston State University. He has published twenty books and more than two hundred articles on a variety of criminal justice-related topics. His publications have appeared in *Justice Quarterly*, *Journal of Criminal Justice Education*, *Crime and Delinquency*, *Criminal Law Bulletin*, and *The Prison Journal*.

Joshua Hill is an assistant professor at the University of Southern Mississippi. He researches the public policy of crime and criminal justice, cybercrime, and research methods. He is the co-author of *Introduction to Homeland Security* with Dr. Willard Oliver and Dr. Nancy Marion.

Kenneth Leon is a PhD student in the Department of Justice, Law, and Criminology at American University. He received an MA degree in criminology from George Washington University and a BS degree in criminology from Florida State University. His most recent project involves a refocusing of criminological inquiry on non-prescribed stimulant use among adolescents.

David A. Licate earned a PhD in political science from Kent State University. He is a professor of criminal justice and associate director of the Center for Emergency Management and Homeland Policy Research at the University of Akron. Licate is a consultant and research partner on several federally funded grant programs involving the implementation of data-driven and evidence-based policing strategies.

Nicholas P. Lovrich is Regents Professor Emeritus and a Claudius O. and Mary W. Johnson Distinguished Professor of Political Science at Washington State University. He is the series editor for *Criminal Justice: Recent Scholarship* for LFB Scholarly Publishing, LLC.

Nancy Marion is a professor of political science at the University of Akron who specializes in the interplay between politics and criminal justice. She is the author of many books and articles that focus on criminal justice policy, including *The Medical Marijuana Maze.*

Willard M. Oliver is a professor of criminal justice at Sam Houston State University. He has published extensively in the area of federal crime control policy and his most recent publication, co-edited with Nancy Marion, is *Drugs in American Society: An Encyclopedia of History, Politics, Culture and the Law*, in 3 volumes (ABC-CLIO, 2014).

Brianne Posey is a PhD student in the Department of Criminal Justice and Criminology at Washington State University. A Colorado native, she received her BA in psychology from the University of Northern Colorado and her MA in criminology and criminal justice at Arizona State University. Her thesis is titled *The Effect of Parenting Styles on Substance Use and Academic Achievement among Delinquent Youth: Implications for Selective Intervention Practices.* Her research interests include family dynamics, community corrections, mental health, juvenile justice, and drug and alcohol policy.

Douglas Routh is a PhD candidate in the Department of Criminal Justice and Criminology at Washington State University. His research interests include diversionary and correctional programming, substance abuse treatment, and drug policy within the criminal justice system.

Brooke Shannon is an assistant professor of Security and Intelligence Studies at Embry-Riddle Aeronautical University. Her research interests include information practices and East African affairs.

Kevin F. Steinmetz is an assistant professor in the Department of Sociology, Anthropology, and Social Work at Kansas State University.

Mary K. Stohr is a professor in the Department of Criminal Justice and Criminology at Washington State University. Before academe she worked in an adult male prison in Washington State as a correctional officer (for less than a year) and as a correctional counselor (for about two years). Stohr has published almost 90 academic works of one sort or another, including six books and over 40 journal articles, in the areas of the management of criminal justice organizations and operations, correctional personnel, inmate needs and assessment, program evaluation, gender, and victimization.

John R. Turner received his master's degree in criminal justice from Indiana State University. He is currently teaching and pursuing a PhD in criminal justice and criminology at Washington State University, where he is working on his dissertation, which addresses the implementation of recreational marijuana. His other primary research interests are offender rehabilitation, corrections, life course criminology, and criminal justice policy.

Andrea Walker is a PhD student in the Department of Criminal Justice and Criminology at Washington State University. Her research interests include sex offenders, corrections, and legal issues in criminal justice. She has published articles appearing (or forthcoming) in *Criminal Justice Review* and *Criminal Law Bulletin.*

Ronald Weitzer is a professor of sociology at George Washington University. His has published extensively in the area of sex work, including both ethnographic studies and policy-related essays. He is the editor of *Sex for Sale* (Routledge, 2010) and *Legalizing Prostitution* (NYU Press, 2012), and he co-edited a recent issue of *The Annals* (May 2014) focusing on human trafficking.

Index